Dec '11 – Jan '12.

Deares[...]
It's bee[...]
to shar[...]
adventures together on
your first visit to us.
We haven't seen many
art galleries or gardens.
National Parks more
than made up for it!
Lots love, Jenny &
Brian

THE
PAINTED
GARDEN
IN NEW ZEALAND ART

THE
PAINTED
GARDEN
IN NEW ZEALAND ART

—— Christopher Johnstone ——

GODWIT

To Louise, Isobel and Leo, and in memory of
Maud and Sammy and
Mitzi and Louis.

A GODWIT BOOK published by Random House New Zealand
18 Poland Road, Glenfield, Auckland, New Zealand

For more information about our titles go to www.randomhouse.co.nz

A catalogue record for this book is available from the National Library of New Zealand

Random House International, Random House, 20 Vauxhall Bridge Road, London, SW1V 2SA, United
Kingdom; *Random House Australia Pty Ltd*, Level 3, 100 Pacific Highway, North Sydney 2060, Australia;
Random House South Africa Pty Ltd, Isle of Houghton, Corner Boundary Road and Carse O'Gowrie,
Houghton 2198, South Africa; *Random House Publishers India Private Ltd*, 301 World Trade Tower,
Hotel Intercontinental Grand Complex, Barakhamba Lane, New Delhi 110 001, India

First published 2008

© 2008 text Christopher Johnstone, images as credited on pages 238–261

The moral rights of the author have been asserted

ISBN 978 1 86962 141 4

Text and cover design: Nick Turzynski, redinc., Auckland
Front cover: Karl Maughan 1964–, *Cross Hills* (2004), oil on canvas, 178.0 x 275.0. Collection of the
Te Manawa Museums Trust. Reproduced with the kind permission of the artist.
Frontispiece: Pat Hanly, *Garden Energy* (detail), see page 167.
Printed in China by Everbest Printing Co Ltd

CONTENTS

INTRODUCTION

SOMETIMES THE ONLY idea that we can gain of the gardens and gardening of an early civilisation or culture is a contemporaneous picture by an artist. Whether New Kingdom Egypt, ancient Greece or Rome or Pompeii, there are wall paintings or frescos that illustrate at least aspects of the gardens of their times. Aside from the very occasional eleventh- or twelfth-century Chinese garden painting among the many profoundly beautiful landscapes of that period, it is not until the fourteenth century that paintings of gardens first appear, in Europe. From then on, whether in Renaissance Europe, Persia, Mughal India or the Far East, painted images of gardens become more frequent and therefore the development of the garden in those cultures becomes better documented visually as well as in prose and poetry.

However, the case must not be overstated: paintings which set out to portray the garden *per se* did not appear for another couple of centuries. Until then, painted garden images are usually tucked away in the corners of portraits or religious or mythological scenes or as details in paintings of palaces and castles — and rarely is there even the briefest glimpse of an ordinary citizen's domestic garden. Furthermore, these early depictions are frequently somewhat imaginative constructions, referring to the Garden of Eden and other religious symbologies rather than being accurate and objective documents of real gardens.

By the middle of the eighteenth century — the eve of the European settlement of New Zealand — not only had the garden become fully developed as a cultural artefact but it was also accessible to a growing home-owning middle class with sufficient leisure time and resources to make it an extension of their personal attributes and an expression of their values. Nevertheless, paintings of such gardens remain rare, even in Europe. Two of the earliest English examples date from 1815: John Constable's panoramas of his father's vegetable and flower gardens in East Bergholt in Suffolk.

Less than a year earlier, in December 1814, the Reverend Samuel Marsden had arrived at Oihi Bay, next to Rangihoua pa in the Bay of Islands, aboard the brig *Active*. Rangihoua was already arguably the first place of regular contact between Maori and Europeans; by 1805 at the latest, its people were trading locally grown European potatoes with visiting whalers. Upon Marsden's arrival Rangihoua became the site of the first missionary settlement in New Zealand, and the site of the first properly tended European garden here. This was both a vegetable garden and a flower garden, because the women passengers on the *Active* — the wives of the missionaries — brought with them from Sydney a rose, the first in New Zealand. Despite the poor quality of the heavy clay soil at Oihi, and unlike the wheat the missionaries planted, the rose survived and cuttings from it were later planted in Kerikeri, where the second mission station was founded in 1819. Here gardening and horticulture markedly improved and Marsden planted the first grapevines. Not long afterwards the Rangihoua mission was abandoned.

Visual records of settler gardens begin to increase from the time of the signing of the Treaty of Waitangi and the beginning of formal European settlement, but these are mostly sketches and drawings. The few paintings that exist are invariably by amateurs, the most talented among them William Fox and William Mein Smith. It

JOHN JOHNSON (1794–1848)

THE ARTIST'S HOUSE AND GARDEN ('AND THE
WILDERNESS SHALL BECOME THE FRUITFUL
FIELD' FROM MRS HOBSON'S ALBUM)

1843

SEPIA INK

16.2 X 24.2

ALEXANDER TURNBULL LIBRARY

was Fox who, in 1860, became the first New Zealand artist to paint a garden without a house: his two views of his own garden, Lower Westoe at Rangitikei, are conceived with the grandeur, if not the breadth, given only to landscape, and with a sense of relative modernity.

These Westoe paintings aside, the early period painters Fox, Smith and Charles Heaphy achieve little more than light-hearted description in their house and garden paintings, which are essentially the equivalent of the topographical landscapes of this period. However, Smith's painting of Francis Molesworth's house in the Hutt Valley has an intelligent sensitivity about it that marks him out as one of the finest of the country's military-trained artists. Viewing this painting (and its companion, another view of Molesworth's house) makes it unsurprising to learn that Smith later became a prize-winning gardener.

It would be decades after the two Fox paintings of Westoe before another artist painted a view of a garden alone: it simply did not make sense to paint a garden without a house, because the garden was still considered an extension to the house.

Two of this country's earliest house and garden 'portraits' were almost certainly souvenirs, painted by an occupant of the house on the eve of departure: Fox of his Nelson home, and Mary King of hers, in Jermyn Street in Auckland.

By the same token, some of the early paintings commemorate the completion of a house and were therefore painted long before the surrounding garden had reached any kind of maturity. Fox's view of Westoe is dated before the recorded completion of the house. Molesworth's house had been finished long enough for the creeper (possibly grapevines or roses) to have climbed the rustic veranda posts and for the beginnings of a flowerbed to have been laid out in front.

For most settlers, it was undoubtedly the vegetable garden and crops, if there was enough land, that went in first. However, women especially were likely to think about a flower garden pretty quickly once the practical considerations for living had been addressed. So we find Sarah Mathew, wife of Felton Mathew, the country's first surveyor-general, at the establishment of the new capital of Auckland, having sailed from the Bay of Islands in the *Anna Watson*. In her journal on 3 October 1840 she recorded:

> . . . *the weather, however, is improving, and on shore in our little valley, where I spend the greater part of the day, the warmth is delightful. I have been enclosing a small spot of ground for my bulbs which are all shooting and should be planted.*

The place of her garden plot would soon be called Official Bay, later reclaimed and now in the area of Beach Road.

Another early Auckland resident was John Johnson (1794–1848), the colonial surgeon, whose sepia-wash sketch on this page shows his house below Government House. Among various plants it shows grapevines, a line of willows and pumpkins in the foreground.

The Reverend John Kinder stands alone as the first and finest artist-gardener of real significance in New Zealand. His paintings and photographs document his most important garden, that of St John's College, Auckland, of which he was the master, and to a lesser extent his own Remuera garden.

There is, however, a fine drawing by Kinder of Te Papa Mission Station,

Tauranga (The Elms), dated 1857 (at right). While staying with Archdeacon Alfred Nesbit Brown, Kinder met his future wife Celia, Brown's daughter. In his journal Kinder described the garden, which featured:

. . . yellow cape jasmine reaching a height of a tree. The aloe was just coming into flower. Rose hedges covered with clusters of small flowers some twelve feet high. Apple trees, peaches and other English fruit trees loaded with fruit . . . All this the Archdeacon told me is the growth of some fifteen years. When he first came to settle here the place was an open bank covered with manuka and fern without a tree.

Kinder was also New Zealand's first great photographer and took the country's finest early still life photograph — arguably New Zealand's first photographic work of art: *Pikiarero* (*Clematis paniculata*).

The native clematis, of which there are several varieties, was a very popular plant. Fanny Osborne painted the same variety Kinder had photographed and called it puawhananga, elsewhere named the large-flowered New Zealand clematis, while Sarah Featon's pikiarero is identified as *Clematis hexasepala*. The young Charles Goldie chose to paint clematis for his entry in a section of the 1886 Auckland Society of Arts annual exhibition.

Emily Marshall-White, aka 'A Suffolk Lady', wrote in her chapter on 'Native Flora' in *My New Zealand Garden*, first published in Wanganui in 1902:

Bush Clematis, clinging about on trees in the bush and hanging in snowy wreaths and clusters in early spring, never fails to attract the attention of all, and is in great request for the decoration of rooms; but as it often scrambles up to the height of thirty feet, it is rather beyond the grasp of the flower-seeker.

While botanical paintings do not fall within the definition of garden paintings, the three fine botanical painters featured in these pages — Martha King, Sarah Featon and Fanny Osborne — were directly linked with gardens and their development. King was the country's first resident botanical artist and developed a fine garden in New Plymouth; Featon and her husband Edward encouraged plantsmen and gardeners to grow some of the native varieties they included in their book *The Art Album of New Zealand Flora* (1889); and while Osborne painted only the flora of Great Barrier Island, which was in a way her garden, her husband Alfred supplied Auckland nurserymen with seeds of unusual species.

Competent paintings of town gardens become more plentiful in the late 1860s and 1870s. Another highly talented painter with a military background was Charles Igglesden. His two paintings of his uncle's Wellington house and garden are marvellous in their execution and detail. The paintings of the Ardens, father and son, while varied in quality, are charming and informative records of some of the gardens in New Plymouth. John Hoyte's depictions of Harry Cobley's Devonport garden, while not exactly a town section, represented the grand scale to which wealthier town-dwellers aspired. At the same time they are further examples of views of recently completed houses; one has to imagine how the garden would have looked five or 10 years later.

✻

Not being a well-defined genre of painting nor even a recognised sub-category of landscape, paintings of gardens in New Zealand occur only from time to time and with no regularity or consistency. Nor did changes in gardening styles give rise to any specific documentation by artists. In late nineteenth-century Britain there were popular, if not top-rank, artists who were recognised for their garden 'portraits' such as Helen Allingham, Alfred Parsons, Beatrice Parsons and George Elgood, but they simply do not have their equivalent in New Zealand painting. Even Margaret Stoddart did not accept commissions, and during the short period she painted gardens they were of gardens of her own choice.

One explanation for this, at least in part, may be that with the rising popularity of photography from the 1870s, new home-owners chose to have their houses and gardens documented by means of the increasingly fashionable and ubiquitous technique. There are untold numbers of bland, greyish and unmemorable photographs of houses and gardens from the latter decades of the nineteenth century — wonderful records but hardly art, although there are of course exceptions.

Art historian Ann Elias's study 'New Zealand Still Life and Flower Painting 1880–1940' does not address garden paintings as such but she does touch on closely related issues that are as pertinent to the genre as they are to flower still lifes. While 'flower painting is one manifestation of "floriculture" in New Zealand', its study reveals, she argues:

> the important place that flowers occupied in New Zealand society at the end of the nineteenth and beginning of the twentieth century. Floriculture played a vital role in the economic development and social life of colonials and its history is crucial to an understanding of the history of women's cultural practices in New Zealand.

Floriculture was not only about growing and selling flowers. Elias also refers to the floral sections of horticultural and A & P shows, where prize categories would include not only flower arrangements but also floral decorations, craftwork made with flowers, needlework and flower embroidery and so on, as well as flower painting *per se*. Newspapers of the time devoted regular columns to floriculture, and articles appear on subjects such as writing about flowers, flower symbolism, flower names for girls, pressing flowers, their use in manufactured products such as cosmetics, and even edible flowers. The annual grand floral fêtes — 'large-scale celebrations of acclimatised flowers' — were regular photographic features, and *The New Zealand Graphic and Ladies Journal* recorded in December 1902 that the artist Trevor Lloyd had designed the poster for that year's Auckland event.

Elias states that 'there is a very strong connection between the predominantly female practice of painting flowers in New Zealand and activities such as domestic gardening and flower arranging.' Curiously this gender distinction does not seem to apply to the painting of gardens.

While garden painters may not have consciously recorded garden fads and fashions around the turn of the nineteenth century, coincidental references to them nonetheless occur. One example is chrysanthemums: Mabel Hill and James Nairn painted them with great effect at Bellevue Gardens in the Lower Hutt. Earlier there had been a craze for these flowers which led to annual chrysanthemum days being widely celebrated. Bellevue Gardens was a venue for the annual Chrysanthemum Show — as well as for the Horticultural and Florists' Society Autumn Show.

In Christchurch, the popularity of roses generated the annual Rose Show. In its 'Flower of the week' column, *The New Zealand Graphic and Ladies Journal* of December 1890 recorded that the show was held in the new Canterbury Society of Arts Gallery in Armagh Street: 'the pictures were still up and with the addition of the lovely flowers the room was very pretty.' Later Christchurch experienced an epidemic of 'rose fever' following the establishment of a public rose garden at the Christchurch Botanical Gardens in 1910, apparently the first in New Zealand and the largest in Australasia. Margaret Stoddart painted a striking picture of it in 1916. One of the unexpected consequences of the public's renewed interest in roses was that during the 1920s there was such a demand for Stoddart's paintings of them that despite constantly knocking off potboilers she was unable to keep up.

Today's plentiful and highly profitable garden centres seem such a modern phenomenon but the concept is really a revival of a very old idea. Winsome Shepherd describes the establishment and popularity of tea gardens in Wellington. One of the earliest was Wilkinson Tea Gardens, established in Oriental Bay in 1850. Bellevue Gardens in Woburn, Lower Hutt, was originally the garden of Alfred Ludlam and was painted by Francis Dillon Bell in 1850. When Ludlam died in 1877, James McNab, a nurseryman from Thorndon, bought the property and opened it to the public as McNab's Gardens, and in 1881 the renowned English botanical artist Marianne North made studies of the nikau palm there. In the early 1890s it changed hands again, becoming Bellevue Gardens.

An unusual example of photography and art combining to portray a beautiful garden is the book compiled by Barbara Douglas about her own Oamaru garden: *Pictures in a New Zealand Garden*, printed in Melbourne and privately published in 1921. It intersperses colour reproductions of the watercolours painted by and, one assumes, commissioned from Mabel Hill, with half-tone illustrations by three photographers: B de Lambert, J Wallace and AC Gifford. *Pictures in a New Zealand Garden* appears to be unique in the country's garden literature of the period and for this reason Hill's representation here is largely drawn from her paintings for the book. In this connection it is interesting to note Douglas's dedication 'to all Mothers, Sisters, Wives and Lovers who have lost their dear ones in the Great War, in the hope that the love of flowers and gardens may bring them solace in the years to come.'

For some gardeners, the garden is a living souvenir; a flower planted in someone's memory; a person remembered for giving a plant; a cutting taken from a special place and so forth. Yet little of this is communicated through the paintings themselves.

Memory certainly plays a role in some of Margaret Stoddart's most beautiful garden paintings. Stoddart is the giant of garden painters in New Zealand. She was an exceptional painter at every stage of her 50-year career, from her earliest botanical studies of the mid-1880s to her last atmospheric high-country landscapes. The Stoddart family's connection to Diamond Harbour dated back to the 1850s; when, around 1913, she painted the Old Homestead where she had been born and Godley House where she had lived as a young woman, it was partly because of the imminent sale of the family estate to the Lyttelton Borough Council, marking the end of an era.

When we look at what would be John Oakley's last painting of his large Fendalton garden, is it simply with the benefit of hindsight that we seem to feel the

HARRY HUGO TOMBS (1874–1966)

JUNE DAY, 1941

1941

WATERCOLOUR

51.0 X 66.0

WHEREABOUTS UNKNOWN

intimations of mortality that he must have felt, recuperating from an accident and confined to a first-floor bedroom? Or is there something about his vision, as if he replayed the planting, growth and maturity of each area of the garden in his mind before lovingly painting it?

Few garden paintings were made between the wars, but those that were — by Robert Procter, Colin Lovell-Smith, James Fitzgerald and Olivia Spencer Bower — are all quite different and outstanding in their own way. Some exceptional flower still lifes were made during the same period. Doris Lusk's *Mixed flowers* is simply a stunning early painting and a masterpiece of the genre. Anne Hamblett's and Rodney Kennedy's are rare examples of their work as both soon ceased painting, Hamblett at least in part because of her marriage to Colin McCahon and Kennedy because of his increasing interest in theatre and his incarceration as a conscientious objector during the Second World War.

One war-time garden painting that eluded rediscovery during research for this book is *June day, 1941*, reproduced here from its use as the frontispiece of the December 1941 issue of *Art in New Zealand*. The artist Harry Hugo Tombs (1874–1966) was the magazine's publisher and he exhibited the painting at that year's New Zealand Academy of Fine Arts annual exhibition. A view of the Orongorongos, probably from Tombs's home in Thorndon, it is an early winter scene on a fine day — a Sunday, no doubt, given that Tombs was a very busy publisher and printer.

If Stoddart was star of the genre just before the First World War, Rita Angus shines out in the middle of the century, with the earliest painting in this selection dating from 1943. The two artists are not unconnected; in the 1960s Angus wrote in a letter to Gordon H Brown: 'It was Miss Stoddart's watercolours that impressed me when a Canterbury art student . . .'

Angus was one of New Zealand's finest and most original flower painters but she also produced enough paintings of her parents' extensive garden at Waikanae and of her own gardens to identify her as a garden painter. What characterises Angus's approach to her nature painting is a kind of 'less is more'; indeed, some might wonder if her *Garden, Waikanae* is actually 'finished' — which can be a tricky matter with her work. (In this case the painting seems quite satisfying, given the way the yellowy-orange foliage above balances the 'empty' area below enlivened with the deeper orange flowers.) While the passionflower was painted in the studio or on her sister's kitchen table in Greymouth, we know the iris was done on the spot, in her own garden at Clifton, near Sumner, Christchurch. All the paintings display that visionary intensity — a hallmark of all her work — informed by what her biographer Jill Trevelyan describes as her 'quiet, sustained contemplation of nature'.

Another very keen artist-gardener was Rata Lovell-Smith. She was a teacher at the Canterbury College School of Art at the time Angus was a student but did not actually teach her. Lovell-Smith first exhibited a flower still life, of daisies in a vase, at the Canterbury Society of Arts in 1935 and thereafter increasingly concentrated on the genre. *South window* is unusual because it shows the garden and a hint of landscape beyond. In her 1979 thesis on Lovell-Smith, Ann Elias transcribes a talk the artist gave around 1961–62 to Christchurch florists in which she said:

In dealing with flowers you are working with living things . . . A painter, poor soul, has to create life and light with pigment — an inorganic matter. This is appallingly difficult and when I paint flowers and see the result I humbly beg their pardon.

In this narrative, aside from isolated examples such as Don Binney's student painting *Backyard garden II* and Ivy Fife's exploration of sunflowers in her Christchurch garden, it is only towards the end of the 1960s that a wave of real interest in the painting of gardens begins. In close succession Pat Hanly, Gretchen Albrecht, Philip Trusttum, Alan Pearson and James Ross painted and, excluding Albrecht, showed whole exhibitions devoted to paintings of gardens, in most cases their own.

Pat Hanly's *'Inside' the garden* watercolours, begun in December 1968, were exhibited with huge success at Barry Lett Galleries, Auckland, in May 1969. A small number of oil and enamel paintings followed over the next three years; eventually, in the 1980s, Hanly would return several times to the garden theme in watercolour, all of or inspired by his Windmill Road, Mount Eden garden. Also around 1969, a few steps away in Wynyard Road, Mount Eden, Gretchen Albrecht began to paint watercolour sketches of her garden *en plein air*. They were exhibited in Dunedin in 1973, although the associated acrylic garden paintings that followed would not be shown publicly for several years.

Philip Trusttum's garden paintings in a three-person exhibition at the New Vision Gallery received plaudits from Hamish Keith in 1973, and were followed in 1974 by an Auckland Festival exhibition. Christchurch painter Alan Pearson, who had shown recent garden paintings at the CSA Gallery, now exhibited them at the New Vision Gallery. The gallery had obviously caught the wave, as later that year it showed *The Artist's Garden*, in which paintings by Trusttum and Pearson were joined by a 1974 garden watercolour by Pat Hanly and paintings by Louise Henderson, Philippa Hutchinson (later Blair) and John Papas.

Also in 1974, James Ross painted a group of garden paintings and landscapes at and around his new Titirangi home, though these were not exhibited until 1976. Two years later, a painter of quite a different persuasion, Jane Evans, painted her first group of garden paintings, *My garden*, of her first garden at her new Tasman Street home in Nelson.

The reasons for this veritable efflorescence of garden painting in the early 1970s can only be guessed at: a combination of zeitgeist, coincidence and unconscious borrowing and/or influence — who knows? Yet in a decade that was characterised, generally speaking, by a marked shift towards the avant-garde, some of New Zealand's best younger painters focused on the garden as their part of the modernist project at that time.

There is another, albeit speculative and untested explanation: that young New Zealand painters had to find a way to discover a modernist approach to landscape painting that could not be construed as following in the wake of Colin McCahon, Toss Woollaston or Rita Angus. Since garden painting appears to be alternative to, or at least a sub-genre of, landscape painting, perhaps the threat of the past was neutralised in some way.

What is common to Trusttum, Pearson and Ross is, broadly speaking, their expressionist mode and heavy impastoed surface. Accordingly, they positioned themselves — consciously or not — in the mainstream modernist line of the German expressionists and Emil Nolde. Nolde was one of the twentieth century's finest garden and flower painters who, in turn, continued the Impressionist focus on the garden begun by Monet and Renoir in the early 1870s.

At the end of the 1970s, Claudia Pond Eyley stood alone as a modernist painter of her own subtropical garden in Mount Eden; it would be almost another decade until Karl Maughan burst onto the scene to carry the mantle of garden painting, almost exclusively, into the new millennium. And thus the garden continues as either subject or inspiration for a diverse range of painters in the early twenty-first century.

The last painting in the book, by Auckland artist Peter Hackett, is of Ayrlies, the magnificent garden developed by Beverley McConnell and her late husband Malcolm. Beverley McConnell traces her interest in gardens back to when her father gave her the classic gardening book *Bulbs and Perennials: A Southern Hemisphere Garden Book* by Richmond and Charles Harrison. Inside the cover he had written the lines from Rudyard Kipling's famous 1911 poem 'The Glory of the Garden':

Our England is a garden, and such gardens are not made
By singing:— 'Oh, how beautiful!' and sitting in the shade

The creation of a beautiful garden is hard but satisfying work and part of the garden's reward is the pleasure it gives to others. The same can be said of paintings of gardens.

A NOTE ON STRUCTURE & ORGANISATION

The Painted Garden in New Zealand Art is a selection of paintings (with a few exceptions) of or inspired by New Zealand domestic gardens, by New Zealand painters. In addition there are a few botanical and flower paintings that in one way or another connect to gardens and gardening.

I established some criteria for the selection. Firstly, where possible, I sought out paintings by artists of their own gardens or directly inspired by or related to a known garden. Another criterion was that paintings were to be, in my opinion, of a certain quality and significance, strong enough to stand alone on the page to delight and inform.

I do not make any claims for garden painting as a forgotten or unrecognised genre in New Zealand or indeed western art. Neither do I seek to instruct readers about gardening, gardens or even plants, nor to produce some kind of definitive book of or about garden paintings in New Zealand. The resulting selection is probably more about New Zealand art and artists than about the country's gardeners and gardening. It is more about our art history than our garden and gardening history but I hope it will cast new light on both.

If favourite artists are missing, the most common reason for this is because I could not access a suitable painting. By their very nature, garden paintings — and there are not a huge number of them — tend to become much-loved treasures in

private collections and do not appear in exhibitions or get reproduced in books. Their mere existence is often known only to the owner, their family and friends.

Some paintings I admired could not be located, such as Harry Tombs's *June day, 1941* which was reproduced in *Art in New Zealand* that same year. John Johnson's early sketch of his house and garden at Official Bay, Auckland, in 1843 serves as an example of the many sketches and drawings of this early period, mostly by amateurs, which enrich our knowledge of the gardens of the time but are frequently of limited aesthetic appeal.

Some exceptions to the selection criteria should be self-explanatory. There are two photographs, for example, both by artists who are also painters: John Kinder and Paul Hartigan. There is one print, by Rodney Fumpston, selected because his garden was renowned and this lithograph was begun by the artist using that essential material tusche or lithographer's ink. There is also one painting inspired by a public garden, by William Cumming, included because it has relevance to the garden that Cumming created.

The book is organised chronologically in sections, each with a short introduction. Although the section breaks are somewhat arbitrary, as they are not defined by formal art movements or garden styles, they provide an opportunity for a discussion of a wider range of issues and themes than is possible in the individual texts accompanying each illustration.

The main sequence of paintings is arranged chronologically by artist according to the date of his or her first painting. The artists' biographies, arranged alphabetically, follow on from the main sequence of paintings and text. There is also a short selected glossary of organisations and groups that are referred to in the texts.

Christopher Johnstone
Auckland
August 2008

I. EARLY ARTISTS

1830-1860

THE ANONYMOUS PAINTING with which this section opens was used in its engraved form as an illustration of the location of the Church Missionary Society's first mission station in New Zealand. Though hardly a garden painting, it serves as a striking reference to Maori horticulture and Rangihoua as an early source of European potatoes, as well as showing the site of New Zealand's first tended European-style garden. We can also possibly get an idea of what Ngapuhi chief Ruatara's potato plantation may have looked like from Major Cyprian Bridge's beautifully detailed and atmospheric painting of the pa at Okaihau.

There are no paintings of gardens from the 1830s but on-the-spot descriptions are plentiful, such as Charles Darwin's record of his visit to the Bay of Islands on the *Beagle* in December 1835:

At Paihia, it was quite pleasing to behold the English flowers in the gardens before the houses; there were roses of several kinds, honeysuckle, jasmine, stocks, and whole hedges of sweetbriar.

Generally speaking, Darwin had a dim view of his short visit to New Zealand but he recorded his visit to the mission station at Waimate as the 'one bright spot' because of its 'Christian inhabitants'. He also described what he saw there, including:

large gardens, with every fruit and vegetable which England produces . . . and English oaks; also many kinds of flowers . . . All this is very surprising, when it is considered that five years ago nothing but fern flourished here.

In 1826, almost 10 years before Darwin's visit, the great Sydney-based botanist Allan Cunningham spent several months in the Bay of Islands. The results of his botanical work were published in detail first in 1836, in *Florae Insularum Novae Zelandiae Precursor*, and then in the *Annals and Magazine of Natural History* in 1838. It is conceivable that the list of 40 plants commissioned by the New Zealand Company to be painted by the country's first resident botanical painter, Martha King, was compiled with the help of these descriptions.

Five of King's paintings were reproduced in *Illustrations to 'Adventure in New Zealand'*, published by Edward Jerningham Wakefield in 1845; the more expensive copies had hand-coloured plates and in some only King's were coloured. King was in good company, because among the other artists in the book were Charles Heaphy and Captain William Mein Smith.

There are very few subsequent paintings and drawings by the talented King, and it seems her creative energies were diverted towards her noteworthy garden. A Taranaki friend and later a community leader, Maria Atkinson (née Richmond), described a visit to King and her sister Maria in a letter in 1855:

We went to an early tea that we might enjoy the lovely evening in their beautiful garden, the latter was in finer order than I have ever yet seen it, glowing with choice flowers . . . Miss King is a wonderful woman: besides doing all the cooking and household management and assisting at the school three days a week she has found time to make a wilderness at the extremity of their garden blossom like a rose . . . clearing away all the ugly undergrowth from a number of beautiful fern trees, draining a little swamp and confining the water . . . then making terraced paths and beds on the steep side of the gully from which you can look down on their spreading fern trees and get glimpses of the flower garden, thatched cottage and sea beyond.

Sadly, King herself did not record her garden but we are fortunate that as competent a painter as Charles Heaphy was in Nelson to record the garden of Mr and Mrs William Bishop in the Maitai Valley. His painting is the best record we have of a mature flower garden in a rural setting in the 1840s. Katherine Raine points out in her discussion of settlers' gardens in *A History of the Garden in New Zealand* that the garden was 'remarkably sophisticated and spacious for the time' and 'the very epitome of the gardenesque style, with its fine lawn and paths, curved flowerbeds and widely spaced clumps of plants.'

'Gardenesque' was the term given to the style of garden design adopted for domestic gardens in Britain in the first half of the nineteenth century, which featured flowerbeds around and in front of the house and ornamental shrubbery. According to the garden historian Richard Aitken, the term was coined by John Loudon in the first issue of *Gardener's Magazine* in 1826, where it was used 'to describe a style that distinguished gardens as works of art rather than imitations of nature.' It is interesting to note, however, that Loudon, in his influential book *The Suburban Gardener and Villa Companion* (1838), advised a geometrical garden style for countries 'in a wild state because gardens should be recognisable as works of art and not mistaken for wild nature.'

William Fox was also in Nelson. His production varied in quality from the most sublime landscapes of the era to the somewhat naïve but charming and informative record of his house and garden.

When one looks at a painting like that of the young miller Francis Molesworth's house in the Hutt Valley in 1844, it is arguable that William Mein Smith was a better artist than both Heaphy and Fox. This painting looks forward to the works of Alfred Sharpe with such references to the recent clearing of the bush as the tree stump in the foreground. It also is ominously prophetic: Molesworth died tragically young following a tree-felling accident. In the short time he was in the Hutt Valley, Molesworth, who was vice president of the Horticultural Society, developed a fine garden enclosed by a thorn hedge.

Francis Bell's painting of the house that Molesworth's business partner, brickmaker Alfred Ludlam, built for himself in the Gothic revival style at the same property is also a reminder that the bush had to be cleared — by Ludlam himself — and tamed: Ludlam has planted young nikau at the corners of the terrace, on either side of the steps and along the drive. He has put in new flowerbeds, on the left a vegetable garden with fruit bushes and, almost dominating the house, an impressive conservatory. Ludlam's intention to be the serious gardener he became is signalled. To the right of the conservatory, through the trees, Bell has included a glimpse of two buildings that are probably associated with the windmill Ludlam and Molesworth built as a joint venture.

The most developed garden painted in the period, certainly in Auckland, is that of Captain William and Mary King in Auckland. The substantial house on Jermyn Street the Kings owned at the time of the painting had been built by former harbourmaster Captain David Rough in 1840–41 and subsequently extended. Its large, well-maintained garden has a pleasant, informal symmetry, epitomising the gardenesque; King painted it as a souvenir of her stay in Auckland.

The missionary settlement Rangihoua on the north side of the Bay of Islands, New Zealand

before 1832

ARTIST UNKNOWN

RANGIHOUA WAS ARGUABLY the first site of regular contact between Maori and Pakeha in New Zealand, and the site of the first post-contact garden planted for produce. By 1805 Maori at Rangihoua were growing excellent potatoes, to trade with visiting whalers for axes and other goods. The extraordinary-looking eminence on the left is a pa; the anonymous artist, informed by knowledge of the tidy enclosures of the English countryside, has imagined the pa and its gardens being organised into neat rectangles.

In 1814 the bay adjacent to Rangihoua pa became the site of the first Church Missionary Society settlement, the group of houses to the right in this small painting. *The Missionary Register* of 1832, illustrated by an engraving identical to this painting, describes the first sale of land:

It consists of about 200 acres, and was transferred to the Society for the consideration of twelve axes, by Ahoodee O Gunna [Te Uri o Kanae], King of Rangeehoo, as the name was first spelt.

The sale was negotiated by the Reverend Samuel Marsden and was 'signed by the Chief with a facsimile of the tattooing on his own face'.

Whether the painting or the engraving came first, it indicates that an artist, amateur or professional, had visited the area and sketched what he saw in sufficient detail for the painter or engraver to copy, with some artistic licence. Probably the work of a journeyman painter, given its old-fashioned style, the treatment of the waves and the boat suggests that the artist was copying an eighteenth-century engraving. The boat flying the Red Ensign probably represents HMS *Dromedary*, the first Royal Navy ship to officially visit New Zealand.

Garden historian Professor Helen Leach records that when the missionaries established their station in 1814, 'They raised poultry, grew wheat (though with little success) and tended gardens, but none of these activities flourished.' A Commission of Enquiry in 1821 ascertained that since Marsden's arrival aboard HMS *Dromedary* in the Bay of Islands in 1820, bringing a bullock team, the gardens had improved. The settlement was on clay, however, and in 1830 Marsden recorded that the area was 'not fit for cultivation'.

The missionaries' attempts at gardening and horticulture markedly improved at the second mission station to be established, at Kerikeri, where viticulture would also be successfully introduced. One plant that we know survived at Rangihoua, even if it may not have flourished, was the first rose brought to New Zealand. A cutting struck from this rose was later planted at Kemp House, Kerikeri.

Rhabdothamnus solandri or New Zealand gloxinia

1842

MARTHA KING 1802/3–1897

MARTHA KING HAS the distinction of being New Zealand's first resident botanical artist, yet virtually nothing is known about her life before she emigrated from Ireland with her elder sister and brother. They arrived in 1840 and two years later took up land in Wanganui purchased from the New Zealand Company.

Emma Wicksteed, who travelled with King from England to New Zealand on the *London*, painted a panoramic view of New Plymouth and her husband, John Wicksteed, was the New Zealand Company agent there. He probably informed the New Zealand Company about King's artistic abilities.

Martha had also previously painted a portrait of William Wakefield of the New Zealand Company, so her reputation as an artist had reached Wellington upon her arrival. In September 1842 Wakefield made a donation of £50 to the Wellington Horticultural and Botanical Society and the following week the society commissioned King, for 'a sum not exceeding £10', to produce 'two sets of drawings of the most interesting indigenous botanical specimens', one for the New Zealand Company and one for the London Horticultural Society (the Royal Horticultural Society from 1861).

King completed the two sets of 40 paintings each in breathtaking speed in January 1843, and in September the New Zealand Company in London received its set with 'universal admiration'. Two years later, William Wakefield's nephew Edward Jerningham Wakefield published his two-volume *Adventure in New Zealand* and separately issued the *Illustrations to 'Adventure in New Zealand'*, three of its 15 lithographic plates reproducing five of King's paintings. There are no precursors to King's paintings; Joseph Hooker's *The Botany of the Antarctic Voyage: Florae Novae Zelandiae* was not published until 1853–5. Neither do we know how or why King selected the plants she painted.

Her pencil inscription on the painting of *Rhabdothamnus solandri or New Zealand gloxinia* — called matata by Maori — reads 'This grew from a cleft of rock in St John's Wood, Wanganui. It is not a creeper as its appearance would indicate'. The plant was originally described by Joseph Banks and Daniel Solander on 29 October 1769 when Captain Cook's *Endeavour* arrived at the Coromandel Peninsula, but Sydney Parkinson's drawing of it was not published until much later. However, the great botanist Allan Cunningham, who had collected in the Bay of Islands in 1826, described it in *Florae Insularum Novae Zelandiae Precursor* (1836) and in the *Annals and Magazine of Natural History* in 1838. It is likely that a copy of either or both of these was held by the New Zealand Company in Wellington and therefore would have been available to assist King in her selection.

S.L. C No 16

The home of
Mr & Mrs William Bishop,
Maitai Valley

1844

CHARLES HEAPHY 1820–1881

AS AN ARTIST, Charles Heaphy is best known for his many topographical watercolours and portraits, as well as charts and coastal profiles, made while an employee of the New Zealand Company. However, the highest praise is reserved for his earlier paintings, made following his arrival in the country, foremost among them *Mount Egmont from the southward* (Alexander Turnbull Library).

By 1844 — the year he painted this watercolour, ascribed to him on stylistic grounds — Heaphy had abandoned his attempt to farm near Motueka. Having lost what capital he had, he began a series of explorations of the hinterland of the fledgling settlement of Nelson.

The painting shows William and Anna Bishop (née Fyfe, 1826–1894) in front of their new house. They were married in September 1844 and it is probable that Heaphy was commissioned to paint the watercolour as a record of the occasion.

Bishop owned land in the Maitai Valley but is not known to have built there. It has been suggested that the house pictured here may have been on Nile Street, Nelson, where the Bishops had a home, but the hills behind the house rule out this location.

It is an interesting conundrum because, leaving aside the poorly drawn and out-of-scale couple, the detailed observation of the garden leaves us in no doubt that the artist painted it from life, if not in situ. The planting around the house, the flowerbeds and the vegetable garden are reasonably mature; even the sapling in the foreground has seen at least a season in the ground.

William Bishop (1817–1884) was one of Nelson's early settlers. He and Isaac Coates had traced the Maitai River to its source, east of Nelson, and published a diary of the 'excursion' in the *Nelson Examiner and New Zealand Chronicle* in February 1843. Later, when the Bishops moved to Wellington, Bishop was a director and sometime chairman of the New Zealand Steam Navigation Company.

The painting was given to the Alexander Turnbull Library by a granddaughter of William and Anna Bishop, who had 11 children. The Turnbull also holds a charming oval portrait by Heaphy of Anna Bishop from the same donor, showing a pretty woman with ringlets in a green dress holding a posy, assumed to be painted in the same year.

F A Molesworth, Newry, Port Nicholson, NZ

1844

WILLIAM MEIN SMITH 1799–1869

THIS PAINTING BY William Mein Smith is one of the finest early paintings of a New Zealand homestead, and is a fascinating record of early building and gardening. The house was built by Francis Molesworth (1818–1846), who had purchased several 100 acre (40 hectare) blocks of land in the first New Zealand Company sale in Wellington. He established a farm in the Hutt Valley which he called Tetcott, probably after a small settlement in Devon. The house was renamed Newry after its purchase in the mid-1840s by Alfred Ludlam.

Molesworth emigrated to New Zealand in 1840. He was born in Cornwall, where the family's seat is at Pencarrow, on the other side of Bodmin Moor from Tetcott. Pencarrow, with its 20 hectare heritage garden, is still owned by the Molesworth-St Aubyn family. Molesworth's brother, Sir William Molesworth, was a banker and one of the directors of the New Zealand Company.

Botanical writer Winsome Shepherd has described Smith's painting:

The wooden house with its steeply sloping shingled roof, had been brought out [from England] ready to erect. The forest trees and undergrowth around the house have been cleared as a precaution against fire. Wheat is ready for cutting. There are glass frames for cucumber and melons, and circular flower beds. The garden is well stocked with fruit trees and other plants from England.

The prefabricated house probably did not have a veranda, which would explain the rustic roof supports made out of forked tree-trunks. In due course Molesworth had a fine garden enclosed by a thorn hedge, the only one in the colony.

Shepherd also draws on HW Petre's *An Account of the Settlements of the New Zealand Company* (1842) to point out that trees, shrubs and other plants from Sir William Molesworth's Pencarrow were sent out to his brother, including camellia seedlings, the first to be grown in Wellington. In return, Francis sent home seeds including those of the New Zealand fuchsia, ramarama, red kowhai (better known nowadays as kaka beak), totara and karaka.

Smith has shown the supplejack hanging from tall trees and a tree stump in the centre to symbolise the clearing of the land. There is a companion painting of a view closer to the cleared bush, with wheat growing around it and a haystack.

Molesworth contributed significantly to the horticultural development of the fertile Hutt Valley. In 1845 he also finished building a flour mill as a joint venture with his neighbour Alfred Ludlam. Molesworth was later injured while felling a tree and returned to England, where he died in 1846. Ludlam took over the management of Molesworth's property and eventually bought it, the final payment being in 1847.

View of an ordinary New Zealand pa with potato plantations around it

1845

CYPRIAN BRIDGE 1807–1885

BEFORE EUROPEAN SETTLEMENT, the introduction of the European potato and other vegetables began with a gift of potatoes from Captain James Cook to a chief in Mercury Bay in 1769. The French explorer Marc-Joseph Marion du Fresne also planted potatoes, wheat, maize and nuts on Moturua Island in the Bay of Islands in 1772.

By the time of this painting by Major Cyprian Bridge, the European potato was widely and successfully cultivated by Maori. The painting shows a pa with fenced potato plantations at the front and to the right in the middle distance, with several people working in them. To the right of the path is a swampy area with fern or bracken and mangroves. The pa has strengthened palisade walls and loopholes to enable the firing of muskets around the base.

Cyprian Bridge was one of a number of military artists working in New Zealand in the middle of the nineteenth century, of which Horatio

Robley and the Prussian-trained Major Gustavus Ferdinand von Tempsky are the best known. British military officers usually had drawing lessons as part of their training, especially after the Napoleonic Wars, so they could draw the terrain for operational purposes.

Military historian Chris Pugsley suggests the subject of this painting is Tamati Waka Nene's pa at Okaihau, inland from Kerikeri in the Bay of Islands. Nene built the pa in March 1845, and Bridge and his force arrived the following month. Later Nene, who was pro-British, defeated Hone Heke at Pukenui. In January the following year, after the British occupation of Ruapekapeka pa, Nene, Heke and his ally Te Ruki Kawiti agreed on peace.

This painting comes from a sketchbook of paintings of various military actions during the Northern War, by both Major Bridge and Lance-Sergeant John Williams.

WILLIAM FOX 1812–1893

IN 1843 WILLIAM Fox was appointed resident agent for the New Zealand Company in Nelson, succeeding Arthur Wakefield, who was one of those killed in the skirmish between settlers and Maori at the Wairau. Fox held the position until 1848, the year of this watercolour, which he may have painted as a souvenir.

Fox took over his predecessor's house overlooking Blind Bay. The painting documents Fox's developing interest in gardening and horticulture, which also had a socio-political context in his work. As well as having to work on complex land claims, Fox also had to deal with the results of the New Zealand Company back-down from its original commitment to employ working-class settlers. To defuse the immigrants' anger, Fox introduced a scheme to employ them part-time and allocated them small sections on which to grow their own produce on their days off. He became interested in social reform and believed that gardening improved the mind and body of the gardener.

Fox practised what he preached, and while one suspects that his charming watercolour is somewhat idealised, even idyllic — he did, after all, send watercolours back to the New Zealand Company in London as a record of successful settlement — there is no reason to doubt the essential veracity of this garden view. The artist-gardener seems to be admiring the results of his efforts: on the left two grapevines, in the centre a flowerbed and presumably vegetables to the right.

The grapevines would be among the earliest in Nelson. Some Germans (mostly Silesians) from the Barossa Valley in South Australia stopped off at Nelson in 1843 and a few settled and planted vines. As the original growers died, the vineyards became neglected and died too. However, FHM Ellis & Sons made wine near Takaka from 'grapes and sundry fruits' between 1868 and 1939.

In May 1846, an article in the *Nelson Examiner and New Zealand Chronicle* gave 'Hints for colonial wine growers', which extolled the growing of vines on espaliers, as we see in Fox's painting. Grape-growing did not, however, seem to be successful; a writer to the same paper 20 years later was still exhorting Nelsonians to persevere with viticulture because of the similarity of the region's climate and soil to the German wine districts of the Rhine and Moselle. Fox went on to plant grapes for wine at Rangitikei.

Lower Westoe Rangitikei, 1860

1860

WILLIAM FOX 1812–1893

IN 1849, A year after moving to Wellington, William Fox bought a 5000 acre (2023 hectare) property on the Rangitikei River near Marton. He named it Westoe, after his birthplace, and built a house on the river flats which he called Lower Westoe, selling off the other half of the property. In 1860, when these two watercolours of Lower Westoe were painted, Fox was elected to Parliament as the member for Rangitikei.

It has been suggested that Fox's watercolours of his garden tell us more about the 'aristocratic' aspirations of an English country gentleman than its portrayal in aesthetic terms. Nevertheless, these paintings are unique in their era for their romantic mood, however idealised.

The Reverend Canon JW Stack, in his *Further Maoriland Adventures*, recorded his visit to Westoe in 1861:

Here everything that refined taste and artistic skill could accomplish had been done to enhance the natural beauty of the situation. It was a pleasant surprise to find in such an out of the way part of New Zealand a miniature reproduction of an English gentleman's country house, with all its comforts and conveniences both inside and out.

Certainly, the more charming of the two views of the garden at Lower Westoe (at left) supports Stack's perception, with its vignette of two elegantly dressed women occupied with some flowers. Completing the image is the watering can and the basket or possibly flax kete. Beyond them, in the middle ground, is the gardener, probably Maori, next to a wheelbarrow, and Fox has set the entire scene against an impressive though fanciful backdrop of wooded bush.

The wheelbarrow and gardening tools also appear in Fox's other, equally dramatic, Lower Westoe garden view (at right), but this time they are in the foreground and without the gardener. At the end of the vista established by a broad path, a couple is seated on a rather large-looking garden seat, a vivid sunset sky behind them. Fox has included a few flowers on the right of the path.

Following his two weeks as premier in 1856, Fox spent most of 1857 to 1859 working on the Westoe property. In 1859 he came out of virtual retirement when he was appointed commissioner of crown lands for the Wellington province and in 1860 he became unofficial leader of the opposition, leading to his next premiership in 1861. It may be that the paintings record a tranquil period just preceding his return to politics. However, there is no indication of what specific purpose Fox had in mind when he painted his garden views.

Fox was a busy politician and spent some time back in England during his ownership of Westoe. The property was managed by Arthur Halcombe, who represented Rangitikei on the Provincial Council. Letters between them reveal that they shared common interests in horses, racing and viticulture, with Fox writing in the 1860s: 'the kind I rely on most for wine is the seyraz [shiraz]'. The correspondence also shows that Fox did not always agree with Halcombe's estate management or his accounts.

WILLIAM FOX 1812–1893

BECAUSE IT WAS built on the river flats, Lower Westoe was prone to flooding, so William Fox eventually decided to build a new house on higher ground. Designed by Charles Tringham, later the architect of the Italianate tower of Queen Margaret College, Wellington, the new Westoe was apparently not finished until 1874, suggesting either that Fox made a mistake in his dating of this painting or that he chose to render it in the manner of an architect's 'perspective' — there certainly is a touch of the ruler about its style. The elegant homestead still stands and remains in private ownership.

A photograph by William Harding, taken ca. 1875 and held by the Alexander Turnbull Library, shows a very similar view of the house, though closer, shortly after its completion.

Later in life Fox, who had become increasingly concerned with social reform, became very active in the temperance movement. He founded the New Zealand Alliance in 1886, the year after he sold Westoe 'at a considerable loss', art historian Jill Trevelyan tells us, and retired to Auckland.

The house of Alfred Ludlam Esq., River Hutt, New Zealand

1850

FRANCIS DILLON BELL 1822–98

IN THE MID-1840s, Alfred Ludlam (1810–1877), who had arrived in New Zealand in 1840, purchased a farm in the Lower Hutt from his business partner, Francis Molesworth (see page 26). He named it Newry after his birthplace in County Down, Ireland, and in 1850 completed the building of the new house in this painting. Ludlam then established a significant garden for produce and plant sales. One of his orders, from Camden Nurseries in Sydney in 1848, emphasises fruit trees but also includes various viburnums, roses (Banksia and Perdita) and a *Crinum capense*.

For the New Zealand Exhibition in Dunedin in 1865, Ludlam wrote an important 23-page essay which was published in the *Transactions of the New Zealand Institute* in 1868. Describing himself as 'a lover of plants' and 'no botanist', he called it 'Essay on the Cultivation and Acclimatisation of Trees and Plants'. It describes the development of his garden, listing most of the major plants and trees he planted there. Ludlam was a fervent advocate for the establishment of a botanical garden for Wellington, and concludes his essay with his regret the government had not established such a facility, writing 'Perhaps, when peace is once more restored to the Northern Island, we may hope to see some advance made in that direction.'

In 1868 Ludlam opened his extensive grounds to the public, and after his death in 1877 the property became McNab's Gardens, a tea-garden popular with daytrippers from Wellington. After 15 years it was bought by a Mrs Ross, who changed its name to Bellevue Gardens, and its popularity peaked during the 1890s. Open to the public, it was a venue for dinners, picnics and events, including the annual Chrysanthemum Show. In the 1890s it was painted by Mabel Hill and James Nairn (see pages 85 and 95).

Ludlam's wishes for a botanic garden were eventually fulfilled. His obituary in the *Evening Post* on November 15, 1877 read, 'To him Wellington is principally indebted for the Botanical Gardens, which, although far inferior to what they should be, form nevertheless an agreeable recreation ground.' The piece praised his selection of the site and noted his financial contribution used 'to stock this domain with choice and rare trees and plants'.

Bell's painting of Ludlam's house and garden was made in 1850, the year of Ludlam's marriage to Sydney woman Fanny Minto. Besides the house and impressive conservatory, the very beginnings of the extensive gardens can be seen against the background of the partially cleared bush. We can see that Ludlam has planted nikau at strategic points and later photographs show the now large nikau on either side of the drive, as well as conifers planted in the 1860s and 1870s. Through the trees on the right of the conservatory Bell has shown two buildings which may be adjacent to Ludlam's flour mill.

House of Captain King, R.A., Jermyn Street, Auckland

1858

MARY KING 1829–1907?

THIS PAINTING OF the home of Captain William King of the Royal Artillery, the commander of the British army in Auckland, and his wife Mary was painted not long before the couple left Auckland for Malta. *The Daily Southern Cross* recorded King's departure on 26 August, 1859:

We are losing a valuable man at a critical time. Captain King has served in New Zealand during nine years, both here and in the Taranaki and Wellington Provinces, in all of which places his departure will be a source of regret to many friends — military and civilian.

The Brigade Orders published in the same newspaper describe Captain King's 'intelligence, zeal and ability' and the high regard in which he was held by the former commander of the military forces in New Zealand, Colonel Robert Henry Wynyard.

Captain and Mrs King lived in this house on Jermyn Street, Auckland, essentially the continuation of Custom House Street, east of Britomart Point. The house had been built by Captain David Rough, the former Auckland harbourmaster and customs collector. It was drawn by Wynyard in 1849 in a view from Official Bay which also shows the colonel's own house (formerly owned by surveyor Felton Mathew) and that of the former colonial secretary Willoughby Shortland. St Paul's church is shown above. Wynyard's drawing shows the house very much as it appears in King's painting.

In *The Lively Capital*, Una Platts quotes a description of the house in 1842:

a very small white weatherboarded cottage with a verandah & creeping plants . . . entwining thereon, quite in keeping with a garden wherein the useful & ornamental were elegantly blended by the hand of taste.

In the Kings' era it was a very good address: Sir John Logan Campbell had built his home Logan Bank in Jermyn Street in 1842. The Kings' house was demolished in 1907 and after further land reclamation Jermyn Street was torn up in 1918 to make way for what is now Anzac Avenue.

In November 1858 *The Daily Southern Cross* recorded the auction by Connell & Ridings of 'the whole of [the Kings'] household furniture' including an Erard double-action harp and a rosewood cottage piano, 'nearly new'. There can be little doubt that King painted this colourful and descriptive watercolour as a souvenir of their home and garden. She may also have been the gardener as well as the artist, as the commander of the British army in Auckland would no doubt have been a busy man.

The Kings' gentility is reflected in her painting of the garden and the house beyond. There is loving attention to detail. The garden is formal but not overly so, with flowers and shrubs and pleasantly laid-out beds and paths. The Red Ensign, indicating Captain King's position as commander, is prominent, while less so are the two soldiers on the far right. In front of what we would today call the picture window, two well-dressed gentlemen are viewing the drawing room, where the piano and harp were no doubt important features.

II. LATER NINETEENTH CENTURY

1860–1890

THE INCREASING DIVERSITY of New Zealand painting in the second half of the nineteenth century is reflected in the variety of approaches to the paintings of gardens shown in this section. We also start to get a better feel for some different garden styles around the country: Albin Martin's farm cottage garden at East Tamaki; Mrs Hamar Arden's tidy garden in New Plymouth; Captain Sharp's city garden overlooking Wellington Harbour, and the grand design of Harry Cobley's beachside acres at Devonport.

Opening the section, however, is a view by Irish-born Richard Kelly of the developing hillside suburbs of Dunedin, with some glimpses of gardens. Kelly moved to Otago in 1862 as part of the gold rushes, describing himself as 'a passing visitor from Melbourne'. However, he worked until his death as a draughtsman in Christchurch and in Palmerston, Otago. Kelly's meticulously detailed depiction of trees and plants, as well as the buildings and the prominent blue fence, matches for skill and technical brilliance fellow professional draughtsman Charles Igglesden's views of his uncle Captain Sharp's house and garden in Wellington. Sadly very few other paintings by either artist are known.

Of particular interest are the large gardens of Henry Tiffen in Napier and Sir George Grey on Kawau Island, north of Auckland. Both were planted with exotic species, especially trees, sourced from around the world. These two gardeners represent the fashion for what was called acclimatisation — essentially the introduction of non-native species — which brought about the establishment of acclimatisation societies around the country.

One of our finest painters at that time was Alfred Sharpe. As a conservationist, he was distressed by the kauri logging and destruction of the native bush around Auckland and further afield. Given that he was totally against acclimatisation, it is a little paradoxical for Sharpe to have painted Grey's garden at Kawau. With Constance Cumming's painting from a slightly different viewpoint, a good visual record of Mansion House during Grey's residence has been preserved. The flowering *Agave americana*, a feature of the Mansion House garden, also appears in Joseph Annabell's painting of Henry Tiffen's garden in Napier.

The works of the Reverend John Kinder — gardener, painter, photographer and antiquarian — straddle these three decades. The earliest of his paintings included here is dated 1856. However, because the Whatman paper Kinder used for some paintings is watermarked 1886, it is generally held that many, if not most, of Kinder's paintings in this, his signature style, were not painted until much later in his life. Indeed, many were probably painted after his retirement in 1880, when he would have had more time for art.

By all accounts the garden at St John's College, Meadowbank, which Kinder designed and developed, and for which he employed a gardener at his own expense, was exceptional. Kinder painted it several times. He then created his own garden at Woodcroft, Remuera, about which less is known.

Albin Martin, a farmer, was another exceptional artist, though not as prolific as either Kinder or Sharpe. Martin is one of the few New Zealand painters from this period whose artistic pedigree is well documented. He had been a pupil of the renowned English painter John Linnell, who subsequently became a great friend, and he knew other prominent English artists such as Samuel Palmer and George Richmond.

Martin's *Garden at East Tamaki* is small masterpiece. The flower garden it depicts, along with the essential vegetable garden, was important to the Martin family. Its beginnings were mentioned in a letter from Jemima Martin to her sister:

> . . . [flax] is a very handsome plant & very useful. I can give you but little idea of it as it is so unlike ordinary flax. If we want a piece of string for any purpose we have nothing to do but to go out & cut a leaf of this handsome plant & take a strip of it . . . We are just making a garden & I hope to be able to do a little in it . . . the children mean to do a great deal.

From other letters we know that the garden had at least hydrangeas, brought from England, roses and belladonnas.

Botanical painting in this period is represented by Sarah Featon's *Pikiarero (Clematis hexasepala)* of around 1880, one of the original paintings for *The Art Album of New Zealand Flora*, the first New Zealand book to feature colour reproductions. The project to publish all 40 paintings was never completed; the first three parts issued were published together in 1889. Featon's husband Edward wrote the text, which includes advice to gardeners and nurserymen about which plants are suitable for gardens and commercial propagation.

In addition to Kinder's striking photograph of pikiarero from around 1865, there is one more image of clematis from around the same time as Featon's. By Charles Goldie, at the time a 15-year-old schoolboy, it was painted for the 'Hand-painted door panel' category of the annual exhibition of the Auckland Society of Arts in 1886.

The young Goldie was already on his way to being one of the best professionally trained painters of his generation; the skills of Winifred Kerr Taylor, two years his junior, could call on little more than the instruction of a governess. Her tentative though delightful painting shows Alberton in Mount Albert, Auckland, where she was born, raised and died. It was painted before Taylor's mother began to develop the extensive flower garden and orchard on the slopes below the house for which Alberton would become renowned.

Dunedin 1862 from the zig-zag of Graham Street, between High and Maclaggan streets

1862

RICHARD KELLY 1820–1873

THE EARLIEST RECORDED painting by Ireland-born Richard Kelly is an 1858 watercolour of the bridge over the Yarra River in Studley Park, Melbourne (State Library of Victoria). Three years later, Kelly moved from Sandridge (now Port Melbourne) to Dunedin. There, in 1862, the year he painted this painting, he was recorded as 'a passing visitor from Victoria'.

This painting shows both Richard Kelly's profession as a draughtsman and his vision as an artist, albeit one with a fascination for detail. His professional leanings are apparent in the structure of this striking watercolour, with the blue-green fence lining the footpath and the finely rendered chimney and roof at the bottom right.

Kelly's title indicates his viewpoint on Graham Street, which intersects with Maclaggan Street at the far right, below the quarry. The artist's view is to the west towards Mornington and Belleknowes.

The painting is interesting for the record it provides of the development of suburban gardens in Dunedin. There is a young cabbage tree in the foreground and a tall, mature specimen just to the left of the middle of the composition. There are punga ferns in the gully and the fence which begins in the foreground takes our eye to the rather oriental-looking rata.

Kelly has taken great pleasure in recording the tidiness of the gardens, including the herbaceous border of the path on the left, the well-kept lawn above the lower house at the bottom right corner and its plantings of shrubs. There are some other nice touches such as the fence bordering Graham Street, which is in the process of being built. Perhaps it's Sunday morning, which is why neither the artist nor the fencer is at work.

Auckland, from the veranda of Mr Reader Wood's cottage

1856

JOHN KINDER 1819–1903

READER WOOD (1821–1895) and his wife May (née Holland) were close friends of the Reverend John Kinder. Wood was an architect and politician — the MP for Eden and Parnell, where he lived. He was also colonial treasurer and commissioner of customs in the Fox ministry, and was later a member of the Auckland Provincial Council and served on Sir George Grey's Provincial Executive before retiring from politics in 1881.

Wood arrived in New Zealand in 1844 and saw active service in the Volunteer Artillery. He practised as an architect in Auckland and was appointed to a succession of government positions, including government architect. Wood assisted Kinder in the design of St Andrew's Church, Epsom, and supervised its construction.

Wood probably both designed and built his relatively modest house, halfway down what was then called Hobson Bay Road, and is now Brighton Road. However, notwithstanding the title adopted by the Auckland Art Gallery, Auckland is not visible from Brighton Road; the magnificent view, therefore, is across Parnell towards the northeast, with a glimpse of Hobson Bay, towards Devonport and Rangitoto.

The watercolour is in Kinder's distinctive style, meticulously composed with nice touches of detail. The late afternoon sun casts shadows across the veranda, delicately catching the leaves of the climbing roses, just coming into flower, on either side of the steps down to the lawn and the undeveloped parklands beyond: a very satisfying blend of architecture and landscape, Kinder's passions.

One can imagine the artist sitting at a table in the main reception room, a little back from the veranda, where the sun would have been in his eyes, taking down the view just as he saw it.

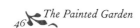

1856

from Veranda
of Mr Reader Wood's Cottage

Pikiarero (Clematis paniculata)

ca 1865

JOHN KINDER 1819–1903

JOHN KINDER WAS one of New Zealand's earliest photographers. His reputation as an artist is based on both his landscape paintings and his photographs. His first photographs date from 1859, around the time of his marriage, while the last dated photographs were taken in 1888 at his home at Woodcroft in Remuera. According to photography historian Ron Brownson's book on Kinder, *Pikiarero (Clematis paniculata)* is a rare example of a close-up still life photograph by Kinder, and an equally rare interior. As a photograph by an early gardener and pioneer photographer — and one who knew his native flora as well as his European botany — this image is unique and perhaps the first true photographic work of art in New Zealand.

Kinder gave careful thought to the set-up of the still life. He selected a Parian ware jug that features a petalled flower similar to the clematis in its moulded decoration; it can be seen just below the kaka beak flower that Kinder draped over the handle of the jug, partly obscuring the classical figure whose leg alone can be made out. The striking effect of the cream flowers and jug silhouetted against the dark obscurity of the background makes this a masterpiece.

Kinder used Maori names when referring to indigenous plants. There are several native bush clematis variously referred to as pikiarero, as by Kinder, or puawhananga. A tree-climbing vine, for Maori its flowering marked the beginning of spring and the eeling season. On special occasions, Maori girls wore wreaths made from a smaller variety, *Clematis hexasepala*, as painted later by Sarah Featon (page 73).

Saint John's College

1878

JOHN KINDER 1819–1903

JOHN KINDER CAME to New Zealand to take up the position of headmaster of the Church of England Grammar School established in Auckland by the Bishop of New Zealand, George Selwyn. Selwyn had appointed Kinder to the post while on a visit to England in 1855, when Kinder was a curate and master of a grammar school in Uttoxeter, Staffordshire. Kinder duly arrived in Auckland in October that year to take up his post at the school, for which land had been purchased in Parnell.

Kinder did not enjoy teaching boys very much and in 1869 applied for the position of master of St John's College. Although successful, he did not take up residence at the Anglican theological college, in the Auckland suburb of Meadowbank, until 1872.

The college, established by Selwyn in 1842 at Waimate North in the Bay of Islands and moved to Auckland in 1844, had been closed for several years. Kinder was responsible not only for renewing its functions and its upkeep but, using his own money, he also undertook the landscaping of the grounds and the establishment of its gardens.

His design and plantings are described in J King Davis's history of the college, published in 1911:

Year by year under the loving and artistic care of the new Master, garden and glen became, more and more, places of delight; indeed, no student or visitor in those times will ever forget the terrace on the north side of the stone building, with its well-trimmed box hedge, the tiny lawn below, the flower beds rich with bloom, and below them the maze of the pathway, now running round the head of the gully, with pretty glimpses opening out of Rangitoto and the sea, now diving into the recesses of the glen and bordered by the native trees and ferns, here winding to take advantage of a nook that a little care has converted into a fairy bower, here to follow the banks of a tiny stream, while it penetrated further and further into the small bush, always beautiful, marked also in parts with dainty and delicate loveliness.

Kinder's fondness for St John's College is demonstrated by the 19 sketches and paintings, in addition to photographs, he made of its buildings, gardens and chapel. This is one of the most charming because it includes the gardener at work and a small figure walking along the path, probably the master himself. The wooden building on the left is the dining hall and to the right is the dean's house, a two-storeyed stone building.

Kinder resigned from his position at the college in 1880 because of a false accusation by a board member. When he resigned he made a point of stating that he could no longer be responsible for the garden, and unfortunately the gardener was dismissed at the same time.

View from Woodcroft, Remuera, August 16, 1888

1888

JOHN KINDER 1819–1903

THOSE FAMILIAR WITH the Auckland suburb of Remuera will find it difficult to conceive of a time when a view like this was possible from the neighbourhood of Arney Road. John Kinder had the house Woodcroft built after his resignation from St John's College in 1880. He had expected his resignation to be rejected but once accepted he negotiated an extension of his notice until the construction of his new house in Arney Road was completed in 1882. The handsome two-storeyed wooden building had spacious rooms and an extensive garden, with a view from upstairs to North Head in Devonport and Rangitoto beyond, as shown in this painting taken from the small balcony.

Kinder drew on the experience he had gained at St John's College when laying out the garden at Woodcroft. Art historian Michael Dunn, in *John Kinder: Paintings and Photographs*, writes:

Judging by the photographs and paintings he made of the house and garden, he again linked house and grounds by pathways and steps. These led down from the elevated position of the house to spacious lawns, shaped flower-beds and plantings of large trees, and one of his favourite evergreens, the Norfolk Island pine.

Kinder lived at Woodcroft with his wife Celia until his death in 1903. Here, besides gardening, Kinder painted the beautiful views of New Zealand for which he is best known, based on the many sketches and photographs he had made during his travels over the previous 25 years. The last paintings and photographs of Woodcroft are dated 1888. He also catalogued his extensive library, and in 1900 completed a short autobiography for his family, called *A Brief Account of My Life*.

Kinder is likely to have chosen the name Woodcroft because of a connection to the England of his youth. It may refer to the fourteenth-century Woodcroft Castle near Peterborough which Kinder and his antiquarian-leaning student friends at Cambridge could have visited.

Garden at East Tamaki

ca 1865

ALBIN MARTIN 1813–1888

GARDEN AT EAST Tamaki is the best painted record of Albin Martin's home and garden. As an oil painting of a garden it is unique in New Zealand art of this period. Its painterly style — reviewers criticised Martin for painting too small and with too little detail — is very idiosyncratic but Continental in influence. It probably dates from the 1860s, as it was acquired by Martin's friend James Mackelvie before his return to Britain in 1871.

When they emigrated from England on the *Cashmere* in 1851, Martin and his wife Jemima brought plant material with them, including hydrangeas. Cuttings from these original plants were planted in their later Ellerslie garden, where they continued to flourish.

Even in the earliest months after their arrival, gardening and flowers were on their minds. Jemima Martin wrote in August 1852:

We were in Auckland in the summer & saw but few wild flowers & those very small & poor & I believe this is the general character of the wild flowers. Some of the flowering trees are beautiful & the way in which our English garden flowers flourish & grow like weeds is wonderful. Anything everything grows without care.

Albin wrote to John Linnell in September of the same year:

As far as a beautiful country, climate and soil goes, we have made a most decided change for the better, the only thing we want, is the society of our friends in England. Just as the summer is beginning to decline with you, our spring is commencing, and we are now very busy in getting our garden in order. I hope the place which last year was but a wilderness, will soon have roses blossoming in it . . .

And by May 1856, the Martins' eldest daughter, Mary Mergellina, wrote to her aunt in England:

I had to leave off yesterday to get the tea whilst Mama went out for a few minutes to plant some roses in her new garden.

In this undeniably pretty painting we see family members perhaps picking flowers or pruning in the flower garden of Stour House, named after the river in Martin's birth county, Dorset — highly appropriate given the garden's site on the banks of the Tamaki River. Martin has indicated the presence of the Tamaki with a thin white brushstroke at the base of the slender central tree. The sunflowers are distinctive.

The Martins also had a vegetable garden on which they were highly dependent because of the distance they lived from any markets. It had its own enclosure in the back yard, fenced to keep out the chickens, goats, pigs and dogs. The flower garden may also have been fenced, but perhaps for aesthetic purposes and to emphasise the romance of the scene, Martin omitted it.

View looking from Captain Sharp's garden, Wellington

1868

CHARLES IGGLESDEN 1832–1920

FOLLOWING SERVICE WITH the British Army in India, Captain Charles Sharp (1806–1880) arrived in Wellington in 1841. He was appointed customs officer at Wanganui and harbourmaster and pilot of the port of Wellington from 1854 to 1860. Later he became a trustee of the Permanent Equitable Building and Investment Society of Wellington.

His house was one of the first on Woolcombe Street — later Wellington Terrace and now The Terrace — near where it joined Salamanca Road. The garden was so extensive that 25 houses were built on it when the estate was subdivided.

Charles Igglesden was Sharp's nephew. His professional eye for detail and skill as a painter, together with his personal connection with the subject, combine to ensure that this and the following house and garden views are unequalled.

Painting in December 1868, Igglesden has paid as much attention to the planting, colour and variety of this ordered and well-kept garden as

he has to the landmarks, both built and natural, from close to hand — there is a 'To let' sign in the window of the house on the other side of the road — to Lower Hutt in the far distance. The weeding gardener, who also appears in the companion painting (on page 59), could be Captain Sharp himself.

Many features in the painting have been identified. The neighbouring house, with the galvanised iron chimney flue, belonged to Joseph Nancarrow, who was the first examiner of engineers for merchant ships and must have been known to Sharp. On the right is Wellington harbour with a pier projecting out from Lambton Quay, with Midland Point beyond. The building on the left with the spire is the Wellington Grammar School (later Wellington College), and beyond it St Mary's Church on Hill Street. On the crest of the hill, where Wadestown is today, is the The Grange, the home of renowned pastoralist, politician and Wellington community leader Captain William Barnard Rhodes.

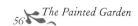

Captain Sharp's residence

1868

CHARLES IGGLESDEN 1832–1920

TO TAKE THIS view of Captain Sharp's house, Charles Igglesden has positioned himself in the vicinity of the bottom of the circular drive as it turns down to Woolcombe Street, as depicted on the previous page. The steepness of this part of the section is clear in both paintings. Igglesden has more scope for his sense of humour in this view, with its phenomenal number of interesting details. Indeed, it is almost as if the view from the house is the formal view and this view of the house the informal, though no doubt both were painted for his uncle. It is a substantial house with two storeys in the rear section.

While the garden view is very much a late spring or summer view, in this painting the leafless tree on the right suggests that it is late autumn, as do the recently acquired young trees, still in their bright green boxes.

Captain Sharp was clearly a keen gardener, or at least keen on his garden. On the far right of the veranda he has built a lean-to potting shed. The planting and trees on the left are beautifully observed and meticulously recorded.

The gardener, wearing his distinctive hat, reappears here, sharpening his scythe while Captain Sharp's red-jacketed pet monkey chews on something as one of several dogs looks on. Another dog on the veranda is on his hind legs begging to a woman in a bonnet, perhaps Mrs Sharp. Igglesden has painted objects reflected in the glass panes of the French doors and to the right of the open front door is a green portfolio stand above which are two bird cages.

On the left side of the house there is a rainwater butt, positioned under the end of the veranda gutter, with some yellow lilies nearby and beyond it, a palisade fence.

Untitled [House and garden]

ca 1870

HAMAR ARDEN 1816–1895
& FRANCIS ARDEN 1841–1899

THIS DELIGHTFUL AND carefully observed painting has been attributed to the father-and-son painters Hamar and Francis Arden. It shows a well-established New Plymouth settler's house, believed to have been on Powderham Street, in the centre of the city today, with a view due south towards Mount Taranaki. There is an extensive, newly planted vegetable garden and what appears to be a summerhouse under construction.

Hamar Arden was quite prolific, painting views of the New Plymouth township and surrounding landscapes. He frequently featured Mount Taranaki, including in the painting (now sadly deteriorated) of his single-storey Bell Block house from around 1860, recording his charming garden with circular flower beds, lilies, various shrubs and a cabbage tree.

The New Plymouth community had high expectations of Francis Arden's potential as an artist according to the *Taranaki Herald*, which in April 1871 announced:

Our readers may have noticed an advertisement in our columns for some time past, announcing that an exhibition of works of art would be held in Auckland during the present month. For this exhibition Mr. F. H. Arden, jun., has finished two large watercolour drawings, which were exhibited in the Taranaki Institute a short time since, previous to his forwarding them to Auckland. Both pictures were greatly admired. One of them consists of a view of Mount Egmont taken somewhere near the Waiwakaiho bridge. It is about the truest view of the mountain we have seen; and the river is very picturesquely drawn, although perfectly true to nature. The other picture represents H.M.S. Barrosa taking in sail off Tiri-tiri . . . Both pictures cannot but help attracting considerable attention from connoisseurs in Auckland . . . Mr Arden's views of the Armed Constabulary Redoubt at Waiiti, and Captain Messenger's Redoubt, give an excellent idea of the land in that part of the Province, and the beautiful views that exist there for an artist to depict. We may state that Mr. Arden, jun., intends to follow the profession of an artist, and from the sketches we have seen, we should imagine that with such talent as he has exhibited, he will attain in a few years a prominent position in the profession he has chosen.

If Francis Arden did, as has been suggested, spend time as a painter in Auckland, there is little to corroborate it. Following his death in 1899 his obituary in the *Taranaki Herald* described him as having been a printer, working for the *Herald* and newspapers in Timaru and New South Wales. Back in New Plymouth, Arden 'for many years lived quietly at his home on the Frankley Road where he indulged in his favourite hobbies of aboriculture and painting, for he was no mean artist'.

Dear Granny Arden's home in Courtney Street, New Plymouth

ca 1880

HAMAR ARDEN 1815–1895

THIS ELEGANT HOUSE and beautifully kept garden was the home of the artist and his wife Alice on what is now called Courtenay Street, the continuation east of Powderham Street in the centre of New Plymouth. The informality of their first garden at Bell Block, recorded by Arden soon after their arrival (Puke Ariki), has developed into a formal, ordered plan with strong lines, lawns and pretty flowerbeds with roses and overhanging ferns and trees. The veranda is entwined with flowering creepers. The late afternoon sun casts long shadows and bathes the house and garden in a warm, soft light, creating a peaceful atmosphere.

As this was Arden's own home and a haven after the rigours of early settler life, it is not surprising that its depiction is redolent of a much loved and cherished place. It also seems to express the character of his wife, aged around 61 at this time who, according to her obituary in the *Taranaki Herald*, 'possessed a most amiable disposition, and was never wearied of performing acts of kindness and benevolence, which endeared her to a large circle of friends and acquaintances.'

Auckland Harbour and Rangitoto Island from the garden of Harry Cobley's house

ca 1870

JOHN HOYTE 1835–1913

SOMERSET-BORN WILLIAM Henry Cobley (1839–1913) — known as Harry — had been unsuccessful on the Otago goldfields, but struck it lucky when he moved north. In August 1867 he was one of four men who discovered the Shotover gold claim on the Hurunui Creek, Thames. A year and half later, having made his fortune, he moved to Auckland, married the young Louisa Penman and built this mansion on Cheltenham Road, Devonport. Cheltenham Beach was originally called Cobley Beach, and he named the nearby areas of Cheltenham and Vauxhall. Cobley then launched a new ferry service for Devonport in 1869.

John Hoyte was teaching at Auckland Grammar School when he painted this view and the one on page 67 of Harry and Louisa Cobley's home, presumably as a commission. Hoyte had arrived in New Zealand in 1861 and by the late 1860s had achieved a good reputation as a competent landscape painter.

On viewing these watercolours of Cobley's garden and house (see page 67), there can be no doubt about their exact location. In this painting, the artist is looking due north from the house, with Rangitoto to the right.

By the time these pictures were painted, the Cobleys had achieved quite a lot in terms of landscaping and planting. The house and garden are surrounded by a white-painted picket fence and much of the new planting is along this fenceline. The fine view over the pond and its fountain, the wide shell paths and shrubs to the Hauraki Gulf and Great Barrier Island, visible in the distance, is a classic Auckland vista.

Because of the rise and fall of the land, the fence on the beach side of the house dips down from left and right to give an uninterrupted view from the house, a kind of ha-ha.

Harry Cobley's house, Devonport, Auckland

ca 1870

JOHN HOYTE 1835–1913

FOR THIS PAINTING, John Hoyte has moved to the rear of the Cobleys' block, towards the southwest corner, far enough back to include North Head on the right, with the line of trees indicating Cheltenham Road and just the summit of Rangitoto on the far left.

Three levels of terracing with connecting flights of steps are visible. The artist has shown the family on the veranda; the Cobleys had six children, the first four of whom were born in this house. The third child, their first boy, was named William Henry after his father and became a gardener. The house was demolished in the 1970s.

Tiffen House and the original St Paul's Church

ca 1870

JOSEPH ANNABELL 1815–1893

JOSEPH ANNABELL, a Hastings artist, painted a good number of portraits in the area, many of which were based on photographs by Samuel Carnell (1832–1920). However, Carnell's photograph of the Tiffen house does not show the neighbouring St Paul's Presbyterian Church which Annabell has added in, perhaps explaining its odd perspective. Another Carnell photograph, a closer view, includes four women playing croquet, as are the figures in the painting.

The painting shows the Napier house and garden of Henry Tiffen (1819–1896), surveyor, pastoralist, land commissioner, politician, community leader, horticulturist and entrepreneur. Tiffen came to New Zealand in 1842 as an assistant surveyor for the New Zealand Company. In 1852 he took up and later purchased the Homewood run, near Otane in Hawke's Bay. As Wellington provincial surveyor, in 1856 he took on the responsibility for the Napier land office and laid out the townships of Clive and Havelock North. Tiffen was a philanthropist and had a high profile in community affairs. He was elected to the first Hawke's Bay Provincial Council in 1859, was involved with the Napier harbour improvement and was the first chairman of the Hawke's Bay County Council.

Tiffen imported many plants and exotic trees to plant on his property, one of which has survived: a white kurrajong (*Brachychiton populneum*), recognised as a fine example and retained by the city council when the Tiffen house was removed in the 1950s to make room for a car park. (The Napier Borough Council had purchased the Tiffen property in 1907 to build the Municipal Theatre in Tennyson Street, which was destroyed in the 1931 earthquake.)

Tiffen did not have any children, but his brother Frederick and his wife Lucy had many. Their property was called Elmshill, and they also had a house in Clyde Road not far from Henry Tiffen's house. While the identity of the figures in the painting is not known, they are likely to be Lucy Tiffen and four of her daughters.

CONSTANCE CUMMING 1837–1924

THE REMARKABLE GEORGE Grey (1812–1898) was twice governor of New Zealand, premier from 1877 to 1879, and was also one of the finest scholars of his era resident in New Zealand.

He was an antiquarian, scientist, linguist, connoisseur and collector of art, manuscripts and books and an author of scholarly books on Maori language and culture. His gifts of books, manuscripts and art ensured the establishment of Auckland's library and art gallery.

In 1862 Grey purchased Kawau Island in the Hauraki Gulf, 50 km north of Auckland. Over the next 26 years, until he sold it on his return to England in 1888, he spent a fortune turning Kawau into a botanical garden and zoological park. The island was also the location of New Zealand's earliest copper-mining enterprises, and Grey enlarged and embellished the mine superintendent's house to create what is known as Mansion House.

In January 1877, the Scottish travel writer and artist Constance Cumming visited Grey, who would become premier of New Zealand in October that year. She had been a guest of her cousin Sir Arthur Gordon, governor of Fiji, and she recorded her experiences there and over several months in New Zealand in her second book. *At Home in Fiji* was published in London in 1881 — a combination of diary, travelogue and letters to family and friends.

Her detailed, enthusiastic descriptions depict a paradise island created by Grey:

So palms and pines of many sorts here grow side by side, with all kinds of indigenous hard wood; hops and vines festoon orange trees, while mulberries and loquats, apples, quinces, pears and strawberries all flourish. Peaches, apricots and figs grow into luxurious thickets wherever they are once planted and bear fruit abundantly. Flowers are equally luxuriant — and one tithe of the care bestowed on a garden in Fiji is here rewarded by a glow of blossom: sweet-peas, jessamine, mignonette, and many other well-nigh forgotten delights, make the whole air fragrant. The house stands at the head of a lovely little bay, and only a green lawn and a belt of tall flowering aloes intervene between it and the shore. This bay, like all the shores of the isle, is fringed with large trees, called by the Maoris Pohutukawa — ie, the brine-sprinkled — because it loves to outstretch its wide boughs over the salt sea.

Sir George Grey's home on the Kawau was one of a large number of finished watercolours Cumming made in New Zealand, and one of 27 displayed in the New Zealand section of the Colonial and Indian Exhibition in London in 1886.

Prominent features of Cumming's painting include the magnificent pohutukawa in flower, the plantings of pines on the hill and the agaves, some of which are in flower, along the high-water mark. These are *Agave americana* — sometimes called American aloe — which take many years to flower and then die.

Pikiarero (Clematis hexasepala)

ca 1880

SARAH FEATON 1848-1927

OVER 40 YEARS had passed since five of Martha King's botanical paintings, many hand-coloured, were published in London in 1845 (see page 22) and yet the book of Sarah Featon's paintings, published in the late 1880s, was the first colour publication to be produced in New Zealand. This advance was made possible by the invention of chromolithography.

The Art Album of New Zealand Flora, being a systematic and popular description of the native flowering plants of New Zealand and the adjacent islands was written by Featon's husband Edward with quotations from Joseph Hooker's *Handbook of the New Zealand Flora*.

Volume One — in the end the only volume of the three planned to appear — was itself initially issued in three parts, the first in 1887, parts two and three in 1888 and finally as one volume in 1889. With its decorative frontispiece and 40 fine chromolithographic plates, *The Art Album of New Zealand Flora* is a handsome volume and at the time of its publication was favourably compared with Walter Buller's *A History of the Birds of New Zealand*. Featon's lively and accurate watercolours were described by art writer Janet Paul as 'bold and strongly decorative'.

Edward Featon's text, which may occasionally be a little high-flown and florid, reveals his extensive botanical and traditional Maori plant knowledge. He was especially keen on native plants and not only consulted nurserymen in Auckland and Christchurch but also exhorted them to widen the range of native plants they sold.

In the book he offers domestic gardeners practical advice on selection and planting to encourage their successful propagation. For example, his text accompanying this plate concludes:

As an addition to our gardens, the graceful 'Pikiarero' is well worthy of attention; and few enclosures are without a secluded corner, or a lattice, where it would be a worthy addition, as it is hardy, quick-growing and beautiful. If the young plants are transplanted in the autumn, there is no difficulty in obtaining a successful growth.

The first part of the book was advertised in December 1887 with the following endorsement by governor-general Sir George Grey, to whom it was dedicated: 'A most interesting and beautiful collection of paintings'.

Two further volumes were planned, and the majority of the paintings were completed, but whether because of the cost or Edward Featon's death, they never eventuated. The next we know of either Featon or her paintings is that in 1918 she was so poor that she felt pressured to sell the original paintings to reduce the mortgage her son and daughter-in-law would inherit when she died. Although she felt they were worth £1000, she sold them to the Dominion Museum, now the Museum of New Zealand, for only £150 because she felt strongly they should remain in New Zealand and not go to the South Kensington Museum (now the Victoria and Albert) or the Smithsonian Institution in Washington DC.

PIKIARERO

Clematis Hexasepala.

The garden front of Sir George Grey's mansion at Kawau

1884

ALFRED SHARPE 1836–1908

ALFRED SHARPE'S VIEW of Mansion House provides an important record of what the house and garden looked like when Sir George Grey was still resident. The original mine superintendent's house is on the left, though Grey's architect Frederick Thatcher had embellished the garden façade by adding the bay windows. He also extended the house by adding the two wings, creating a courtyard in between. The 'Juliet steps', seen here, allowed direct access to the garden from the two principal bedrooms upstairs.

Grey planted many exotic trees on Kawau, one of which stands just right of centre: a coral or flame tree (*Erythrina lysistemon*), called a kaffir boom in its native South Africa, a variety which flowers when in leaf, as in Sharpe's painting. On the left edge is an oak and the branches of another oak are visible on the right, below which is a mulberry. Along the path on the left Sharpe shows some young palms, although these are not the tall Chilean palms that are a feature of the garden today.

The English historian and biographer James Froude, in *Oceana* (1886), gives this description of the garden:

He has oak and walnut, maple and elm, poplar, ash and acacia. A clump of immense cedars stands close to the house, and round the grounds are groves of magnolia and laurel and bay. From the Cape he had brought the mimosa and the Caffre-baum, and the whole air is perfumed with orange blossom and citron and stephanotis.

To these can be added olives (a grove of around 5 hectares), cinchona trees (a source of quinine), agaves and yuccas, camphors, magnolias, cork trees, Indian deodars, spider lilies, loquats, custard-apples, almonds, pineapple and cinnamon trees, among many more.

Another writer enthused, 'There is hardly a country under Heaven from whence Sir George had not obtained a plant of some kind or other.' As early as July 1863, Grey wrote to his friend Ormis Biddulph: 'You have no idea what a beautiful place I am making of Kawau: all who see it declare it to be on of the most beautiful things in the world.'

It is a little ironic that Sharpe painted Kawau, given his fierce support for native fauna and flora, especially the kauri, and his staunch opposition to introduced exotic species such as 'sparrows, chaffinches, greenfinches and other hard-billed vermin, brought here by those wise men of Gotham, Messieurs the Acclimatisation Society.' In at least one respect he was to be proved right: the wallabies Grey introduced multiplied so greatly that they became pests.

In 1884 *The garden front of Sir George Grey's mansion at Kawau* was one of Sharpe's entries in the second annual exhibition of the Fine Arts Association of New Zealand in Wellington, and on its return it was displayed in the new exhibition window of the Queen Street stationers Phillipps and Son in Auckland.

Charles Goldie 1870–1947

THE YOUNG CHARLES Goldie had a privileged upbringing in Velitoa, the mansion his father had built at 47 Pitt Street, Auckland. As art historian Roger Blackley records in *Goldie*, his artistic talent was recognised early, while still a schoolboy at Auckland College and Grammar School.

Goldie's first official success was at the Auckland Society of Arts (ASA) annual exhibition in April 1885, when he was awarded second prize for a drawing of an ornament in the 'Shaded study from the round' category. Later that year he was a second prize-winner for a drawing in the New Zealand Art Students Association exhibition. The following year his first exhibited oil painting, an entry for 'Study of still life, in oils' gained him a third certificate, while he did better at that year's New Zealand Art Students Association exhibition with a bronze medal for his brilliant watercolour: *Still life: Maori carvings, mere, baler, matting and tui-bird.*

This provides the context for Goldie's *Clematis*, a panel painted in oils on a red ground. A partly torn label on the back of the panel indicates that *Clematis* was entered for a competition in the 'Hand-painted door panel' category and that Goldie was 15 years and five months old. His age perfectly matches the ASA's annual exhibition in April 1886, so this must have been his submission

for that category, which received 10 entries that year. He was not the winner; the first certificate was awarded to Miss AR Gardner. Entries might have been anonymous, with the artist being recognisable only by their 'motto' on the label. Unfortunately, the label is torn where Goldie's motto was written.

Goldie exhibited other comparable works around this time. In 1887 he showed a painting of roses at the ASA in the 'Study of still life, in oils' section, which earned him a prize of one guinea. The following year his entry was a painted plaque of a convolvulus on a gilt background.

Clematis, especially the native varieties, was a popular plant, although whether the 15-year-old Goldie was aware of the plant's association by Maori with the coming of spring is not known. However, indigenous plants and flowers such as the kaka beak appear in some of his later Maori portraits.

The butterfly Goldie has placed at the top of the panel is perhaps a foretaste of the humour he showed at the ASA in 1890. The pundits believed his *Still life* of two snapper on a marble slab, a goldfish bowl and some flax leaves should have won but he received only an honourable mention. One of the reasons for his failure, the *New Zealand Herald* suggested, was that Goldie had included two goldfish in the bowl and so it could not legitimately be a still life.

WINIFRED KERR TAYLOR 1868–1964

THE KERR TAYLORS were a well-off Auckland family. Allan Taylor named his farm Alberton after the adjacent volcanic cone of Mount Albert, and his original two-storey farmhouse, built in 1863, was extended in the 1870s to the form shown here. Features such as the turrets and veranda were introduced by the architect to reflect Taylor's childhood in India, where his father had been in the army.

Allan and his wife Sophia liked to entertain and Alberton became renowned for its social gatherings, including garden parties, balls, tennis and croquet matches. The home farm, as the land around the house was called, was big enough for shooting parties and hunt gatherings and the garden alone was 2.4 hectares.

The Taylor daughters, Winifred, Mildred and Muriel, would have learned drawing, and perhaps painting, as part of their education at Auckland Girls' High School — sketches by all three exist. Winifred also enjoyed tennis, singing and horse riding.

The charming, somewhat naïve, painting of Alberton and its environs, which is dated 1888, is ascribed to Winifred. It shows the garden front with Mount Albert and its scoria pit behind. Winifred's high viewpoint indicates that she probably made her initial on-the-spot drawing at St Luke's Anglican Church (on the corner of New North and St Lukes roads); the family donated this land and worshipped at the church.

After her husband's death Sophia Kerr Taylor — the family added Kerr to their name in the 1880s — became a member of the Auckland branch of the Women's Franchise League. She had yet to fully develop her garden but considered herself a farmer. She raised prize poultry, sending their eggs to market along with flowers, fruit and vegetables grown on the estate, which she ran for 40 years until the three unmarried daughters took over.

The garden that Sophia created was recorded as it was in the 1920s by family members. There was a large variety of plants including violets, geraniums, iris, azaleas and camellias. Paths led from the house to the circular fountain — the only man-made garden feature still existing — and then a single path led to an arched gate. A croquet lawn was on either side of the path and a tennis court away to the left.

The rectangular paddock we can see in the painting was divided longitudinally into three sections: the vegetable garden on the left, the flower garden — which featured a similar fountain to the remaining one — in the middle, and the orchard on the right. The whole was bounded by a scoria wall. From the bottom of the garden it was a short walk to Meola Creek, where there was a bathhouse by a swimming hole. Named by the family after a glacier in India, the creek remains as the culvert that meanders along the east side of Mount Albert Grammar School, built on 6.5 hectares of land bought from Sophia Kerr Taylor.

III. EARLY MODERN

1890–1940

James Fitzgerald, *Summer evening in the city* (detail), see page 121

UNLIKE BRITAIN AT the turn of the century, New Zealand did not witness the appearance of specialist garden painters such as Helen Allingham, who painted the great Gertrude Jekyll's garden, and Beatrice Parsons, whose detailed paintings of distinguished gardens were later used by Suttons to illustrate their seed catalogues. Margaret Stoddart is probably New Zealand's best known painter of gardens yet it was only for a relatively short period, around 1911–15, that gardens were her main focus. She began her career with botanical studies, then developed her talent as a flower and landscape painter when in Europe. After her series of stunning garden watercolours, Stoddart once again concentrated on landscapes until the end of her life.

In this section we see the beginnings of modernist painting in New Zealand — and its poor reception! For example, Stoddart sent works from Europe to Christchurch for exhibition but in 1902 *The Press* commented that 'her taste for a woolly misty impressionism has fallen upon her to the detriment of her work.' Note this is impressionism with a small 'i'; a kind of shorthand signalling that a painting was 'modern' or influenced by European art.

The Scot James Nairn was the most important of several foreign artists to settle in New Zealand around the turn of the century. Nairn, sometimes erroneously credited with the introduction to New Zealand of French Impressionism, was one of a loose grouping of progressive Scottish painters dubbed the Glasgow Boys following their exhibition at London's Grosvenor Gallery in 1890, just a few months after Nairn arrived in New Zealand.

Though Nairn's style and his dedication to *plein air* painting made him the most advanced painter working in the country at the time, he is unlikely to have had any direct experience of French Impressionism before leaving Scotland. However, a painting such as *Garden scene. Woman beneath trees* is reminiscent of Impressionism: its subject is a figure in the garden lit by dappled sunlight and the painter's touch is light, with visible brushstrokes animating the painted surface. Nairn's slightly earlier *Autumn blooms* is one of New Zealand's finest flower paintings. It was painted at the Bellevue Gardens at Woburn, not far from Silverstream in the Hutt Valley, where Nairn had established a base for members of the Wellington Art Club.

Mabel Hill, Nairn's talented younger colleague at the Wellington Technical College, had painted her *Chrysanthemums* at Bellevue Gardens and exhibited it four years before Nairn's painting. Hill's paintings of the Oamaru garden of Dr Alexander and Barbara Douglas from 1917 provide an interesting comparison and counterpoint to Stoddart's garden works. They had a specific *raison d'être*: they were to be illustrations in a book written by Barbara Douglas, *Pictures in a New Zealand Garden*, published in 1921 and the first illustrated book to be published about a New Zealand garden. Stoddart's paintings were large, impressive exhibition pieces; Hill's, in comparison, were miniatures, concentrating on a selection of discrete areas of the Douglas garden.

The first non-illustrated garden book to be published in New Zealand was Emily Marshall-White's *My New Zealand Garden*, published under the *nom de plume* 'A Suffolk Lady' in Wanganui in 1902. It may be fanciful but not impossible that Minnie Izett, who painted *A New Zealand Garden* in Wanganui around 1905, would have known Marshall-White and her extensive garden on St Johns Hill. Coincidentally, the Wanganui garden that concludes this section, painted by a little-known artist, Violet Whiteman, was at the top of Durie Hill, across the Whanganui River to the southeast.

The other foreigner who came to New Zealand in 1890 and who, with Nairn, is generally credited with revitalising New Zealand painting was Dutchman Petrus van der Velden. While Nairn's tragic early death robbed New Zealand of one of its most influential and colourful early modernists, van der Velden did not achieve the long-term success he felt he deserved. When he came to paint *A garden in Tinakori Road, Wellington*, he had no fixed abode and was struggling to sell his work. His view of the wild, wintery back garden of his Thorndon lodgings may reflect his mood as well as his emotional response to the scene but it is also a fine poetic sketch that epitomises the northern European romantic tradition that van der Velden brought to this country.

While van der Velden's influence on New Zealand painting is difficult to characterise, he taught some of the next generation of Canterbury artists. One was Robert Procter who, perhaps encouraged by van der Velden's example, went to Europe to paint. *The verandah* was painted on his final return to New Zealand and represents a European sensibility that is quite rare for New Zealand painters — light years apart from Olivia Spencer Bower's *Untidy veranda* of a decade or so later.

If Nairn signalled the beginnings of modernism in Wellington in the 1890s, a later arrival from overseas, Robert Field, engaged under the La Trobe Scheme, brought modernism to Dunedin in 1925. Field taught at the art school at King Edward Technical College, where Anne Hamblett, Doris Lusk and Rodney Kennedy benefited from his teaching and inspiration. All three are represented here by flower still lifes. Kennedy's and Hamblett's output was curtailed by the war and marriage respectively, though fortunately not before they had demonstrated their abilities as innovative artists. Lusk, one of the finest painters of her generation, established her credentials early but the outstanding *Mixed flowers* was to be the only significant still life that she painted.

In Christchurch, to where both Hamblett and Lusk would shortly move, modernism was also gathering adherents. Although not so prolific because of his teaching and administrative responsibilities, Colin Lovell-Smith turned out some brilliant paintings of which *Canterbury garden* is a fine example.

Twenty-five years Lovell-Smith's senior was the Edinburgh-born and London-trained commercial artist James Fitzgerald. His equally brilliantly coloured, bravura rendering of irises in the early evening, an isolated example of a pure garden painting at this time, seems strikingly modern.

Painters in Auckland do not seem to have been very interested in gardens as a subject during this period. However, on Great Barrier Island in the Hauraki Gulf, northeast of Auckland, the talented Fanny Osborne produced the last examples of traditional botanical painting of her era.

In her Tryphena garden and around the island, Osborne identified and painted a wide range of native flora, some unique to the island, such as the houhere reproduced here. Since Osborne painted for pleasure and to supplement her income, not for reproduction, she has not received the same recognition as her approximate contemporary Sarah Featon, but she is arguably her equal as an artist.

Chrysanthemums

1896

MABEL HILL 1872–1956

THE SUBJECT OF this brilliant watercolour — a tour de force — was almost certainly Bellevue Gardens (formerly McNab's) at Woburn in the Hutt Valley. It was a popular tea garden and a venue for dinners, picnics and events, including the annual Chrysanthemum Show.

It was painted by Mabel Hill, who studied art at Wellington Technical College until 1891. She then became an instructor and a colleague of Scottish artist James Nairn, who had joined the staff that year to teach still life painting and life drawing. Hill and fellow teacher Mary Richardson (later Tripe) attended his life drawing classes.

Hill first exhibited at the New Zealand Academy of Fine Arts in 1892 and at the Otago Art Society and Canterbury Society of Arts in 1893. *The New Zealand Mail* reported on the eighth annual NZAFA exhibition in July 1896 that:

Autumn, *No 3, and* Chrysanthemums, *No 43, could almost be classed together. In these Miss Hill has exercised her powers in the production of two of the finest watercolours which she has yet given us. The latter is the more important; and shows power in treatment of colour, though inclined to spottiness. The former is full of atmosphere and light.*

The *Otago Witness* in November 1896 reported in its third review of the OAS exhibition:

That Miss Hill does not confine herself to figure subjects is evident from two very choice landscapes which bear her name — 'Chrysanthemums' (No 207) and 'Autumn' (No 217). The first-mentioned of these is a landscape into which the lovely blooms that give the title to the picture have been introduced — a rustic flower garden in point of fact — and the picture positively blazes with the rich colour of these noble specimens of garden flora.

Hill's painting, with its abundant colour and main features parallel to the picture plane, appears adventurous and innovative to the modern eye, though apparently not to the contemporary reviewer.

Hill painted frequently with Nairn in the Hutt Valley at his artists' retreat at Pumpkin Cottage, Silverstream, and at Bellevue, which she referred to as 'a garden at Petone'. The partial view of the house beyond the flowers, especially its gable end and chimney, leave little doubt that this painting was made at Bellevue, accessible by the same train from Wellington as they took to Silverstream.

Hill would have painted much of her picture *en plein air*, as encouraged by Nairn. It is tempting to surmise that the good notices Hill received for *Chrysanthemums* inspired Nairn to 'have a go' at a similar scene (see page 95).

MABEL HILL'S CHARMING European and New Zealand flower pieces, landscapes and portraits were popular in their day. Some of her earlier house and garden watercolours have an old-world charm reminiscent of English painter Helen Allingham and Australian Percy Spence.

Sometime around 1915, a friendship with an Oamaru couple resulted in Hill's contribution to a unique and captivating privately published portrait of a garden. *Pictures in a New Zealand Garden* was written by Barbara Douglas, the wife of surgeon Dr Alexander Douglas, and published in 1921.

The best-known written New Zealand garden portrait up to that time was *My New Zealand Garden* by 'A Suffolk Lady', the *nom de plume* of Emily Marshall-White. It was not illustrated when first published in Wanganui in 1902. It was very popular and is likely that Barbara Douglas knew of it.

The Douglases bought an old weatherboard house at 43 Reed Street, Oamaru in 1898. In 1907 they commissioned talented young Dunedin Arts and Crafts architect Basil Hooper to enlarge and modernise it. Little of the original house was retained: a second storey was added and the alterations were made in Oamaru stone, rough-cast externally, with a Marseille tile roof.

The Douglases were both gardeners and they created 'a glorious garden', according to their granddaughter Barbara Simpson. From the dates of her paintings, Hill's first visit was in 1915 when she painted *Reed Street, Oamaru* and some other local views. It is not known whether Barbara Douglas already had the idea for a book or simply commissioned Hill's paintings; what is known is that the artist returned to paint the garden two years later, in 1917.

At the end of the First World War, Barbara Douglas was active in raising funds for returned servicemen and war widows. She also embarked on the preparation of *Pictures in a New Zealand Garden*, which she dedicated 'to all Mothers, Sisters, Wives

and Lovers, who have lost their dear ones in the Great War, in the hope that the love of flowers and gardens may bring them solace in the years to come'. Although the book was not published until 1921, it is possible that copies were sold as a fundraiser.

Hill's watercolours were reproduced in colour with half-tones of photographs by the Oamaru-educated astronomer Algernon Charles Gifford and Basil de Lambert, who later became a radiologist in Christchurch and Dunedin. The third photographer was J Wallace.

The 30-page book was printed in Melbourne by Alexander McCubbin, son of the great Australian painter, Fred McCubbin. It had 11 tipped-in colour plates of Hill's 'watercolour Sketches' and 19 monochrome halftone photographs.

Douglas's brief foreword explains her objectives in producing the book:

> *This book is not a book of instructions. It makes no pretensions to special gardening in New Zealand. Its object is by a series of pictures to share with others the pleasure derived by a garden-lover from one small garden.*

The combination of photographs and paintings reveal a very large and complex garden with mature trees, vines and climbers, architectural and decorative features, paths, raised beds, lawns and bowers and native bush.

This view is of the north-facing façade of the house, showing the tiled roof, green gables and open balcony upstairs, which was off their young granddaughter Barbara Douglas's room. Below was the dining room, in front of which was a sundial. Barbara Douglas (now Simpson) lived with her grandparents at 43 Reed Street while attending Waitaki Girls High School until 1942. She recalled peonies and daisies and perhaps a cherry tree in the garden, as Hill depicted in her painting. The house was demolished in 1976.

Asters and arabis

1917

MABEL HILL 1872–1956

ASTERS AND ARABIS is Plate II and the first of Mabel Hill's watercolours in *Pictures in a New Zealand Garden*. In a relatively small watercolour Hill achieves a lot of detail, using delicate strokes with the brushpoint for the asters and giving form to the arabis (rock cress). Barbara Douglas wrote:

Every woman who is interested in the beauty of her garden must realise the important part played by the judicious massing of colour. She may not be an artist with canvas and brush, but in her carefully-planned garden she will be the possessor of a gallery full of exquisite pictures — pictures which charm and satisfy completely. We look to midsummer and autumn to give us gorgeous colour effects. In this country we scarcely have time to tire of grey twigs and bare stems, ere we find these same twigs and stems bursting into bud once more. The fast lengthening days and sunshine quickly change our surroundings from grey to gold.

Mabel Hill

For the passer-by

1917

MABEL HILL 1872–1956

THE GATED ARCHWAY depicted in *For the passer-by* is one of the few features of the Douglas property that remains today. A photograph of the archway is the first plate in *Pictures in a New Zealand Garden*. 'Lift the latch and walk in,' the author invites the reader, 'and we shall talk of many things that interest us in our everyday gardening work. The treasures we love most are not rare plants; for truly there are none in this garden, but just the common-place things which thrive well and please us with their elegant manners.'

Douglas's writing style may sound old-fashioned and even stilted to the modern reader, but it conveys an elegiac mood, appropriate to the book's apparent purpose. The text for Plate VI reads:

Some years ago a stone wall was built on the south side of the garden. Roses, Clematis and Vines were planted and trained to grow up and over the wall, so that the Passer-by might have a picture to enjoy, as he goes to and fro.

Conrad F. Meyer is the earliest Rose to bloom. Afterwards comes Souvenir de Léonie Viennot — one of the most beautiful climbers we have; the other Roses are American Pillar, Fortune's Yellow, Climbing Liberty and Climbing American Beauty.

Clematis paniculata, C. flammula, C. Jackmani [sic], Lathyrus pubescens, Ipomoea, and a glory-vine (Vitis coignetiae) — these also, with the Roses, are all scrambling up the stone buttresses, jostling each other in their efforts to be first 'over the top'.

I like to think that the Passer-by loves them all, and each day looks for a bright flower that will nod to him 'Good-morning' and 'good-night.'

General McArthur

1917

MABEL HILL 1872–1956

IN *PICTURES IN a New Zealand Garden,* Barbara Douglas lists some of the many roses in her garden, fragrant, climbers and:

. . . a group of well-known soldiers, General McArthur [sic], General Jacqueminot, Captain Hayward, Lieutenant Chaure and Commandant Felix Faure . . . Robust, brilliant and dependable, General McArthur is one of the most popular red roses that we have. The bright crimson flowers are fragrant, and are produced on strong handsome stalks. The habit of growth is stiff for bedding, but it makes a fine half-standard. A low hedge of General McArthur is effective, for there are always many blooms and well-shaped buds to be had for cutting . . .

General MacArthur (the more usual spelling), a hybrid tea rose, was hybridised in 1905 by EG Hill. It was illustrated as a colour plate in HH Thomas's *The Rose Book*, published in London in 1914, which suggests that the Douglases were up to date with their plant selection.

Autumn blooms

JAMES NAIRN 1859–1904

THE SUBJECT OF this painting is the same as Mabel Hill's *Chrysanthemums* (see page 85): Bellevue Gardens at Woburn, Lower Hutt, not far from Silverstream where he and members of the Wellington Art Club painted. It is unlikely to be a coincidence that these two colleagues at Wellington Technical College painted at the same location, but one can only speculate that Nairn, impressed by Hill's watercolour, was inspired to visit Bellevue himself the following autumn, resulting in a no less spectacular painting. Nairn has placed the large white and yellow chrysanthemums in the foreground plane, with the two gardeners leaning on their hoes behind them.

Nairn painted chrysanthemums — 'the Queen of the Autumn' as the flower was then called — a number of times and although Nairn inscribed 'Autumn Blooms' on the back of this painting, it has also been known as *The Chrysanthemum Garden*. Another version, now lost, shows a similar view except the figures were on the right. It was probably owned by the Johnston family, tea merchants prominent in Wellington in the 1890s.

Autumn blooms was first shown at the Auckland Society of Arts annual exhibition in November 1899, priced at £25, where it was called *Autumn blooms, Petone*. It was then exhibited at the Suter Art Gallery, Nelson, in August 1900, as was recorded in a review in the magazine *Triad*:

The Ninth Annual Exhibition of the Bishopdale Sketching Club, assisted by artists in the principal centres, was opened by His Lordship the Bishop of Nelson on Monday evening, June 11th, in the Suter Art Gallery. Mr J M Nairn (Wellington) had two large canvases — 'Autumn Blooms' and 'Noon' — most successfully painted; he also had two excellent tinted pencil sketches of an old man and woman and four watercolours — good examples of this clever artist's work.

Later the painting represented Nairn in the Centennial Exhibition at the National Art Gallery in 1940. It was owned by John Newton, a major soap manufacturer, whose portrait Nairn painted in 1898.

Garden scene — woman beneath trees

ca 1900

JAMES NAIRN 1859–1904

JAMES NAIRN WAS one of the Glasgow Boys, a group of progressive painters in Scotland in the 1880s who were influenced by European painting, particularly French artist Jules Bastien-Lepage. He had also exhibited with the somewhat progressive New English Art Club in London the year before he left Scotland for what was planned as a round-trip to visit to New Zealand and return to Europe via Japan to pursue his interest in Japanese art.

While the Glasgow Boys were interested in painting modern life and the everyday and had rejected the conservatism of the Royal Scottish Academy in Edinburgh, they were not Impressionists. Nevertheless, Nairn's paintings such as *Garden scene* do suggest Impressionism, especially its subject, particularly associated with Renoir, of a woman in a sunlight-dappled garden.

The woman is probably Nairn's wife Ellen, and the location their Woolcombe Street garden. Nairn married the 19-year-old Ellen Smith in March 1898 and they had two daughters. Here Ellen, her hat catching the sun, is seated in what looks like an upholstered cane chair, reading, with vividly painted flowers beyond.

Coincidentally, one of the first paintings exhibited by Nairn, *Old garden in Glasgow*, also featured a figure in a garden. It was exhibited in 1890 at the annual exhibition of Wellington's New Zealand Academy of Fine Arts, of which he was elected a member late that year. The small oil painting is listed in Nairn's *catalogue raisonné* by Vickie Hearnshaw, and in an article published in 2004 she quotes a review in the *Evening Post* describing it as the 'cleverest piece of painting' in the exhibition.

Mount Victoria, Wellington

1900

JAMES NAIRN 1859–1904

JAMES NAIRN WAS as proficient in watercolour as he was in oils. This view looks approximately southeast to the peak of Mount Victoria, visible through the tree, with the spire of St Peter's Anglican Church (1879), on the corner of Willis and Ghuznee streets, just to the right. The peak and flanks of the mountain and the top of the church spire are caught by the evening sun, while the city below is obscured by the deepening purple dusk. Nairn shows the moon on the rise just above the tree.

A note on the painting explains that it is a copy of an oil painting that Nairn made for Dr JH Scott, a professor of anatomy at the University of Otago. Called *Landscape* or *Mount Victoria, Wellington, evening*, it is now in the Museum of New Zealand Te Papa Tongarewa.

Nairn has followed the composition of the oil painting quite closely except that he has pulled back a little to show the lawn and inserted the figure of the woman. The oil is also more richly coloured overall and the sun bathes the entire north-facing hillside.

Around 1897–98, before his marriage, Nairn lodged with his friend and patron Dr Kington Fyffe in Willis Street, near where another friend and patron, Dr Walter Fell, also lived and had his practice. By 1901, the year after he painted *Mount Victoria, Wellington*, he and his wife Ellen were living nearby in Woolcombe Street, an extension of The Terrace — and, coincidentally, where Petrus van der Velden would also lodge a few years later (see page 102). This view is therefore most likely to have been painted from around this neighbourhood, probably from a house further up The Terrace.

MINNIE IZETT 1862–1924

IN 1896, FREQUENT advertisements were placed in the *Wanganui Herald* for art lessons, of which this is typical:

MRS LEONARD JONES (pupil of Sir James Linton) Will give Lessons in Oil, Water Colour and Pastel, Free Hand, and Model Drawing. — Studio: Over Old Colonial Bank, Avenue.

The classes appear to have been popular; an article in the *Wanganui Herald* in August 1902 reports 'The exhibition of students' work which has been on view at Mrs Leonard Jones' studio closes tonight at 10 o'clock', followed by a lengthy commentary. In 1903 we learn that there is a new incentive to study with her: 'Being registered with [the] Minister of Education, country pupils secure the advantages of reduced railway fares.'

Mrs Leonard — or Minnie — Jones was a founding member of the Wanganui Arts and Crafts Society. Following her first husband's death, she remarried, and as Minnie Izett remained active in the society throughout her life, including being its secretary. She was also a prolific exhibitor at the society's exhibitions. Examples of Izett's works include, in March 1904, oil paintings titled *Fruit* and *River scene* and watercolours *Wanganui river* and *Chrysanthemums*.

In April 1905 there is the following mention in the *Wanganui Herald*: 'Mrs Izett shows some good work, her best being a garden sketch and a basket of primroses.' *A New Zealand garden* is possibly the painting referred to here; 'sketch' could refer to a finished painting in watercolour of this type of subject. The title the artist gave to this reasonably large painting suggests that she may have had an international audience in mind. Prominent in the painting are hollyhocks, with a path perhaps leading past the punga to the countryside beyond.

Following her first husband's death, Izett travelled to Europe, probably first to London, where she studied with Sir James Dromgole Linton (1840–1916), an English painter who ran a private art school called the Linton School. He was president of the Royal Institute of Painters in Watercolour and was involved in the establishment of the Tate Gallery. Izett then travelled to Europe: watercolours in the collection of the Sarjeant Gallery indicate she visited Florence, Naples and Monte Carlo.

A garden in Tinakori Road, Wellington

1908

PETRUS VAN DER VELDEN 1837–1913

THE DUTCH PAINTER Petrus van der Velden arrived in Christchurch in 1890 and quickly established his reputation with his striking paintings of the Otira Gorge, one of which was bought for the Dunedin Public Art Gallery in 1892. His growing renown, however, was not matched by increased earnings, and in 1898 the family moved to Sydney in search of greater financial success.

After the death of his wife, van der Velden stayed in Sydney until January 1904, when he returned to Wellington accompanied by Australia Wahlberg, whom he married in February that year. Van der Velden continued painting, including a posthumous portrait of Richard Seddon that was destroyed in a fire in Parliament Buildings in 1907. Later he produced several self-portraits and landscapes, some with cattle, but most were versions of the Otira Gorge paintings that established his reputation. One of the latter was bought by the Auckland Art Gallery in 1913, and this sale may have been the reason for his visit that year to Auckland, where he fell ill and died.

In these last difficult years in Wellington van der Velden became increasingly reclusive. The couple frequently moved lodgings and are recorded at Karaka Bay (1906), c/o Mrs Matheson, Woolcombe Street (1908), Duppa Street (1909–10) and 56 Derwent Street, Island Bay (1912). Another lodging was the Bellevue Hotel, Lower Hutt; around 1906 van der Velden ended up owing £73 for board and lodging and appeared before the Wellington Magistrates' Court regarding the debt.

Tinakori Road had a number of boarding and lodging houses, which rented rooms mostly to single labouring men. *A garden in Tinakori Road, Wellington* is probably a view from one of the van der Veldens' lodgings, either before or after their residence with Mrs Matheson in Woolcombe Street, now The Terrace. A small wooden footbridge indicates a stream running down between the sections and may provide a clue to the location of the view.

This watercolour sketch of a back garden in winter well conveys the northern European energy and expression that was found so novel and refreshing when van der Velden first began exhibiting in New Zealand. The sketch is reminiscent of those made in Otira in which he caught the atmosphere, mood, life and movement of nature — sketches that represented an essential element in van der Velden's artistic process.

🌿 Garden, Christchurch

ca 1912

MARGARET STODDART 1865–1934

MARGARET STODDART'S earliest successes were her botanical paintings. She exhibited 35, all of native flora, between 1883, when she was a student at the Canterbury College School of Art, and 1889. Twelve were acquired by the Canterbury Museum in 1890.

In 1893 she met Ellis Rowan, the leading Australian flower painter, who was visiting New Zealand, and through her had a successful exhibition in Melbourne the following year. In 1897, Stoddart travelled to Europe, spending time in Italy, Norway, France and England where, in 1902, she met up with Frances Hodgkins and Dorothy Richmond in St Ives, which she made her base.

Stoddart exhibited in St Ives from 1902–1904 and 1906, and during these years she developed into a superb landscape painter. However, her most striking paintings from this period are paintings of trees in blossom and spring flowers such as bluebells in the woods, as well as still lifes.

On her return to New Zealand in 1906, Stoddart was sufficiently well established to become a full-time professional painter. She developed a range of approaches to her painting, including garden and orchard views in which the flowers and blossoms take precedence. These would remain her forte for the next decade or so.

The location of *Garden, Christchurch* is not known but it was exhibited at the Canterbury Society of Arts Annual Exhibition of 1912, for 5 guineas. It has a directness of observation that suggests it was painted *en plein air*.

Old homestead, Diamond Harbour

ca 1913

MARGARET STODDART 1865–1934

MARGARET STODDART'S PARENTS were important early settlers in the Lyttelton area and Diamond Harbour was first referred to as 'Mr Stoddart's Bay'. Diamond Harbour, possibly named by Stoddart's father, Mark, is on the south side of Lyttelton Harbour, opposite Lyttelton itself. Mark Stoddart purchased 20 hectares here in 1852, and by the time he married Anna Schjött in 1862 had purchased a prefabricated house from Australia and erected it on a sheltered site overlooking the bay.

This is where Margaret Stoddart and her brothers and sisters were born and grew up. Stoddart would have been immensely influenced by her surroundings and by her father's knowledge of the land, plants and trees.

She would also have been familiar with the popular and nostalgic genre of English painting of the rustic country cottage surrounded by flowers, epitomised by Victorian artists such as Helen Allingham. However, Stoddart was a more modern painter, less minutely detailed — indeed, more what one might loosely term Impressionist, appropriate to the romantic depiction of her old home, overgrown with flowers.

The homestead still belonged to the Stoddarts in the 1910s and this painting is one of several in which the house features. It was exhibited at Canterbury Society of Arts in 1913.

Godley House, Diamond Harbour

ca 1913

MARGARET STODDART 1865–1934

GODLEY HOUSE AT Diamond Harbour was built in 1880 by the builder of the Lyttelton Harbour breakwater, Harvey Hawkins, to whom the Stoddart family trust had sold their Diamond Harbour estate in 1876. In 1897, Margaret Stoddart and her mother and sisters returned to live at the house, as Hawkins had been declared bankrupt and the house had reverted to the trust. One of the sisters and her husband occupied the old homestead nearby, which the family also still owned. Here at 'the big house' the Stoddarts grew flowers that were sent to the market, with Margaret's sister Agnes responsible for the garden. In 1911 Margaret's mother Anna died and, after protracted negotiations, the Lyttelton Borough Council eventually purchased the house and land in 1913. The council continued to sell flowers grown on the property.

Also in 1911, Stoddart arranged an exhibition of 50 paintings at the Canterbury Society of Arts. A review in the *Lyttelton Times* of 24 Ocober 1911 stated:

The old homestead has evidently been one of Miss Stoddart's favourite resorts. A spreading almond tree in full bloom is shown in one picture, and in others there are trees which must have been planted soon after the settlement of Canterbury began, and which have found at Diamond Harbour good soil and a congenial climate.

Julie King, an expert on Stoddart, later succinctly summarised the painter's achievements:

It was during her years at Diamond Harbour that Margaret produced some of her most memorable images, completing a succession of paintings of places that had been familiar since childhood — the old wharf, the farm, fruit trees and the orchard, and the cottage that her father had brought from Australia before his marriage, and where she was born.

House in a summer garden

ca 1928

MARGARET STODDART 1865–1934

THIS IS ONE of the most spectacular of Stoddart's garden paintings from this period. It was purchased by the North Otago Art Society in Oamaru, probably from one of its annual exhibitions. Neil Roberts, a specialist in Canterbury art, suggests that the house depicted in this painting may have been on Clifton Hill, near Sumner, where Stoddart frequently painted in the 1920s, or near her home on Hackthorne Road. It is one of the most spectacular of her garden paintings from this period and may be the work she exhibited as *Gateway Clifton* in 1928.

Margaret Stoddart continued to paint and exhibit at the Canterbury Society of Arts into the early 1930s, by which time she had returned to landscape as her primary subject. These late Canterbury landscapes endure being as among her finest works.

Art critic James Shelley and painter Sydney Thompson jointly wrote a tribute to Stoddart after her death, published in *Art in New Zealand* in December 1935:

Her paintings were intimately personal, and in them her very way of life was expressed; they were fine because she was fine, and the deliberate composition and firm technique spoke truly of the high principles and clearly defined character of the woman.

In a further tribute, some 30 years later, painter Rita Angus was to record in a letter to art historian Gordon H Brown: 'It was Miss Stoddart's watercolours that impressed me when a Canterbury Art Student'.

Houhere, lacebark (Hoheria populnea)

ca 1916

FANNY OSBORNE 1852–1934

FANNY OSBORNE (NEÉ Malcolm) was a botanical artist whose works are all of plants and flowers found on Great Barrier Island, where she was brought up and lived with her husband Alfred following their elopement and marriage in 1873. Fanny did not start to paint her stunning botanical studies until well into the twentieth century, when her youngest children were old enough to attend the island's school, which had opened in 1884 with Alfred as its first teacher.

We do not know the inspiration behind Osborne's paintings and, furthermore, she seems to have had no scientific training. She was painting groups of paintings of native flowers from the early 1900s; the earliest date to be directly associated with her paintings is 1916, the date of her two albums in the Auckland Museum, possibly compiled by Osborne herself. Just over 150 of Osborne's paintings have been recorded.

Osborne was born on Great Barrier, and after her marriage returned to the island to settle at Tryphena, where her husband took over a land grant from his father. The Osbornes were self-sufficient; as well as farming and beekeeping, they planted mulberry trees and imported waterlilies — apparently the first New Zealanders to do so — planting them in hillside pools. Alfred Osborne was very interested in plants, especially natives,

and he supplied nurserymen in Auckland with seeds of unusual species.

In her book on Fanny Osborne, Jeanne Goulding described this painting of houhere (lacebark):

An unusual form with bluish stamens (as painted here) found on the Osborne property at Tryphena about 1910. This form cultivated by nurserymen became known to horticulturists as Hoheria populnea *'Osbornei'.*

Goulding adds that 'It was claimed to be a handsome and striking tree'.

Osborne's paintings are all of plants she had grown up with and knew intimately, painted from fresh examples that she had gathered herself. Most importantly, they were never sullied by poor lithographic reproduction.

Goulding writes that by the 1920s, 'it was well known that Fanny Osborne had painted many delightful studies of native flowers which she sold at the homestead at Tryphena'. Her reputation was such that Lady Alice Fergusson, wife of the then governor-general of New Zealand, visited and sketched with her and bought some of her paintings.

HOUHERE
(LACEBARK)

ROBERT PROCTER 1879–1931

SCOTTISH-BORN ARTIST Robert Procter is probably best known for his colourful Italian market scenes, featuring lots of figures in traditional dress, and clichéd views of tourist spots such as Venice, with lantern-lit gondolas. However, he had a more serious and less market-driven side to his art, revealed by his calm, nostalgic and contemplative oil studies of forgotten corners, ranging from old sheds to quiet Venetian lanes.

The verandah is a fine and magical example of Procter's art in this mode but set in New Zealand. Procter's true subject, however, is the late afternoon sunlight; its rays catch the flowers but are not strong enough to penetrate into the veranda, where the light is filtered and softened and the colours in the shadows muted. A light summer breeze lifts the blind, emphasising the attraction of this pleasant retreat.

None of Procter's exhibited paintings have titles that fit *The verandah*. Art historian John Perry suggests that it depicts a Canterbury scene, painted around 1926 when Procter exhibited in Christchurch. Another option, though less likely because of the setting and the architecture, is Rotorua, because Procter exhibited a number of paintings of that region between 1921 and 1926.

Details of Procter's life and travels are sketchy, but in his book on the artist Leo King has gathered most of the information we have about this talented painter, particularly using the subjects and locations of his paintings.

Before going to Europe, Procter had painted a range of New Zealand subjects. Examples include his fine Impressionistic *Sunset and boats* (Auckland Art Gallery) which compares favourably with similar subjects by fellow Scot James Nairn, and figure paintings such as *Sunny hours*, of a Maori woman from Kaiapoi (Christchurch Art Gallery).

However, when he returned with a suitcase of European paintings, there was some disappointment. In 1911 the reviewer for the *New Zealand Times* felt moved to comment on *The last gleam* — a Venetian scene — in the New Zealand Academy of Fine Arts annual exhibition: 'I should like to see this young New Zealander discarding his European sketchbooks and turning his attention to the beauties of his native land.' Whether Procter read the review or not, *The verandah* would certainly have been an appropriate response.

Flower piece

RODNEY KENNEDY 1909–1989

RODNEY KENNEDY WAS a talented painter whose studies with William Allen and Robert Field at the Dunedin School of Art confirmed him in the direction of modernism. His developing passion for theatre and his detention as a conscientious objector during the Second World War resulted in his giving up painting, but not his support and encouragement for painters such as his friends Toss Woollaston and Colin McCahon. Art historian Peter Entwisle has also suggested that Kennedy might have been dissatisfied with his own work when confronted by that of his friends, which he considered superior.

There are only six known easel paintings by Kennedy, of which two flower still lifes are in the Hocken Collection. *Flower Piece* has an unusual, contemplative stillness despite its bold design. It is essentially a harmony with curves in yellow, orange and green with the sharply angled purple table on which the vase of marigolds is standing.

The composition is somewhat theatrical because of the illusory and ambiguous space. There are no shadows to indicate the direction of the light but the artist has highlighted in turquoise the right edge of the vase and the curve of the table. The flowers at the top of the canvas are dramatically cropped for effect and to emphasise the high angle of the view.

In the late 1950s Kennedy inherited his aunt's house in Alva Street, Dunedin. It had an overgrown back garden that Kennedy, with help from friends on the heavy work, managed to turn into a beautiful garden. He was especially fond of white flowers such as lilies.

While touring rural Otago and Southland with a theatre company he would gather not only plants but also manure and compost. One friend remembers:

> . . . the garden was an eclectic mix of rambling bits and pieces that were popped in as they were collected. The garden seemed to be bulging with a myriad of different climbers, shrubs, bulbs, roses etc all striving against each other.

One story has it that Kennedy was not averse to climbing over the railings at the Botanic Garden to steal plants.

Canterbury garden

ca 1934

COLIN LOVELL-SMITH 1894–1960

COLIN LOVELL-SMITH'S artistic output and reputation as a painter suffered partly as a result of ongoing health problems from war injuries and partly because of his administrative responsibilities at the Canterbury College School of Art and the Canterbury Society of Arts. However, the quality of his painting — he was a consummate technician — was not compromised, as evidenced by *Canterbury garden*.

Probably dating from the late 1920s to the early 1930s, according to art historian Neil Roberts, the subject of this painting is most likely to be the home and garden of one of the Lovell-Smith family. Neither the cottage nor the woman can be identified but one possible candidate is Kate Lovell-Smith, formerly the suffragist Kate Sheppard, who married Colin's father William in 1925 at the age of 78. (William died in 1929 and Kate in 1934). However, she lived next door to Colin Lovell-Smith on Riccarton Road and

her house was not a cottage. The Lovell-Smith family owned and lived in a number of properties in Riccarton, to the west of central Christchurch, which was still a rural area in the 1930s.

It is possible that this is the painting Lovell-Smith called *The elderberry tree*, exhibited at the CSA in 1938, because the tree with white blossom, which could be an elderberry, is in the centre of the composition and is the focal point for the path and flowerbed.

Location and occupant aside, there is plenty in the painting to have attracted the artist's interest. Overall the scene is uniformly lit by bright sunlight, including the flowers and blossom on the central tree, and the principal forms — the house and large trees — stand out crisply against the mostly clear sky. The flowers are deftly flicked on with one or two brushstrokes. There are also enough shadows to give variety and contrast to the surface and to emphasise depth.

Summer evening in the city
1935

JAMES FITZGERALD 1869–1945

THIS BRILLIANT, BRAVURA painting depicts the garden at Wai-iti, the property at 42 Ennis Road, St Albans, owned by the renowned Christchurch barrister and personality Charles Stewart Thomas (1889–1988), who lived there from 1916 until his death.

Wai-iti means 'little water', and alludes to the stream running through the property that is featured in the painting. Fitzgerald has given us a late afternoon scene, almost a nocturne, with the last rays of sunlight dramatically brightening the irises in the foreground and casting a few long shadows on the lawn. The clever composition further accentuates the diagonal by the positioning of another rustic bridge just in front of the trees.

Both Scottish, Fitzgerald and Thomas were probably friends. Fitzgerald lived at 69 Browns Road, a couple of minutes from Wai-iti, and his Medusa Studio was next door to Thomas's firm in the city.

When exhibited at the Canterbury Society of Arts (CSA) annual exhibition in 1935, *Summer evening in the city* was priced at 18 guineas — one of the most expensive paintings Fitzgerald had ever shown at a CSA exhibition. Fitzgerald also showed another garden painting that year entitled *Lake Mona Vale*.

In his biographical sketch of Thomas in *Brief Encounters*, writer Glyn Strange reports that he:

developed an absorbing interest in gardening, propagating his own seedlings and pricking them out in neat, military rows which were labelled, catalogued and tended with the same passion for accuracy that had characterised his work in the law.

Thomas imported and grew 300 varieties of irises. He presented bulbs from Wai-iti to the Christchurch City Council which were planted in the garden of Mona Vale, acquired by the city in the late 1960s.

Wai-iti itself no longer exists; Thomas subdivided in the 1950s, retaining his street number for the new house he built on Ennis Road.

The untidy veranda
ca 1935–38

OLIVIA SPENCER BOWER 1905–1982

OLIVIA SPENCER BOWER painted *The untidy veranda* at Claxby Farm, her family's property at Swannanoa, near Rangiora, a few years after returning there.

Spencer Bower was born in England but had emigrated to New Zealand with her family at the age of 15, and studied at the Canterbury College School of Art before returning to England to study at the Slade School and the Grosvenor School of Modern Art in London.

On her return to New Zealand in 1931, she lived at Claxby. The farm was being worked by Spencer Bower's brother, who had bought it after selling the family home in Fendalton. Spencer Bower found it a little difficult being back in New Zealand; in a letter to a friend she wrote:

Here I was back from England with my pretty clothes and self confidence I hadn't had before, and I was incarcerated in the slump [the Depression].

However, she exhibited eight works, mostly of European subjects, at the annual exhibition of the Canterbury Society of Arts the following year. By 1933 the subjects of her paintings reflected her home farm environment. *The untidy veranda* was exhibited at the Canterbury Society of Arts in 1938 and reproduced in colour as the frontispiece to *Art in New Zealand* in March 1938.

One can easily understand why publisher Harry Tombs thought this an appropriate painting for a colour plate in his magazine. By this time Spencer Bower was at the top of her game, as this confident, strong and engaging watercolour attests. Depression or no, the late summer or early autumn painting records a plentiful crop of fruit and flowers from the garden and suggests the enjoyable domestic activity of their gathering.

When her brother married in 1942, Spencer Bower and her mother moved back to Christchurch. Nevertheless, she would have been a regular visitor to Claxby, and in the 1960s she again painted several views of the veranda; the painting in the Christchurch Art Gallery is from a similar position but with mature trees and shrubs growing around it.

Later in life Spencer Bower was an innovative gardener and painted her two Christchurch gardens, though she referred to the paintings of Memorial Avenue, Fendalton (1942–1969) as 'a little thin'. Her house and studio at Leinster Road, Merivale, were built to her own requirements and there she planted tussock grass, some years before native plants became fashionable.

Poppies

ca 1937

ANNE HAMBLETT 1915–1993

ANNE HAMBLETT WAS a talented modernist painter but her at times challenging marriage to Colin McCahon and bringing up four children made it difficult for her to pursue her career.

Her exhibited paintings were favourably noted on several occasions in *Art in New Zealand* and in newspaper reviews of Otago Art Society annual exhibitions.

In 1922 Hamblett's father became vicar of St Matthew's Church in Dunedin. He and her mother Ellen (née West) created a fine flower and vegetable garden at the vicarage on Stafford Street, near the city centre. Hamblett's daughter Victoria Carr remembers that the flowers were very important for decorating her grandfather's church, and the extensive vegetable garden was equally as important, to grow food for the six children.

Hamblett lived at home while she was a student, which is where she probably set up this still life on a corner table; the surroundings look more like a domestic room than a studio. The poppies presumably came from the garden.

Hamblett's painting style is bold and sure without being flashy, and the rich red poppies contrast strongly with the blue vase and yellow tablecloth. Art historian Peter Entwisle characterised Hamblett's aesthetic when he wrote:

> *There is a toughness about the way these works are painted and a stubbornness about their refusal to be elegant.*

Poppies is arguably Hamblett's best known surviving painting and has her own hand-carved frame. Entwisle says she valued it highly herself, pricing it at £40 in the 1937 Otago Art Society annual exhibition, a very expensive painting for the time.

Entwisle proposes that the characteristics of Hamblett's paintings could be seen as:

> *a natural expression of the artist's personality. Laconic, unsentimental and intelligent, Anne Hamblett painted a few things that will endure despite having given over most of her adult life to being the wife and helpmeet of another artist.*

Mixed flowers

1940

DORIS LUSK 1916–1990

WHEN DORIS LUSK began art school at the King Edward Technical College in Dunedin in 1934, her teacher for landscape painting was Charlton Edgar. However, Robert Nettleton Field, who had earlier taught at the college but was away in England at the time, had introduced earlier students to the British modernist art theory of Roger Fry and Clive Bell, and Lusk became conversant with it. No doubt on Field's return in 1935 she absorbed his ideas (eventually published in 1940 in *Art in New Zealand*) at social gatherings at his home, although what she learnt from him directly as a teacher was pottery.

Whatever theory and influences might lie behind it, Lusk's *Mixed flowers* is refreshingly idiosyncratic, precocious, sophisticated and beautifully painted. It reveals that Lusk was as original in her still life painting as she had already demonstrated in her landscapes.

By this time Lusk was just managing to make a living from her various part-time jobs in Dunedin. With some friends, including Anne Hamblett, she had rented a former photographic studio on Moray Place, and this became the focus of their social life as well as being a busy workplace. A contemporary photograph shows Lusk seated on a divan in the large studio with raked, south-facing glazing, her 1940 exhibition hung around the walls. *Mixed flowers* was one of six flower and still life oil paintings in the selection.

The show was reported in *Art in New Zealand* (September 1940):

An exhibition in August of paintings by Miss Doris Lusk provoked much interest . . . Mr Charlton Edgar drew attention to a very attractive example of decorative work, 'Mixed Flowers.' So charmed was he with its beauty that he was purchasing and donating it to the Dunedin Art Gallery. There is much breadth of treatment in Miss Lusk's work and a strong sense of design . . . That Miss Lusk has produced such strong and attractive work this early in her career augurs well for future exhibitions.

The composition could be summarised as an exercise in counterpoint. Lusk has daringly chosen a paisley-patterned cloth for the lower half of the picture to set off the centrally positioned cream jug, while the tulips and other flowers, whose colours are picked out in the paisley below, are shown against the pale wall. To top off her playful composition she has placed some lavender flowers at the point where the top of the jug meets the top edge of the paisley, and just above that is the geometrical centre of the painting.

Lusk's painting bears virtually no relationship to seventeenth century Dutch flower still lifes except for her choice of the tulip. Rather, this is a traditional subject seen through a modernist filter, with possibly a nod in the direction of Matisse, to the extent that she would have seen his work reproduced in books.

The Painted Garden
126

View of the Duncan family garden, Durie Hill, towards Wanganui

ca 1940

VIOLET WHITEMAN 1873–1952

ENGLISH-BORN ARTIST Violet Whiteman (née Sells) is considered one of New Zealand's finest animal painters in the British tradition that has its beginnings in the early horse painters and runs through to Alfred Munnings. Whiteman was familiar with horses as she and her husband had bred and raced thoroughbreds in Herefordshire before coming to New Zealand.

As Whiteman's reputation grew, she received commissions to paint numerous animal portraits. The last of these was probably that of the 1948 New Zealand Derby winner Beau Le Havre, by which time her eyesight was failing and she suffered from arthritis in her hands.

She also painted Silent Bill, a horse owned by Sir Thomas Duncan (1873–1960), a pastoralist and racehorse breeder, who gave it as a present to Prince Henry, Duke of Gloucester, on his visit to New Zealand in 1934–5. The duke then rode Duncan's horse Black Man to fourth in the Ladies Bracelet at the Marton Jockey Club's New Year meeting before rejoining his ship in Wellington.

This painting is of the flower garden of the Duncans' family home on Durie Hill, Wanganui, across the Whanganui River from the town. As Whiteman knew Sir Thomas and Lady Duncan, this delightful painting may well have been a commission or, more likely, a gift from the artist to her friends and patrons.

A 1919 photograph held in the Alexander Turnbull Library shows the Duncans' large house when it was new, with a wide, circular drive at the front. Beyond, the Whanganui River widens towards the sea below. To the right of the house are the path and gate as can be seen in Whiteman's painting, though the magnificent flower garden has yet to be created. Whiteman's view is across the river to the city, where the brown roof of the Royal Wanganui Opera House and the spire of St Paul's can be seen.

The Duncan family home has been demolished, but a small stretch of the white fence with its distinctive fenceposts remains as a reminder of what was once an elegant mansion on the top of Durie Hill.

IV. MODERN

1940–1970

THIS SECTION OPENS and closes with two of the country's best-known painters — Rita Angus and Pat Hanly respectively — and in between demonstrates a range of styles and approaches to garden painting, perhaps to be expected in the post-war era when painting found itself at a crossroads. We find painters such as Lois White, Cedric Savage and Rata Lovell-Smith, who would soon be approaching the tail end of their careers, and Don Binney, who was just starting out on his, as well as Hanly, who had already hit his straps and was searching for a new direction. The garden was an answer.

Two gardeners, Angus and Lovell-Smith, represent the 1940s. Lovell-Smith was a very active gardener, perhaps especially after she retired from teaching at the Canterbury College School of Art in 1945, not long before *South window* was painted. Her still life in front of a window with carnations, cornflowers and hydrangeas suggests that colour played an important role in her garden, a presumption that would appear to be confirmed by talk about flowers and colour that she gave to a group of Christchurch florists in the early 1960s.

Lovell-Smith was a recent convert to Roman Catholicism. Angus, too, was interested in religion and read widely on the subject, including books on Eastern religions and philosophy. 'Rita's spirituality was mystical and deeply personal,' Jill Trevelyan explains in her biography of the artist, adding that it was 'derived from a blend of Western and Eastern beliefs, including a classical pantheistic tradition that finds the presence of God in all living things.' The singular and intense vision that characterises Angus's watercolours, emphasised by her use of symmetry, can be seen to project and reflect her spiritual relationship with nature.

A fellow student of Angus's was Ivy Fife, who received her diploma in 1931 and, following a short break, returned to the school as a teacher and colleague of Lovell-Smith. *Sunflower*, an example of Fife's paintings of the sunflowers in her garden which brought her a degree of popular success, dates from much later in her life, however Fife had never had a solo exhibition and sadly she died while her retrospective exhibition was being organised.

The only virtually gardenless painting included in these pages is of the house in Titirangi belonging to Colin McCahon and his wife Anne (née Hamblett). McCahon painted it soon after the family moved in. Artistically McCahon was far more interested in the bush, specifically kauri, but the McCahons' garden was nevertheless very important to them economically.

Just along the Manukau Harbour from French Bay, above which the McCahons lived, is Blockhouse Bay, the home of Lois White. White was a painter and teacher at the Elam School of Fine Arts, from which she retired the year before McCahon began to teach there himself. White's painting is a self-portrait, showing herself surveying her small vegetable garden after some planting. At first its title *Back door* seems curious, because the door is a relatively small element in the painting. However, since the door extends the vertical of her own figure, it becomes a compositional device, helping to stabilise the unusual zigzag composition and at the same time emphasising the golden section.

Another painting of a figure in the garden is Auckland artist John Holmwood's *The gardener*, which appears to be inspired by Grant Wood's *American Gothic* (1930), a painting that was certainly known in New Zealand from the 1940s. One can understand why it might have been one of the artist's favourite paintings but what the ordinary Russian made of it when it toured the USSR in the late 1950s is not recorded.

Auckland artist Eric Lee-Johnson was a near contemporary of Holmwood's, and shared a commercial design background with him. The nearest Lee-Johnson usually came to painting a garden was the wild vegetation and bush often shown encroaching upon his characteristically dilapidated rural buildings. In his attractive record of Pompallier, formerly the French Catholic mission's printery at Russell in the Bay of Islands, he has paid special attention to what remained of its late-nineteenth-century garden. It is probable that with some of the grant money that financed his tour of Northland to make a painted record of its old buildings, Lee-Johnson bought himself another camera; he had sold his Leica to buy a motorcycle some years before. The view of Pompallier in his black and white photograph (Museum of New Zealand Te Papa Tongarewa) is identical except for the front door, which is open.

Two very different inside–outside garden views by markedly different contemporaries stand out for their charm, skill and originality. One was painted by Stewart Maclennan, then the director of the National Art Gallery, and the other by Cedric Savage, one of the country's most popular painters, then living near Nelson.

Savage probably conceived his painting to commemorate his friendship with the woman he shows in his garden, the British artist Mabel Annesley, for several years his close neighbour in Motupipi. She was about to return to the United Kingdom and perhaps Savage also felt he would soon leave for Europe himself. Few paintings give such a strong sense of the presence of the artist: the brilliant fuchsia still life, the beckoning open door, the close friend and neighbour in the sunhat, the cat in the deckchair and the sun- and blossom-filled terrace.

Maclennan's prize-winning watercolour of his Wellington garden is in quite a different mode to Savage's fine oil but it nevertheless shares some of its elements: the open door, looking out to the garden, strong sunlight and shadows, and the deckchair and some birds in place of the cat.

Unusually, the birds for which Don Binney is so well known do not figure in either of the artist's garden paintings. However, he points out that pipiwharauroa or shining cuckoos did come to his parents' Parnell garden, and in 1962, the year after he painted his student work *Backyard garden II*, the pipiwharauroa made its first appearance on one of his canvases. *Farewell, Cecil Road* is, as its title makes clear, another valedictory painting, like Savage's and several others in these pages.

The other Wellington painter in this section is Gwen Knight. Knight spent much of her adult life in Europe, where she studied at leading art schools in London, Munich and Paris. On her return to New Zealand in 1948 she settled in Wellington and *Suzie's garden* is a typical example of the colourful landscapes that made her such a popular artist in the 1950s and 60s.

The garden paintings of an accepted old master of New Zealand contemporary art, Pat Hanly, which straddle three decades, are positioned at the end of this section but could equally have been the starting point of the next. *'Inside' the garden* is one of Hanly's earliest oil and enamel garden paintings, inspired like all his garden paintings by the Windmill Road, Mount Eden garden made by his wife Gil. It followed the *'Inside' the garden* watercolours that were exhibited with great success in 1969, the first of several garden-themed watercolour exhibitions that Hanly held until the mid 1980s.

RITA ANGUS 1908–1970

RITA ANGUS REFERS frequently to gardening in her letters to friends, at times going as far as to say that she wanted to be left alone to paint and garden. She loved nature, especially all aspects of flowers, and her delicate watercolours of passionflowers, irises and waterlilies are among her most admired works.

As well as painting blooms alone, Angus often included flowers in her paintings in other ways; portraits feature them and self-portraits show flowers embroidered on a piece of clothing of which she was particularly fond. They are not only decoration but symbolic, most obviously of fecundity, an underlying theme of many of her paintings.

The year 1943, when Angus painted this exquisite, tiny watercolour, was a turning point for the artist. Her parents purchased a cottage for her at 18 Aranoni Track, Clifton, near Sumner, Christchurch, in which she settled in the autumn of 1943. It was a time for renewal after a period of poor mental and physical health. She wrote to her friend, composer Douglas Lilburn:

I am letting my past slip away from me, as I rest in the sun and work in the garden, my brain is less cluttered with useless problems, my brain is free and clear for the present.

Having her own house allowed her, probably for the first time, to plant a vegetable garden.

Art materials were increasingly hard to obtain because of the war, so Angus drew and painted in watercolour. Her sister, Jean Jones, recalled that Angus painted this passionflower while was staying with her in Greymouth in 1943, but it is probable, as these works could take a long time to complete, that Angus had begun the painting at Clifton and completed it in Greymouth.

Another exceptional painting of this period, *Tree* (Museum of New Zealand Te Papa Tongarewa) was certainly painted in Greymouth: it is of the cherry tree in Jean and Fred Jones's garden. The visionary intensity about these early nature paintings by Angus may reflect her interest in mysticism and spirituality, both eastern and Christian.

Although Angus was interested in indigenous plants, this is not the New Zealand passionflower — *Passiflora tetrandra* — but one of the many cultivated exotics such as *Passiflora racemosa*.

RITA COOK /43

Waterlilies

1950

RITA ANGUS 1908–1970

IN OCTOBER 1949, Rita Angus experienced a serious psychotic episode that, she later admitted to her mother, was caused by self-starvation. After two months in Sunnyside Mental Hospital, where she received electroconvulsive therapy as part of her treatment, Angus was able to leave on condition that she stayed for a year in the care of her parents.

William and Ethel Angus had lived at Waikanae on the Kapiti Coast since 1943 and Angus was a regular visitor to their home. William Angus added to the already extensive property with the purchase of some native bush and turned it into a very large garden. Jill Trevelyan, the artist's biographer, describes it as having 'a cherry-tree walk, leading to a waterlily pond and a magnificent central rosebed'.

Angus had frequently painted the garden on previous visits, but *Waterlilies* is a *tour de force*, particularly given that she was recuperating. She sent the painting to that year's exhibition of The Group. Though painted in an entirely different style from Monet, it is interesting that Angus used the French Impressionist's approach to the overall composition: the waterlilies are viewed from above, thus avoiding a horizon line. However, Angus goes one step further and avoids all but a hint of perspective.

Garden, Waikanae

ca 1952

RITA ANGUS 1908–1970

GARDEN, WAIKANAE WAS painted on one of Rita Angus's visits to her parents in Waikanae. The centrally placed tree in a symmetrical composition is a recurring motif for her.

A 1946 painting made at her parents' house, *Tree in blossom*, shows the garden in its early stages. *Garden, Waikanae*, painted some six years later, is of a similar view, towards the Waikanae Hills, but reveals a mature, more densely planted and colourful garden, lit by the morning sun. The painting's bright colours suggest happiness and optimism and Angus had plenty to be optimistic about; she was fully recovered from her illness and back living at Clifton.

In 1952 Angus was included in Wellington gallery owner Helen Hitchings's extremely important London exhibition *Fifteen New Zealand Painters* and she would soon begin a four-year stint making plant illustrations for the *School Journal*.

RITA ANGUS 1908–1970

IN THE LATE 1930s and early 1940s, Rita Angus painted detailed watercolour studies of numerous flowers including crocuses, aquilegias, nasturtiums and carnations. Her earliest significant painting of irises was in 1942 when she painted some of the flowers in a vase (Christchurch Art Gallery). The following year, Angus went so far as to compare the iris with herself and her talent as an artist when she wrote in a letter to composer Douglas Lilburn, quoted by Tony Mackle in *Rita Angus: life and vision*:

It is only in the last few months that I've begun to know mine, as a tiny New Zealand flower it grows, I think I may belong to the iris family one day.

Later the iris became one of her favourite flowers to paint, also appearing in paintings of other subjects as the *Sun Goddess* watercolour of 1949. Angus painted this watercolour, *Iris*, in her garden at Clifton near Sumner, Christchurch. The painting can be dated precisely because a friend of Angus's, a young man called Robert Erwin who had modelled for her, wrote to Lilburn in November 1953:

I see a good deal of Rita. I spent the afternoon gardening and basking in the sun on the brick terrace. She is doing a water-colour of flag irises — painting them 'in situ'.

Angus exhibited *Iris* at the 1955 New Zealand Academy of Fine Arts annual exhibition, priced at 15 guineas.

South window

ca 1948—9

RATA LOVELL-SMITH 1894–1969

IN THE 1920s and 1930s, Rata Lovell-Smith became known for her modernist Canterbury landscapes. While from the mid-1930s she increasingly painted still lifes with flowers, in 1939 she won the Bledisloe Medal for Landscape at the Auckland Society of Art.

At the time she painted *South Window* she and her husband, painter and art school administrator Colin Lovell-Smith (see page 118), were living at 299 Riccarton Road in a house they built in the mid-1920s, not long after their marriage. Rata Lovell-Smith had recently retired from teaching at the Canterbury College School of Art.

Painting a south-facing view meant the sun was behind the artist and, in Christchurch, facing south means facing the Port Hills. In the top left-hand corner Lovell-Smith shows the distinctive peak of the Port Hills generally known as Castle Rock or Te Tihi o Kahukura — pinnacle of the rainbow. From the upper south-facing window of the house on Riccarton Road she could probably not quite see Castle Rock, although there is a small peak visible which, a little playfully, the artist has given the form of the far better-known landmark.

One can imagine a scene where, having picked the cornflowers and carnations in the garden and put them into a glass vase, perhaps destined for a bedroom, the artist saw the hydrangeas through the window. She would have noticed that they were essentially different tones of similar colours and, with the Port Hills peeking through, worthy of a picture.

Lovell-Smith was a very keen gardener. In her master's thesis on the artist, Ann Elias reprints a review from the *Evening Post* about her first exhibited flower painting, at the CSA in 1935, which is described as 'a distinctly original, if somewhat wiry little statement'. Elias adds that a characteristic of Lovell-Smith's flower paintings is that 'the edges of flowers, the petals and stalks are precisely delineated', as is the case in this painting.

South window was exhibited at the Canterbury Society of Arts annual exhibition in 1949.

View through to Savage's garden

ca 1953

CEDRIC SAVAGE 1901–1969

CEDRIC SAVAGE WAS one of this country's most popular painters of his generation. After serving overseas in the Second World War, he returned to settle near Takaka, Golden Bay, where he cemented his position in the artistic scene. He served on the committee of management of the National Art Gallery from 1945–1953 and showed in art society exhibitions around the country to generate income.

Savage built a house on Packards Road just south of Motupipi and established a very fine garden. He was generous with the fruit and vegetables that he grew there. 'Stepping into his garden was like being in the Mediterranean' was how one visitor remembered it, an observation borne out by Savage's sun-filled painting.

The woman in *View through to Savage's garden* is his friend and closest neighbour — just 100 metres away — the artist Lady Mabel Annesley. The view is from the doorway between the bedroom and Savage's studio, looking out through the studio's double doors into the garden. Savage may have been attracted by the coincidental juxtaposition of the colours of the fuschia, Annesley's dress and the flowers behind her — wisteria, perhaps? — against the various complementary shades of green.

In an essay on Savage, art historian Dorothee Pauli characterised the relationship between the two artists:

By all accounts, her exchanges with the increasingly sensitive and often argumentative Savage were not always pleasant.

Nevertheless, this is a idyllic scene and, as an interior with figures, an unusual subject for Savage. Therefore, it is tempting to date the painting to the early summer of 1953, the eve of Annesley's return to Britain, painted as a commemoration of her sojourn in Motupipi and their friendship.

Annesley (1881–1959) was the daughter of the fifth Earl of Annesley, an Anglo–Irish peer whose family seat is at Castlewellan, County Down, where she was born. Already a trained artist, in 1920–21 Annesley studied wood engraving at the Central School of Art and Design. In 1941, when Castlewellan was commandeered by the army, Annesley embarked on a round-the-world trip by boat. From October 1941 to at least mid-1942 she lived in Nelson but was back in Britain in 1945. She then returned to New Zealand and by December 1949 was living at Motupipi. In the early 1950s she was a board member of the Bishop Suter Art Gallery but she resigned following a controversy over her acquisition of some advanced British art and returned to Britain in late 1953.

House in trees, Titirangi

1953

COLIN McCAHON 1919–1987

COLIN McCAHON BEGAN this painting not long after he, his wife Anne Hamblett and their four children moved to Auckland from Christchurch, where he believed he had been promised a position at the Auckland City Art Gallery by its director Eric Westbrook. Initially the only job available was as the cleaner but after a few months he was appointed curator.

Meanwhile, he had to find somewhere to live. It was not easy but eventually he found something he could afford in Titirangi, a tiny house at 67 Otitori Bay Road. In reality it was little more than a bach but it was to be the McCahons' home for seven years. The house, on a steeply sloping section, had a small patch of land and was surrounded by native bush, including kauri trees and a grove of nikau palms.

Early in his marriage, McCahon had worked as a gardener at the Wellington Botanic Gardens in order to support his family. A vegetable garden was an important economic necessity wherever they lived; he even grew cabbages in their front garden in Christchurch. Visitors were frequently surprised by the McCahons' gardens. The children gathered cuttings when out on walks and McCahon was generous in offering cuttings to others.

The vegetable garden in Titirangi was essential to their survival, and McCahon began it soon after they moved in. In a letter to a friend, poet John Caselberg, McCahon wrote:

Spent Sat & Sun in the garden — did quite some digging — for vegetables — and some fancy work for my soul. Planted beans & some silver beet & cabbages & about 200 ferns of various sorts in the kauri patch — am planning drifts of ferns in places & drifts of a very softly yellow green small shrub that grows here — a native — it could be a myrtle and a gradual removal of all the wrong things to a safer distance from the native stuff. Have planted 3 clumps of toe-toe to look at themselves in the pond — this tonight — was down there in the dark — in rain & mud it was gently lovely and sweet and so quiet after Barbour St.

None of McCahon's paintings of this period actually show the garden but are views of the house surrounded by bush which McCahon referred to as the 'domestic landscape'. *House in trees, Titirangi*, probably painted in November, is one of these.

Paintings and largely drawings of kauri dominated his work at this time. One drawing was of his wife Anne with kauri behind her which he called *Madame Cézanne at Titirangi*, thus alluding to an important influence.

Pompallier House, Russell
1955

ERIC LEE-JOHNSON 1908–1993

IN THE EARLY 1950s, in his short illustrated biography of Eric Lee-Johnson, Eric McCormick wrote:

Is it now too late to revive the scheme for systematic survey of New Zealand's historic places? Clearly there is urgent need of some graphic record before the surviving relics crumble into dust or are effaced by an ever-encroaching suburbia.

In his autobiography, Lee-Johnson records how this project eventually came to fruition. In 1953 he moved to the Waimamaku Valley, south of the Hokianga Harbour, and the following year he received the first part of a two-year fellowship from the Association of New Zealand Art Societies. This enabled him to fit out a vehicle and travel around Northland making paintings and drawings of early colonial wood-framed buildings. *Pompallier House, Russell* was one of these 'records' and it was first exhibited at the Auckland Society of Arts in 1956, though it was not for sale.

Lee-Johnson was obsessive about the primacy of his work and in his autobiography he lamented this series:

They attracted attention, setting off a romantic movement that soon had imitators adding a popularising touch of disintegration to every kind of country or city dwelling, early or late. Where my drawings were informed architectural studies accurately recorded by one who well knew how wooden buildings are constructed, most imitators would only produce superficial pictures that sagged in the wrong places.

The Catholic mission printery at Russell in the Bay of Islands, now known simply as Pompallier, did not have a garden. The mission was disestablished in 1850 and in the 1880s, Pompallier's new owner, Hamlyn Greenway, converted the building into an elegant home. His widowed sister, Jane Mair, designed and developed the garden.

Kate Martin, manager of Pompallier for the New Zealand Historic Places Trust, reports that a leading garden writer of the time described Mair's garden as 'promiscuous',

a casual mixture of annuals, perennials, shrubs and trees contrasting with the then more fashionable geometric style of planting. [Mair planted] the deep and curvaceous flower borders that follow the garden path and the scented elaeagnus hedges as windbreaks, then inter-planted them with colourful tecoma.

There was also shell ginger, bougainvillea, pyrostegia, potato vines, whau and cabbage trees, making a typical 'tropical' garden of the era. In addition there was a vegetable garden and an orchard planted with the popular cultivars of Mair's time, which are rare today.

The Stephenson family took up residence in 1905 and in addition to erecting the flagpole, they planted the Poor Knights lily soon after the species was discovered in 1924. They turned a neglected hillside into a parkland of native and exotic trees, including a totara avenue that is now reaching maturity.

Lee-Johnson painted a phoenix palm where originally there was a fan palm, which was probably planted after the government took over Pompallier in 1943. His view shows the sash windows that were installed in the late 1870s and the balcony that was removed in the 1990s as part of the restoration of the building back to its 1840s form and function as the mission's printery.

JOHN HOLMWOOD 1910–1987

JOHN HOLMWOOD WAS a painter of landscapes, urban scenes and subjects with figures, all very much of their time: brightly coloured, direct and expressionist in their handling. His figure paintings especially were wittily observed and lively and, as a result, popular.

It is tempting to call the painting *New Zealand Gothic* because it seems to be an ironic version of the famous painting *American Gothic* (1930) by American regionalist painter Grant Wood, in which a middle-aged farming couple, the man holding a pitchfork, stand in front of a weatherboard house. Here Holmwood has a single figure, holding a rake in his left hand and the handle of another implement in his right. Like Wood's man, Holmwood's is largely bald, but the remaining hair on either side of his head sticks up and gives him a slightly devilish look. In place of the jacket worn by Wood's man, Holmwood's gardener wears a jerkin. Behind the gardener is an orange tree in front of a red garden shed; a red barn appears in the background of *American Gothic*.

The gardener has all the characteristics of Holmwood at his idiosyncratic best: humorously observed, defined by firm outlines and painted with lively brushwork and vivid colours. One feels absolutely certain that this is a portrait of someone that Holmwood knew well.

Holmwood's first solo exhibition was in 1957,

the year after he painted *The gardener*. He showed 26 paintings, mostly oils, at the Architectural Centre Gallery in Wellington. The *Evening Post* reviewer thought Holmwood 'a gifted artist, imaginative, sensitive and, in many ways, quite original in his approach'. He concluded with the advice that Holmwood 'has the skill to become a brilliant landscape painter, but', he added, 'there are times, especially in his figure studies — an example is *The Gardener* — when he sacrifices quality for the bizarre.'

Peter Tomory, the then recently appointed director of the Auckland City Art Gallery, included the painting in the first of his ground-breaking annual exhibitions *Eight New Zealand Painters* (November–December 1957). Holmwood recorded that *The gardener* was also included in the Tomory-selected exhibition sent by the New Zealand government to tour the Soviet Union in 1959, along with his *Landscape with a sawmill* (1952). Although it is not on the list of exhibits, a letter in the gallery's exhibition file from Colin McCahon, then keeper of the gallery, states that 'permission has been given for the John Holmwood picture to be included', and this may well have been *The gardener*.

Holmwood thought *The gardener* one of his best works, and it was included in his *Retrospective Exhibition 1946–1976* at the Auckland Society of Arts in 1984.

A LOIS WHITE 1903–1984

FOR MOST OF her life, artist Lois White lived at 5 Richardson Road, Mount Albert, Auckland, in a house her father had designed and had built for his family. The Mount Albert area had yet to be extensively subdivided and the Whites had a large garden and an orchard surrounded by a scoria wall to keep out the grazing animals.

It was not until 1952 that the Whites — Lois, her sister Gwen and her mother Annie, known as Ma White, then aged 88 — moved for the first and last time; they returned to Taunton Terrace, Blockhouse Bay, where they had lived close to her mother's uncle when Lois was a toddler. It was a small, fibrolite-clad house, overlooking what is now Blockhouse Bay Beach Reserve. White later built a studio in the garden of which there is an interior photograph by Marti Friedlander from around 1980.

In 1950, the Elam School of Art became part of the University of Auckland, and White was appointed as a lecturer in figure painting. She still showed annually at the Auckland Society of Arts: usually figure compositions, mainly of religious subjects, and sometimes landscapes. She also sent works to the Otago Art Society. Her paintings were not mentioned by Auckland reviewers, although reviewers elsewhere occasionally singled out her work. In 1958 *Gethsemane* was bought by the Sarjeant Gallery, though not without controversy.

In 1959 White exhibited two paintings at the Manawatu Art Society in Palmerston North: *By the waters of Babylon*, a major figure composition of 1954, priced at 40 guineas, and *Back door*, a

painting of the previous year, modestly priced at 14 guineas.

Back door is a self-portrait, with the artist standing in an almost military or at least rather defiant pose, one foot on her lawn, apparently immaculate like the house, a yard brush in place of a paintbrush in her hand. The self-portrait somehow seems to both reflect and presage the growing tensions in her professional life. The ASA was being criticised by Eric Westbrook, director of the Auckland City Art Gallery, and the new wave, represented by the 27-year-old Robert Ellis, a graduate of the Royal College of Art, was starting to make its presence felt at Elam.

White has painted the back of the house and the back door of the painting's title is open. The artist has her back to us and has just tidied up after recently planting some flowers or vegetables, which she is now contemplating.

Back door records the modest but tidy plantings on the left below the back steps and the fruiting tamarillo tree. White has positioned herself immediately below the open back door. She is in shadow while the rest of the scene is in sun, as is her cat, but her two dachshunds — one or the other appears in her arms in several photographs — are absent.

The death of her mother in 1957, aged 93, allowed White to eventually take a sabbatical year. In December 1960 she travelled to Europe for the first time, with fellow artist Ida Eise. After one more year of teaching on her return, White retired in January 1963.

Wellington suburban garden

ca 1960

STEWART MACLENNAN 1903–1973

WELLINGTON SUBURBAN GARDEN was painted at Stewart and Dorothy Maclennan's house in Houghton Bay, Wellington. Designed to their specifications by CJ Fearnley and built in 1952, the house was featured in *New Zealand Home & Building* in October that year, where the writer described it as having 'magnificent views south, east and north' but noted that it was exposed to 'severe' southerlies and northerlies, even for Wellington, 'sweeping up the hill without a break' to the top of Houghton Bay Road.

The pleasant outlook, the nearness to the beaches for the children, and the fact that a bus passing the door will take the owner, Mr S B Maclennan, in 10 minutes to the Art Gallery of which he is Director, were factors in favour of the site.

The photographs illustrating the *Home & Building* article show the grounds totally unlandscaped, while Maclennan's painting, a decade on, reveals a garden of some maturity. Maclennan's son Ian explains that his mother, the artist Dorothy Maclennan (1916–1996), was the gardener and that the garden was 'a pleasant spot sheltered by a hedge and trees'.

Soon after we moved in, a northerly gale blew in two of the lounge windows. The Pinus radiata *were planted soon afterwards for shelter and a trellis windbreak was built which allowed the abutilon hedge to become established and the rest of the garden to flourish. The soil was built up*

from the rocky base with compost and seaweed collected from the southern beaches. The garden was certainly a peaceful and calm haven in most weather. The pines were periodically topped by my father, who usually took a couple of trinitron [a nitroglycerin drug for ischemia] *before climbing the ladder.*

Maclennan's view is towards the north from the living room, which has a door onto a terrace. Beyond the trees one would see Evans Bay. He has captured a charming garden scene, with the strong late-afternoon sun light coming through to a corner of the lawn and catching the edge of the terrace and hedge to the right of the window. This provides a nice contrast with the rest of the lawn and hedge still in shadow. Afternoon coffee things are still on the table, suggesting that while having a cuppa the artist thought the light suggested a good picture and popped inside to get it down — at which point the blackbirds and thrushes appeared on the lawn and bird-feeder, so he included them too. Beyond the garden Maclennan has sketched in a typical Wellington townscape, with the houses seemingly perched on top of each other up the hill.

Maclennan won the National Bank Watercolour Prize in 1962 with *Wellington suburban garden*, and again in 1963 and 1966. The painting was number 13 in Maclennan's retrospective exhibition of paintings, drawings and prints in the New Zealand Academy of Fine Arts rooms in the National Art Gallery in January 1980.

Backyard garden II

1961

DON BINNEY 1940—

IN THE SUMMER of his final student year at art school, Don Binney painted *Backyard garden II* at his family home in Awatea Road, Parnell, Auckland. Earlier that year he had painted a similar view from the same location, *Backyard garden*, which had been exhibited in *Young NZ Artists*, the Auckland Society of Arts' Auckland Festival exhibition.

Binney had probably noticed the artistic potential of the site when up on the carport and garage roof trimming the tecoma hedge. The elevation reminded him of Britain's Camden Town School, and perhaps Victor Pasmore, whose London street scenes were often from an upstairs window.

Binney decided to paint it again 'because the first *Backyard garden* was a relative success: a breakthrough', the artist explains. He adds that his 'first Pipiwharauroa [shining cuckoo] paintings in 1962 were, by association, located hereabouts' because at the end of September they fed on the insects that the cineraria attracted.

For *Backyard garden II* Binney doubled the size of the board and hauled it up onto the roof of the carport, where he blocked in the essentials of the composition in one session. He then took the board into the house, upstairs and through the small hatchway into his studio space under the eaves — he had cut the board to the largest size that would fit through — and the painting was completed there.

Recognisable features in *Backyard garden II* include the incinerator and concrete paving blocks. Much space is given to a prolific grapefruit tree, so typical of damp, ill-drained back gardens in 1950s–60s Auckland. A tecoma hedge forms the termination to the right.

Binney thinks of his approach to painting at the time as being more Canterbury in style than Elam, and cites if not the direct influence of Ted Bracey, then his spirit. It is, however, difficult to avoid being reminded too of Colin McCahon's Titirangi paintings by Binney's treatment of the tree trunk on the left and, superficially, the discretely painted facets or 'patchwork' of the foliage, which Binney associated with the paintings of Keith Patterson in the 1950s.

Binney was also influenced by British painters of the era, perhaps artists such as Peter Lanyon and Terry Frost, whose work Binney had seen in the 'grey and white' illustrations in Pelican books such as Herbert Read's *Contemporary British Art*.

Binney's *Backyard garden II* is very much of its era: perhaps the landscape you paint when you shouldn't paint a landscape! It is somewhat banal, unromantic and almost consciously avoids lyricism. Yet the artist has responded to the specific forms of the shrubs and trees and to fruit or flowers, with the small patches of blue and red and the dotted surface of orange blobs, grapefruit, ripe on the tree.

Farewell, Cecil Road

1985

DON BINNEY 1940–

DON BINNEY'S STUDENT work *Backyard garden II* (see page 157) shows the artist's pleasure in and facility with oil painting. However, besides being in the landscape genre, albeit suburban, there is not much to hint at the direction his painting would take the following year when he introduced for the first time a bird, the subject which would endear him most to his many admirers.

Twenty years later, his artistic reputation secured, Binney married Philippa Moore and they moved into a house in Cecil Road, Epsom, Auckland. The following year, 1982, their daughter Mary was born. Philippa Binney had ideas for the garden, including a sunken garden once they had removed two towering, unattractive cypresses, but their short time there and new motherhood did not allow for much development.

Binney made this carefully worked and detailed picture, using assorted pastels, in commemoration of their stay at Cecil Road, as the title declares. While they did not live in the house for long, they had an emotional attachment to it as their first family home.

Over the scoria rock wall Binney shows Owens Road, with the three white daisy bushes on the near side and some small pittosporum bushes on the other. Philippa Binney recalls that the plants on the garden side of the wall included geraniums, a giant forget-me-not and a single young puka tree, which the artist has recorded.

The Binneys now live in his family home at Awatea Road, Parnell, Auckland, the site of the artist's earliest brush with the garden.

IVY FIFE, whose national reputation was secured by her portrait *Peter* (ca 1943), bought by the Auckland City Art Gallery in 1944, considered herself a portrait painter first and foremost. Landscape was 'her second choice', according to gallery director Brian Muir in his essay in the catalogue to her 1977 retrospective exhibition at the Robert McDougall Art Gallery, Christchurch.

In 1959 Fife became unwell; by 1975 she had developed a serious heart condition and had to stop painting. However, in the earlier stages of her illness, though pretty much confined to home, she could paint but only things 'close at hand'. The sunflower paintings that resulted from this hardship were the apogee of her career, when her skill and technique were matched and rewarded by widespread popular and professional acclaim.

Fife and her husband, Alan Forrester, had planted sunflower seeds that a friend had given them and some grew to a height of 3m. She painted the flowers at different stages, including the dead heads.

The earliest of Fife's *Sunflower* paintings was first exhibited in 1959. The *Christchurch Star*, reporting on the annual Canterbury Society of Arts exhibition, declared:

This year the well known Ivy Fife has gone into the garden for her subjects. One painting features a huge golden sunflower against a dark background.

A later colour photograph captured Fife painting *en plein air* in her garden with masses of tall sunflowers growing in the background, a large board upright on her easel, her right hand on her hip. Her left, not visible, probably firmly wields her palette knife. Her practice was to prepare a ground with two layers of white on the board and then paint the image itself out of doors in front of the motif.

The 1964 *Sunflower* is reproduced in colour on the cover of the catalogue of the 1977 *Retrospective*. Six *Sunflower* paintings were exhibited, as well as paintings titled *Leaves* and *Ferns*. An impressive-looking metre-high painting of her garden with sunflowers in bloom, *Up the garden path* (1959), its current whereabouts unknown, is illustrated in black and white.

Muir, who had the benefit of seeing all the sunflower paintings as he prepared the retrospective exhibition, described their impact in the catalogue:

These pictures, mostly painted with the palette knife, radiate warmth and sunshine, and give to her last major series of painting a brilliant splash of colour and excitement. Their leaves, stems and petals provide wonderful excuses for her love of pattern making and arrangement of shape and colour. There is a boldness and a strength about the sunflower series that quite obscures the rapidly failing physical strength of the painter.

Suzie's garden

ca 1969

GWEN KNIGHT 1888–1974

IN GWEN KNIGHT'S early life painting played second fiddle to music, which she had studied at the Sydney Conservatorium of Music. When she returned to her birthplace of Wellington, after training as a physiotherapist in Dunedin, she was well regarded as an accompanist. Apparently an injury led to her seriously taking up painting. Knight was also encouraged by Frances Hodgkins, whom she met in St Tropez and Ibiza. Hodgkins painted her three times; one of these paintings is *Pinewoods*, which was presented to the National Art Gallery in 1936.

Once based in Wellington, Knight exhibited annually at the New Zealand Academy of Fine Arts as well as in exhibitions of the Group of Nine, the Thursday Group and later the Eastern Bays Group. *Suzie's Garden* was exhibited at the NZAFA's autumn exhibition in 1969 and was later used as an illustration in the history of the academy, *Portrait of a Century*.

An article in the *Evening Post* about Knight's solo exhibition at the Bett–Duncan Gallery in May 1971 noted that the 20 paintings had all been done 'since November from recent trips, her imagination and her travel sketchbooks of years ago'. Accordingly we can assume that *Suzie's Garden* was painted not long before her 1969 exhibition.

It is typical of the delightful, vibrant and expressive painting following Knight's return to New Zealand. It is also a good example of the kind of loose, informal painting — in which strong colour provides structure — that marks the work of New Zealand's European-trained artists of the period, especially those who attended Hans Hofmann's and André Lhote's art schools.

'Inside' the garden

1969–1970

PAT HANLY 1932–2004

WHEN ARTIST PAT Hanly and his wife Gil returned to New Zealand from London in 1962, they bought a house in Windmill Road, Mount Eden, Auckland.

Gil Hanly had little direct experience of gardening, but her parents had a good vegetable garden and she remembers playing in her aunt's large garden as a child. She developed an attractive garden at Windmill Road, although in comparing it to the large, impressive garden she has subsequently made at Walters Road, where the Hanlys moved in 1993, she is a little dismissive; she says it was not planned and the planting was somewhat haphazard, often simply plants friends gave her or plants struck from cuttings she had picked up on walks. Nevertheless, contemporary photographs show a tidy paved area outside the kitchen, a large lawn and beyond it the main planting, screening the back fence. Features included the then-fashionable banana palms, an old plum, a ginkgo and a grapefruit tree. Pat Hanly was not much involved beyond mowing the lawn, yet the Windmill Road garden would both inspire him and be the subject of several paintings from 1968 onwards.

Around 1967 was a watershed for Hanly's painting; his biographer Russell Haley refers to it as 'The Change'. Determined to shake off 'years of useless restrictions of every kind . . . to begin at the literal beginning', Hanly explored all the options, including painting on black canvases in the dark and taking LSD. He wrote a list of 'dos and don'ts' including: 'no cause stuff'

(relating to his stand against nuclear submarines and atomic tests), 'inner nature', 'composition does not exist' and 'do not make *pictures* (any more)!'. The paintings that followed, the *'Inside' the garden, Energy* and *Molecular creation* works, resulted to some degree from this intense period of experimentation.

Hanly's first garden painting, *Interior of garden*, was made in July 1968 then, in December, he began rapidly painting the 42 watercolours entitled *'Inside' the garden* that were shown to considerable acclaim at Barry Lett Galleries in May 1969.

The catalogue cover was of Hanly-paint-spattered black paper. Above Lett's introduction was a paraphrase of William Blake's lines from 'Auguries of Innocence' — 'The universe in a grain of sand and eternity in a flower' — and a quotation from spiritual master Meher Baba. Lett's text concludes: 'The change that has occurred in Pat Hanly's work and ideas is of such importance that in the future any evaluation of his mature work will start with these watercolours', and the uncredited aphorism: 'Those who see only the garden see nothing.'

The *'Inside' the garden* watercolours are of or directly inspired by Hanly's Windmill Road garden. The handful of oil/enamel paintings that followed, like this one, also incorporate elements of the garden but are more generalised. Instead, primacy is given to the forms, paint application — dots or colour blocks — and arbitrary colour.

Garden energy

1972

PAT HANLY 1932–2004

PAT HANLY'S *MOLECULAR* creation series (1968–70)was followed in 1972–74 by the *Energy series* from which *Garden energy* comes. Hanly's biographer Russell Haley has attempted to establish a chronology for the paintings of this period.

What is reasonably certain is that between the Creation Works *and the* Allsorts *exhibitions [April 1974] Pat produced many oil and enamel works on hardboard which examined both the Windmill Road garden and Mount Eden over the whole period of one or several summers. There are twenty or more paintings with titles such as* Garden Awake *or* Mid-Summer Garden. *Several landscape paintings that relate to Auckland's west coast and Huia in particular were painted around this time. A large number of these works also carry the sub-title* Energy Series.

Meticulously painted, and akin to a stage set in its cut-out silhouettes and sharply defined edges, *Garden energy* is the view from the back of the Hanlys' Windmill Road house. The side of the house is on the left, the ginkgo tree appears against the solid blue sky and on the right are the next-door neighbour's pohutukawa, which required cutting back when they overhung the Hanlys' section, as in the painting.

The strong perspectival structure of the composition is unusual for Hanly but extremely effective. It produces a dream-like, almost surreal quality and the flowers deep in the centre, below the floating forms, are magical. Indeed, if *'Inside' the garden* (see page 165) represents that aspect of the psychedelic in which reality dissolves into formlessness, *Garden energy* represents the remarkable, visionary clarity that is also associated with psychotropic experiences.

In Hanly's obituary in the *Listener* in 2004, art writer Gregory O'Brien summed up the garden paintings using this one as an example:

Works like Garden Energy *(1972) owe a lot not only to his idiosyncratic scientific studies, but also to the pointillism of Georges Seurat, the contents of the Psychedelic Poster Shop and the Yates Garden Guide. The garden, in Hanly's art, was certainly a peaceable Eden, but it was also a mechanism storing and releasing energy and colour. The plant life and vegetation were nature's kites and windmills for this quixotic painter.*

Untitled

1981

PAT HANLY 1932–2004

IN 1980 PAT Hanly was awarded a QEII Arts Council grant to study public murals and street art in the United States. However, because of his teaching commitments, the only time the Hanlys could get away for several months was November to January, the northern winter. Not only were they frightfully cold for a lot of the time, there was also not much actual street art happening. However, they travelled extensively, visiting Los Angeles, San Francisco, Washington, Chicago and New York with a side trip to Mexico to see the Diego Rivera murals.

Despite the drawbacks it was an exciting trip. Hanly, who found it very difficult to get back into painting on their return to Auckland, bumped into a friend and mentioned his 'painter's block'. His friend, who owned one of the *'Inside' the garden* watercolours, suggested that it might help if Hanly revisited a familiar subject, such as the garden. A couple of days later he received an excited telephone call from a delighted Hanly, who had followed his advice, with the desired effect. *Untitled* was that first painting, and the friend bought it.

Gil Hanly points out, however, that it was not unusual for Hanly, when he had finished a series, to go through a fallow period before developing a new theme and embarking on the next group of works.

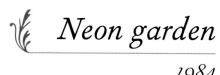

ONCE PAT HANLY had embarked on his new series of garden watercolours in 1981, following his return from the United States, he regularly made groups of watercolours and/or crayon drawings of the garden, usually in spring or summer, for his exhibitions at RKS Art in Auckland.

In 1983, in addition to the *Innocence* series of paintings, he showed *Amazing gardens*, which also went to the Peter McLeavey Gallery in Wellington. In 1984, it was McLeavey's turn to sell that year's garden watercolours, *Incredible gardens*, while in 1987 Hanly was back at RKS Art with *Great gardens*. However, *Incredible gardens* was first exhibited at RKS Art; at the end of his review of the principal RKS exhibition of the time, TJ McNamara added: 'In the smaller gallery Patrick Hanly is showing his incomparably lovely garden paintings. Sadly they are not for sale here but will be sold in Wellington'.

Neon garden was probably one of the *Incredible gardens*. Hanly's reference to neon, together with the dark sky beyond the trees, suggest that we are looking at the garden at night, brightly lit by artificial light. Hanly might also have associated his strong concentric shapes with the structure of neon signs. The artist's sheer delight in getting down the foliage, flowers, fruit and blossom is palpable and the result one of joyful fecundity. More prosaically, the painting documents Gil Hanly's further development of the garden with the addition of a low retaining wall beyond the lawn.

neon garden. Hawley 80

V. CONTEMPORARY

1970–2008

Gretchen Albrecht, *Wekaweka garden* (detail), see page 181

IT SEEMS SOMEHOW paradoxical that there are more artists discussed in the almost four decades to 2008 than there were in the five decades from 1890 to 1940. And not only are there more pure garden paintings in the contemporary period, but there are also more paintings by artists of their own gardens.

Perhaps there was something in the water or simply a case of '*après* Hanly *le deluge*'. For whatever reason, in the early 1970s there was a significant burst of paintings of gardens by a number of progressive painters — both the already established, such as Gretchen Albrecht and Philip Trusttum, and the emerging, such as James Ross. Kees and Tina Hos's New Vision Gallery in Auckland even dedicated an exhibition to the subject, *The Artist's Garden*, in July 1974, which included works by Pat Hanly, Alan Pearson and Trusttum. TJ McNamara's review in the *New Zealand Herald* opened with: 'Predictably, an exhibition called "The Artist's Garden" would be charming and the exhibition at the New Vision Gallery comes up to expectations.' Having noted the single Hanly watercolour and some 'pallid patterns of flowers and leaves' by Louise Henderson, McNamara explains that 'the real energy in the show' came from the two Christchurch painters, Pearson and Trusttum.

On the other hand, the *Auckland Star*'s glum reviewer, Hamish Keith, fed up with Auckland's 'dank' winter, managed briefly to rise to the occasion before sinking back into pessimistic mode:

> *For some odd reason painters are beginning to be happy about something or other. Goodness knows why. The world is such a miserable place . . . all kinds of nastiness looming on every social front, it seems odd that painters should have anything at all to celebrate, particularly gardens at a time when no one can afford one.*

Pointing out that earlier art patrons commissioned illuminations and paintings of great beauty to take their minds off earthly concerns such as wars and the Black Death, he concludes:

> *It may be that our own paintings are doing the same kind of thing for us. Patrick Hanly, for instance, fashions images of miraculous growth, while the rest of us poison the earth and the air. Philip Trusttum paints gardens as delicate as a willow pattern plate while we bulldoze our gentler past and bury it in concrete motorways. Pearson paints luminous gardens, trees and hills in Christchurch, a city which bids fair to become as smogbound in the future as Los Angeles.*

After more in a similar vein — and presciently — he wonders if the painters feel the threat to the environment 'and are trying to open the eyes of the vandals before it is too late'. He concludes with a stanza from the same Kipling poem that ends the introduction to this book:

> *So when your work is finished, you can wash your hands and pray*
> *For the Glory of the Garden, that it may not pass away!*

Keith could, of course, have been onto something. Thirty years later, in his article on the garden in art in *Art New Zealand*, Malcolm Burgess did not reprise the ecological or sustainability issues he so polemically addressed but did raise the affordability issue when looking at radically changing lifestyles as a reason for a renewed interest in the garden as a subject for artists.

Burgess posited 'a new breed of transient, loan-burdened middle class, flitting from flat to flat, cut off from the possibility of home- and garden-owning by a mix of career fixation and addiction to fruitless mobility'. He wondered if 'the suffocating city-dweller clamouring for the garden's beneficial gaseous excretions, seeks to fill a number of urges . . . in a window garden, a pot of herbs, a blade of grass — or a painting of any of these'.

On the other hand, throughout the history of art, artists have frequently turned to subjects close at hand to extend their repertoire — after all, the first Cubist paintings by Picasso and Braque were humble still lifes formed of the everyday objects around them in their apartments. Landscape was fraught territory in New Zealand because of its pervasiveness in the history of our painting and its association with the oft-derided Kelliher Art Award; perhaps the garden, which combined the natural and the man-made, was still neutral enough to explore.

Painter James Ross was the art critic for the *Sunday Herald* in 1974, and he later wrote in *Art New Zealand* that he remembered Trusttum's four small garden paintings in *The Artist's Garden* exhibition as being the most successful of the artist's works since his 1973 visit to Europe. Ross was himself working on garden paintings around that time, inspired by the garden of his new house in Titirangi. The resulting small, intense and thickly painted works would not be shown until 1976 and remain little known despite their originality.

Nevertheless, there were precedents for this kind of painting, such as the work of British artists Leon Kossoff and Frank Auerbach which had been included in the very large, significant and influential exhibition *Recent British Paintings* shown in Auckland in 1971 and Christchurch in 1972. Probably the earliest exponent, however, was the important Viennese proto-expressionist Richard Gerstl, who used similar swirling, sinewy greens and browns in a garden painting of 1908, the year he died.

All things being equal, Gretchen Albrecht's garden paintings from 1971–72 could have been included in *The Artist's Garden*. However, Albrecht did not have an opportunity to exhibit them before they were superseded by her acclaimed landscape-inspired abstracts of 1973–74, so they remained unexhibited until 1978.

Alan Pearson's teacher at Canterbury was John Oakley, a much admired figure in Christchurch and a good friend to a number of artists including Rita Angus. Oakley was also an inspiring gardener. For what would be his last painting he reverted to a timeless, dream-like style. The painting faithfully and lovingly records his own garden, on which he worked for three decades, despite being crippled by childhood polio. The garden was in the glamorous, modern California style so fashionable in the 1960s, inspired by Thomas Church's book *Gardens Are for People* (1955) and featuring a kidney-shaped pool and barbecue area, built to Oakley's design by his sons.

Oakley kept a garden diary and prepared a hand-out for visitors, so the record of his achievements is unusually detailed:

Bulbs are planted on the lawn at the bottom of the garden and make a continuous flowering as follows: August — crocus and English snowdrops; September — daffodils; October — bluebells. The lesser celandine is also establishing itself among the daffodils.

Mowing of this area is done in early December . . . The stone garden at the west end of the pool is planted with Japanese Iris and plants with contrasting leaf forms.

Besides planting an extensive flower garden, Oakley had an extensive vegetable garden, fruit trees (including greengage and quince) and shrubs of all kinds.

In the 1970s the subtropical garden became fashionable in New Zealand. According to landscape architect Rod Barnett, writing in *Botanica*, the trend was stimulated in part by affordable air travel and access to foreign gardening magazines. Artists such as Claudia Pond Eyley, who adopted the style in her Mount Eden garden, also saw its potential for their art and as a result possibly contributed to its increasing popularity.

In the 1980s, the revival of the use of native plants in domestic gardens and an increased awareness of Pacific culture stimulated the colourful paintings that introduced Pamela Wolfe to a wider public. However, a few years later, when she was developing her own garden in Freemans Bay, Auckland, she found her inspiration for painting in seventeenth-century Dutch flower still lifes, using photographs of her own roses as as models.

Rodney Fumpston's striking garden, developed in the 1980s, was the subject of a number of his prints, monochrome and coloured, using a variety of techniques. The garden's longitudinally symmetrical plan featured a verdigris architectural feature surrounded by morning glory, a narrow lily pond and deep herbaceous borders on either side.

Relationships, marriage, parenting, break-ups and death have always played a part in the creative lives of artists, often in conjunction with changes of home environment. Alan Pearson's 1973 garden paintings resulted from the purchase of a house in Lyttelton, the garden of which was a ready subject, paired with productivity galvanised by a new relationship. Jane Evans's excitement at having established her first garden in her new Nelson house inspired the first of several series of garden paintings. The explosion of colourful new paintings from Murray Grimsdale's Pakiri home and studio in 1976 and 1977, represented by the striking painting of his garden, came to an end far too quickly when the artist took on the sole responsibility for raising his two children, eking out a living as an illustrator. Nigel Brown's *Home gardener* paintings mark his rediscovery of domestic happiness with his new partner Sue McLaughlin in their aptly named Aroha Avenue home in Sandringham, Auckland. That same year, 1989, a couple of suburbs away in Mount Eden, Peter Siddell was incorporating elements of his own recently acquired garden in his Turner-inspired sunset painting *Western garden*. And the death of Trevor Moffitt's father inspired an extraordinary body of work of which *Pruning roses* serves as an example.

The gardens of parents or wider family are frequently the subject of an artist's first garden paintings. This was spectacularly the case with Karl Maughan who, since first photographing and then painting his mother's garden some 20 years ago, has established himself as New Zealand's best-known contemporary garden painter. Although he uses photography as a visual reference, Maughan explains that he works 'against the compression of perspective' that occurs in the photograph, and collages different views to achieve his aims. The camera may not lie but the lens of the camera differs to the lens of the human eye, especially the artist's eye.

Maughan's painted gardens range from views of or based on well-known and anonymous gardens, both here and in Europe, to gardens of the imagination, and blends of all of these. As he uses photographs as his basic on-the-spot record, he can and does 'return' to repaint a garden several years later even though the actual garden may have altered, sometimes beyond easy recognition.

Another painter of Maughan's generation — still in his forties — is Paris-trained Peter Hackett, whose colourful paintings of meadows with drifts of wild flowers have widespread appeal. However, in a change of mode, Hackett embarked on a view of the garden at Ayrlies at Whitford, southeast of Auckland, completing it in May 2008.

Susan Wilson's painting of her uncle's garden at Darfield in Canterbury represents a family connection with gardening that reaches back to late-eighteenth-century Scotland. It is a particularly appropriate example of the London-based Christchurch painter's work because family history, especially her father's war service, has played a significant role in her subject matter.

In another part of Canterbury, at Okains Bay on the eastern side of Banks Peninsula, is the garden painted by Nancy Tichborne. It is not far from Diamond Harbour, where Margaret Stoddart painted so many of her garden paintings and in whose tradition Tichborne follows today, delighting in subject and technical skill.

Mary Horlock's essay 'Representing and Intervening', in the catalogue of Tate Britain's *Art of the Garden* (2004), suggests that 'the contemporary garden is a site of contradiction and uncertainty: part conflict, part co-operation; a garden of unearthly delights and earthly imperfections.' While she had in mind the more conceptual garden works in the Tate exhibition, her summing-up sits comfortably with a number of works already discussed but especially with Paul Hartigan's *Big instant #2* (1989) and Leigh Martin's *Noise (Yellow)* (2004).

Although there are a number of painters who base their paintings on photographs, Paul Hartigan's cibachrome print of a multi-exposure Polaroid — already a contradiction in terms — is one of only two photographs in this book. It is included partly because Hartigan is a painter but also because of the painterly way in which he has captured his Lebanese mother's colourful flower garden.

Hartigan, in the pre-digital era of 1989, took his small Polaroid print — a direct print, with no negative — and enlarged it through photographic means. Leigh Martin digitised his original photograph and used a painting machine to translate that digital code back into an image in oil on canvas — essentially removing his hand, his touch from the painting process, except for a final layer of glaze.

Winter trees

GRETCHEN ALBRECHT 1943–

GRETCHEN ALBRECHT'S earliest flower subjects were not paintings but felt and collage works made in the 1960s when she first lived in Titirangi in the Waitakere Ranges, west Auckland, and where she made her first garden. They were not of any particular garden and resulted from 'observing the rambling nature of those plants and flowers around me'.

Around 1969–70 Albrecht made numerous watercolour sketches, mostly from life, of a garden in Wynyard Road, Mount Eden. She then moved into a flat above a shop near the Crystal Palace cinema, where her garden path and circular garden paintings were made, along with paintings such as *Winter trees*.

Here Albrecht enjoyed a view towards the west, 'with the Waitakere Ranges as the horizon, behind which the sun would set, sometimes in spectacular fashion both in terms of colour and sunlit sky contrasting with the dark, often brooding silhouette of the hills'. Looking down, the view was 'a wild garden, in fact, a riot of weeds.'

The garden with its colourful weeds and flowers was inspiration enough for many watercolour drawings and a series of canvases that were a major advance for Albrecht technically and for her growing reputation as a painter to watch.

Wekaweka garden

1971–2

GRETCHEN ALBRECHT 1943–

GRETCHEN ALBRECHT'S garden paintings, of which *Wekaweka garden* is a fine example, were initially painted from, or at least inspired by, a view through a window. This may have unconsciously influenced the upright format of these canvases, rather than the more traditional landscape format. This painting was a gift to her brother in Wekaweka in Northland, hence the title.

The thin, liquid acrylic of these paintings on canvas mimicked the artist's watercolour technique, although on a much larger scale. The choice of colours, too, though richer and applied more intensely, also related to her watercolours. They share a similar structure, with elements at the bottom of the painting that can be read as foreground; the more graphic flicks, pours and brushstrokes of the central area representative of plants, flowers and foliage; and more pure bands of colour at the top that can be read as hills, horizon and sky.

In May 1973 Albrecht moved back to Titirangi. Here she continued to garden, although its direct inspiration for her paintings gave way to the landscape of the west coast beaches and the Manukau Harbour, which eventually took on their own non-objective but no less lyrical intentions.

However, it was not until August 1978 that Albrecht first exhibited her acrylic garden paintings at Peter Webb Galleries: *Gardens — 10 Paintings from 1971*: a specific group of paintings that lined the walls of one room in the gallery.

The artist described it as looking like 'a multi-windowed view of a number of gardens'.

By this time Albrecht's later paintings had been received with considerable acclaim, so it must have been an unnerving exercise to exhibit previously unseen works from several years earlier. The *New Zealand Herald*'s TJ McNamara was enthusiastic:

The whole exhibition projects such a feeling of pleasure in colour and the act of painting that it is fortunate the works have been recalled from the limbo of discarded early experiments.

Experiments, of course, they were not! McNamara and other reviewers had the benefit of hindsight and saw these paintings as transitional works leading to the abstract paintings that brought Albrecht such popular and critical acclaim. The artist, however, recalls clearly that the 18 or so garden paintings were a cohesive body of work but that an opportunity to show them did not occur at the time. Most were painted *en masse* in late 1971, before Albrecht was appointed Teaching Fellow in Painting at Elam and assigned a large studio in 1972. There she continued to paint gardens while becoming increasingly interested in the swathes of colour themselves and less in the marks representing foliage and plants. In 1974 her Auckland Festival exhibition *Paintings* at Barry Lett Galleries secured her widespread reputation.

Albrecht

IN 1972, HAVING separated from his first wife, Alan Pearson bought an ageing, wooden, iron-roofed house in Lyttelton, on a steep section overlooking the harbour. The artist's biographer, writer and poet Denys Trussell, wrote:

From the windows of a studio/living room the rough flanks of tawny hills and the glittering turquoise tongue of harbour waters were visible.

Pearson's new situation had a significant impact on the painter, as he explained:

It was a release, a rebirth, back to nature, a sense of colour, the wetness of leaves — the organic renewal of all forms around me as though I was seeing a new reality.

He entered a very fertile and productive phase of painting. Drawing on his immediate surroundings, gardens, portraits, still lifes and allegories came from his easel in some numbers with 'a density of texture, a fury of colour equal to anything in Expressionism,' explains Trussell, 'so intense they seem almost to boil over the limits of their frame.'

Lyttelton garden epitomises Trussell's description, with its rapid, thick brushwork almost weaving the artist's view from the back of his house of the garden, which sloped down 45 degrees to the fence and on down into the valley to the road below.

While other paintings from this series record the scene more objectively, in this painting there are almost no immediately identifiable elements apart from the clothesline and the fence. The view has been transformed by skeins of paint into rhythmic patterns that, at first glance, the viewer might think abstract. However, the artist explains that the first blue strip beyond the fence is Hawkhurst Road and the next is Ticehurst Terrace, 'on the other side of the hill' — coincidentally, the Lyttelton Tunnel runs underground between them. The artist explains that he introduced the washing line as a device to mark the frontal plane and help to create a sensation of distance, while in the upper part of the painting he showed a 'neurological communication in space with the help of the tree branches and foliage'.

Some of his earlier garden scenes, painted when he lived in Armagh Street, Christchurch, and shown in his 1973 Canterbury Society of Arts exhibition, gave a hint of the direction taken by the Lyttelton paintings. Pearson says:

What did become emphatic after the move to Lyttelton was the expressionist element. Colour became more vivid and lived for itself. The surface texture became impasto and so the focus was on the 'paint' element rather than the 'object' element … This meant that the compositions became more musical and depicted the interconnecting matter and the spirit which lives in matter i.e. leaves, trees, grass and fences etc creating visual, musical sound which gives voice to a larger concern than just the landscape itself.

PHILIP TRUSTTUM 1940—

'McCAHON HAD HIS bible and landscape; Hotere had his poems; I have my chess pieces, my house, my garden,' Philip Trusttum confided to Derek Schulz for his 1980 *Listener* article on the artist.

Trusttum's first paintings with the garden as a subject were his garden-cum-landscape paintings of 1964 which were 2.4 metres by 1.2 metres on hardboard and made in Ashley, North Canterbury. A garden painting was also included in *Contemporary Painting in New Zealand* in London in 1965. These were more abstract than his later garden paintings, loosely based on the works of Chaim Soutine, Jackson Pollock and Asger Jorn.

Trusttum's next extensive group of garden paintings was made between two overseas trips. A QEII Arts Council grant enabled him to travel in Europe and the United States in 1972, and in 1975 he went to Europe with his family.

Trusttum has always been a prolific painter and these garden paintings were as numerous as any of his formally named series of the 1980s. They were painted over a short period and were diverse in appearance, from open and relatively naturalistic garden views to intense close-ups of trees and plants, including dead sunflowers. They were very popular at the time and helped to cement the artist's reputation.

The first of Trusttum's garden paintings to be seen in Auckland were in a three-person show with the works of Don Driver and Brian Reid at the New Vision Gallery in October 1973. They received a hugely enthusiastic review from Hamish Keith in the *Auckland Star*:

On this small showing, Philip Trusttum must surely be counted among the country's best, most exciting and most individual painters. It is certainly one of the year's most important shows.

Keith's review highlighted the key elements of Trusttum's work that struck a chord: the association with Vincent van Gogh, the paint handling, the vivid, expressive and even aggressive colour.

The van Gogh reference is reasonable in some respects, such as the firm, painted outlines of forms including the larger plants and tree trunks and the roofs and chimneys, particularly when the houses are 'deformed' like van Gogh's rustic, thatched houses. The rich, fiery colours and colour contrasts also seem to be more than a nod in the Dutch master's direction. However, the paint handling owes nothing to van Gogh and is quite individualistic. Indeed, as Trusttum's compositions and handling of objects in the landscape become more extreme, the paintings more recall the work of Chaim Soutine, the great French master, at his best around 1920 when living at Céret.

Vanilla tree and houses

1973

PHILIP TRUSTTUM 1940—

IN MARCH 1974 Philip Trusttum had the Auckland Festival slot at the New Vision Gallery, which featured views of the artist's garden from inside the house. Included was *Vanilla tree and houses*, considered by reviewer Hamish Keith as 'the finest' in the exhibition.

The 'vanilla tree' in Trusttum's garden appears in a number of his paintings. The tree is *Azara microphylla*, a small and elegant evergreen that in early spring produces tiny yellow flowers with a very strong vanilla scent. In *Vanilla tree and houses* Trusttum has painted yellow fronds in the foreground plane, suggesting the flowers and the dense perfume that the artist could no doubt smell from his studio.

Back garden no. 47

1973

PHILIP TRUSTTUM 1940—

IN JULY 1974 Philip Trusttum was once again in a group show; he was one of the six artists in *The Artist's Garden* at New Vision and had four paintings in the catalogue: *Black tree, Black lawn, Blue tree* and *The garden*.

Hamish Keith, the reviewer for the *Auckland Star*, opined that Trusttum 'paints gardens as delicate as a willow pattern plate while we bulldoze our gentler past and bury it in concrete motorways'.

It may have been a painting not unlike *Back garden no. 47* that the reviewer had in mind. In this relatively small painting for Trusttum, he has reverted to a more graphic approach. The diluted paint has been absorbed by the canvas rather than sitting on top of it, so we see a lot of white ground and corresponding luminosity, along with short strokes of vivid colour, forms repeated to suggest a three-dimensional effect, trees, plants, flowers and flowerbeds, all seen from above.

IN 1973, AUCKLAND painter James Ross moved from the suburb of Mount Eden to the bush setting of Titirangi. The first group of paintings made following this move were shown at the Barry Lett Galleries, Auckland in November 1976, and included eight entitled *The path*.

In his *Art New Zealand* review of Ross's 1980 exhibition in Wellington, Neil Rowe provided an eyewitness account of the earlier exhibition:

In 1976, James Ross, class of '66–'69, taught by McCahon at Elam . . . hung an exhibition of unabashed landscapes . . . These paintings, with their subject matter, the trees of his Titirangi home, deeply embedded in a thickly-impastoed oil-painted surface, were not well received in the climate of those times. They lost out to fashion on three counts: they were figurative, they were emotively and powerfully expressionistic, and they were painterly — extremely so. It was decidedly uncool to use paint so self-indulgently in this age of austerity.

Nevertheless, TJ McNamara's review in the *New Zealand Herald* of November 1976 received the exhibition well enough, calling the young Ross 'a thoughtful, serious painter' and declaring that oil paint had seldom been spread so thickly in New Zealand art as in these new paintings.

The colours are applied with verve and energy in great thick gouts of paint that give the surface a raised, very textured quality in the manner of the British painter Auerbach . . . the best of them are given life by effects of light.

Ross's paintings in the 1976 exhibition ranged from more naturalistic and objective landscapes with recognisable elements — a roof here, a flash of sky through the trees there — to *The path* series, where the path and steps are not only the focus of the painting but also the sole identifiable features; they take on an almost sculptural presence.

While Ross's extremely thick painting style was unique in New Zealand, it had, as McNamara suggested, a major exponent in Britain, Frank Auerbach, whose *Head of EOW IV* (1961) had been in the Auckland City Art Gallery's 1971 exhibition *Recent British Paintings from the Stuyvesant Collection*.

Ross was not aware of the possible connection at the time but as soon as he was, he stopped painting in the style. He explains:

My idea around these works was to use paint broadly, thickly, subjectively and abstractly, but to use an observed view as some proof of the veracity of the observation. The same ordinary, everyday quality of the chosen site, of say the path down to our front door, or the view through to the neighbour's place might engender half a dozen or so paintings and so became a motif or template. The motif was not selected because it was grand or important in itself. At the time I thought that these works had a quite a strong painterly, but factual, presence.

Garden

1976

WILLIAM CUMMING 1933–2002

WILLIAM CUMMING DREW throughout his life. He first drew professionally as an engineering assistant, then as an artist whose genre was landscape, particularly that of his native West Coast.

In the early 1970s Cumming was painting landscape-derived abstracts featuring hard-edged forms. Later in the decade these gave way to square-format paintings of formal gardens in a neo-pointillist style, which seem to rely on some optical mixing, *Garden* being an example. It is probably one of the five paintings in the *Botanical Garden Series* shown in September 1976 in Cumming's solo exhibition at the Canterbury Society of Arts, *Cumming: Paintings and Drawings*.

This painting's orthogonal structure around a central pathway and its topiaried trees relate to Cumming's later, more graphic, mixed-media works in which hedges and trees take on geometric shapes. The symmetrical composition, sharp colours and clear-cut forms, not only devoid of people but also resisting their appearance, create a surreal and dream-like mood.

This series of paintings appears to have a connection, albeit tenuous, to Cumming's garden design and landscaping three decades later, when he and his wife Jean purchased a gently sloping section on a Heathcote Valley hillside and built a new house and garden. An article in *New Zealand House & Garden* in April 2002 described this major project, in which the sloping section was made into five levels of terraces.

[The design] *is one of magnificent order and restraint, held together by metres of buxus hedging, topiary and sculpture. The garden's five hundred original buxus cuttings were taken from William's great-grandfather's garden in Kokatahi, inland from Hokitika, who was given them by his friend, the late Prime Minister Richard Seddon.*

The Cummings called their house Bloomfield, the name of both the garden at Kokatahi, near Hokitika, and the Cumming ancestral home in Scotland. Apparently Cumming always wanted to create a formal garden. He admired architect Sir Miles Warren's garden at Ohinetahi and his discussions with Warren probably assisted in the making of Bloomfield.

Paintings like *Garden* can now be seen as an attempt to make his dreams manifest long before they became a reality.

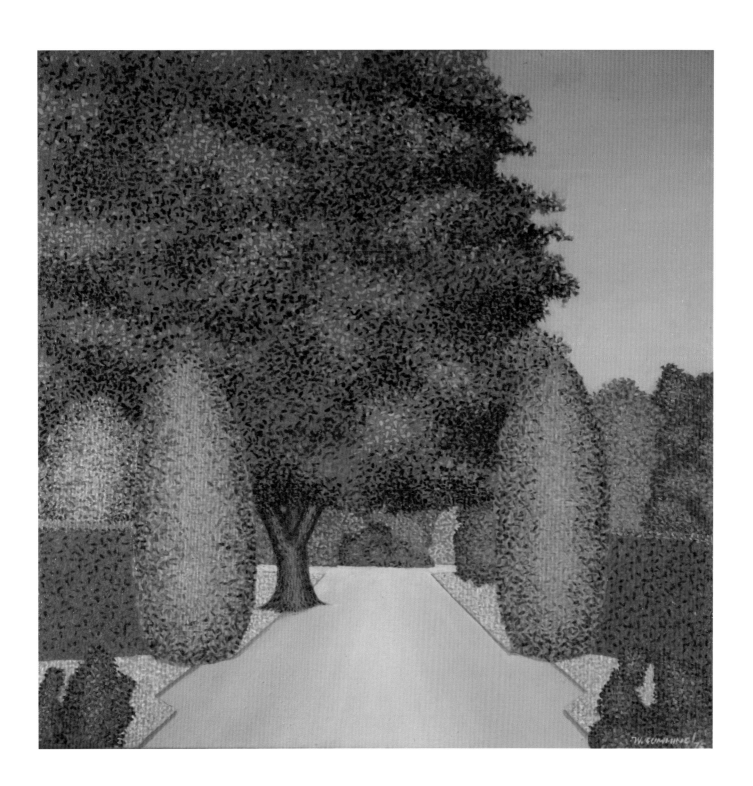

Garden
1976

JOHN OAKLEY 1901–1977

GARDEN WAS JOHN Oakley's last painting. A poignant record of the garden at his Fendalton home of almost 30 years, it is a view from an upstairs room, painted when he was recovering from a broken leg.

During the Second World War the recently married John and Helen Oakley (née Waddy) moved to Christchurch from Napier, and in 1948 purchased a two-storey house on extensive grounds that had formerly been an orchard on Queens Avenue.

The development of their garden over almost three decades is well documented by family and press photographs, Oakley's own garden diaries and the recollections of family and friends. Oakley recorded (in what was probably a hand-out for visiting groups) that his aim was 'to make a pleasant garden which requires a minimum of upkeep'; his proud addition of 'No outside labour is employed' allowed him to discreetly recognise the large contribution of his three sons in its maintenance.

The Oakleys retained some fruit trees and bushes from the original orchard but by the time the house was sold in 1978, despite extensive landscaping and the addition of a family-built pool, there were still 16 fruit trees, a small vegetable garden, an asparagus bed and a permanent runner-bean fence that acted as a screen. In this painting one of the original pear trees can be seen at the rear left of the garden — The Dell — supporting a round table made from a wooden cable reel.

Most of the conifers and many of the shrubs were grown from tip cuttings, and swapping plants and cuttings with visiting garden enthusiasts gave Oakley a lot of pleasure, according to his daughter, Sarah Turbott.

This view, from one of the upstairs bedrooms, looks towards the rear of the section, which adjoined at the far left the property of the famous cricketing family, the Hadlees. On the right one can glimpse the path that bordered the vegetable garden. In the foreground are silver birches.

In Oakley's obituary in the Canterbury Society of Arts *News* (March-April 1977), sculptor EJ Doudney wrote:

I felt in particular sympathy with him in his love and understanding of gardens — his own garden was always a pleasure to see.

Oakley's *Garden* has that strong feeling of being carefully observed, as one would expect, and strongly felt — an emotional investment. The artist may well have sensed that his gardening days were over and that he should record what he had achieved, with the support of his wife and children, over some 30 years.

Another clue to the almost documentary objectivity with which Oakley painted this last painting is in its style. As an occasional exhibiting artist, mostly at the CSA, Oakley's style tended towards the expressionistic, perhaps influenced a little by his friend Toss Woollaston. Here, however, Oakley has reverted to a smooth, slower paint application, reminiscent of his earliest paintings.

In the late 1960s Oakley established the Christchurch Civic Trust to spearhead a campaign to save the historic homestead and garden Mona Vale from destruction, eventually persuading the Christchurch City Council to purchase and preserve the property.

MURRAY GRIMSDALE 1943—

MURRAY GRIMSDALE'S *The artist's garden, Pakiri* dates from a very productive period early in the artist's career, not long after his return from four years in the United Kingdom. He rented a farm cottage — which he later bought — in the small beachside settlement of Pakiri, 90 minutes north of Auckland. There, in 1976, he met and then married May Higgott, and they had two children, Rewa and Bella. While he brought them up, his career as a painter took a back seat.

Grimsdale's new home was the original farmhouse for the area. The farmer's mother had lived there until her death and had developed the extraordinarily colourful front garden that Grimsdale took on with the house, though it had been neglected for five years. His landlord was pretty knowledgeable and in due course introduced Grimsdale to the various plants and shrubs.

In 1976 Grimsdale made two works for an exhibition of painted screens at Barry Lett Galleries, inspired by Roger Fry's Omega Workshop in London. One of the screens was of Pakiri, with his garden on one side and Pakiri beach on the other, and was bought by the writer Hamish Keith and his then wife, the designer Susan Firth. Firth's sister Pamela then commissioned this painting.

It was a halcyon time for Grimsdale, living in a beautiful location with his wife and their first child. His sketchbook, full of drawings, sketches and pastels of happy domesticity, indicates that his first ideas for *The artist's garden, Pakiri* date from December 1976.

Each page is full of lively pencil drawings, mostly of plants, some of which are named. This oil, for which there is no compositional drawing, was completed during the summer of 1977.

The artist points out that not everything in the painting is in season. At the very top right he included the wisteria, which was heavy with blossom when Rewa was born in September. At the top left, in front of the veranda, is some native honeysuckle and near it oleander. The family ate both the fruit of the *Monstera deliciosa* and the nasturtium flowers. Midway down the left-hand side of the painting are pelargoniums and on the other a waxeye sits on the red hot poker.

If Grimsdale had any stylistic inspiration, besides his general graphic approach as an illustrator, it was Henri Rousseau. The French painter was undergoing something of a popular revival in the late 1960s and Grimsdale had seen his *Tropical storm with tiger* in the National Gallery, London.

In all Grimsdale painted some 20 screens over the years, several of which were of gardens or flowers. One is in the collection of the Christchurch Art Gallery.

CLAUDIA POND EYLEY 1946—

WHEN CLAUDIA POND Eyley and her husband Peter bought the old Mount Eden villa where they have lived for some 30 years, it was surrounded by asphalt. Except for some puriri and cabbage trees, there was no garden to speak of. The Eyleys immediately began to establish a garden with brick paths and plantings on a subtropical theme. Ornamental Abyssinian or Ethiopian banana palms, a relative of the edible banana, became the identifying feature. These can grow several metres high and take about seven years to flower before dying, and their heart-shaped leaves became prominent in Eyley's paintings.

Mount Eden garden I, completed in August 1979, was the first of a series of house and garden paintings made by Eyley that continued through the 1980s. It was exhibited at Eyley's show at the Elva Bett Gallery in 1981, and later in her *Unruly Practices* survey at the Auckland City Art Gallery.

In *Mount Eden garden I* the low and close-up viewpoint of the plants allowed Eyley to silhouette them against the sky. Through the use of complementary colours, inspired by the plants themselves, the composition is defined by strong, graphic outlines that take on an expressive, decorative force, suggesting fertility and vitality.

Eyley took this style and applied it to a series of interior/exterior paintings in which the garden is seen from inside the villa, through the window, often including the characteristic top pane of stained glass. In the 1990s Eyley continued the garden theme in a series of *Spirit garden* paintings inspired by meditation gardens in Bali.

Mount Eden landscape

1984

CLAUDIA POND EYLEY 1946—

IN SUMMER, THE view from Claudia Pond Eyley's garden of nearby Mount Eden is obscured by dense vegetation. However, in *Mount Eden landscape* Eyley has made a feature of the extinct volcano.

In her exhibition catalogue *Unruly Practices*, curator Alexa Johnston wrote:

Maungawhau (Mt Eden), ancient pa site and guardian of the area, is a looming presence. Pond Eyley sets this powerful landform with its terraced reminders of earlier inhabitants alongside the more transient liveliness of the domestic garden and asserts the wholeness and continuity of nature.

This three-panel mural was one of several murals or mural-sized paintings commissioned by Pat Hanly for the new Arts–Commerce building at the University of Auckland. In contrast with some of Eyley's other paintings showing Mount Eden, the mural is in high key colours, the mountain, landscape and garden lit with strong sun under a cloudless sky, and the whole vibrates with life.

The view, however, is constructed or imagined, because its elements do not conform to reality. Instead, Eyley has created a dynamic interplay between the red of the man-made — gate, villa roof and chimney — and the green of the natural — plants, garden and mountain. However, close inspection shows Eyley has created many of the plant forms with concentric bands of different colours that blend together at the normal viewing distance.

For compositional purposes, Eyley has repeated a little of the top of the volcano to fill some of the space. She has also substituted what looks like an obelisk (like the monument at the top of One Tree Hill) for what is in reality a rather more prosaic trig point on top of Mount Eden. The bright, positive atmosphere of the painting generates a positive emotion that is underscored by the playful red heart.

TREVOR MOFFITT 1936–2006

TREVOR MOFFITT WAS a keen vegetable gardener and proud of the quality of the produce he put on the family table, especially when there were guests. Moffitt inherited his gardening skills and attitude from his father, Gilbert, for whom gardening was a necessary pastime. Gilbert Moffitt, a rural Southlander, died in 1978 and Moffitt felt his death so keenly that he began a series of paintings about him: *My father's life*.

Moffitt's reputation as an artist was built on his scenes of New Zealand life and character, both imagined and reconstructed, in which he seemed to distil aspects of the human condition. He went about this series in a similar way, though more personally; he explored his family history, consulting family photograph albums and those of friends. The first group of some 30 paintings was shown at the Elva Bett Gallery, Wellington, in August 1979 and the positive response to it, along with a QEII Arts Council grant, gave him the incentive to paint many more. The completed cycle numbered 139 paintings.

Pruning roses epitomises Moffitt's approach: broad and loosely brushed, his father, performing an everyday task, becomes a Kiwi Everyman — an archetype, someone in whom we can recognise elements of ourselves and our fathers or grandfathers. Moffitt's skill transforms his deeply personal experience into something with universal appeal.

Summer garden I

1985

JANE EVANS 1946—

IN 1977, JANE Evans bought her first home, a cottage on Tasman Street near the centre of Nelson. Here she made her first garden, and a QEII Arts Council grant enabled her to convert a lean-to shed into a studio. Her biographer John Coley says the garden was a priority for the artist: she had brick paths and a patio laid, and her friends enthusiastically helped 'to establish the garden she visualised':

On new fence palings they hammered the sides of car crates, which were then painted with a dark fence stain. Against this background a brilliant array of vivid flowering plants soon appeared.

Coley explains that Evans did not consciously design the garden but, rather like her paintings, used her intuition, cultivating 'certain kinds of flowers for their shapes and hues'.

Evans's move to Tasman Street coincided with a period of good health — and a change of medium. Instead of acrylic on canvas she tried acrylic on paper and then gouache, which became her preference. Evans found it much easier to work with physically and its immediacy enhanced her response to her motifs.

The first flowering of her garden inspired Evans's first flower paintings in gouache. The paintings allowed her to be spontaneous and indulge herself with bright colours and dynamic forms. Coley records her as saying:

Suddenly there was this feeling of wanting above all to express the joy of living. Life was full of colour, and that was what I wanted to put down in my painting.

A succession of series of garden paintings appeared from her studio. The first, some 28 gouaches, was simply called *My garden* (1978) and Evans sold them from her home in a matter of weeks. The following year she completed the *Within the garden* series and in 1982 *Flowers growing*.

Summer garden I belongs to Evans's next group of garden paintings, made in 1985. By this time, at least in some of her paintings of the period, Evans reached a greater degree of abstraction than ever before. Few vestiges of identifiable flower detail remained visible as she floated pure colours across wet Arches watercolour paper. Coley describes them as 'intense, lyrical, floating evocations of summer blooms'.

Summer garden I, however, is one of her more descriptive paintings from this time, with identifiable flowers and plants around the brick paving in the courtyard, such as the palm, and the poppies — a favourite subject of the artist's — suggesting vibrancy and movement.

That same year, 1985, she had a sell-out exhibition at the Denis Cohn Gallery in Auckland. These paintings were among the last to be inspired by her garden at Tasman Street, which she sold that year; her next flower paintings were of her current and more famous home, in Russell Street above the port of Nelson.

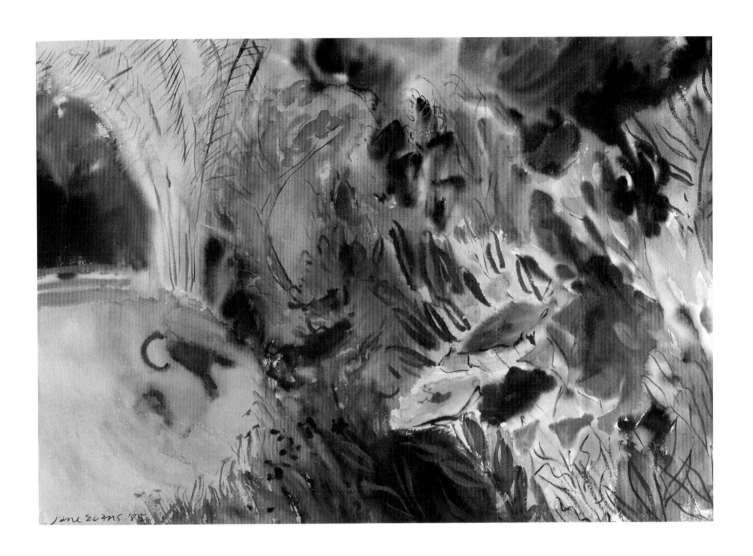

KARL MAUGHAN IS fond of the story of how the garden came to be his preferred subject. In 1986 his parents were living in Guildford Street in Ashhurst, a few kilometres out of Palmerston North. On a trip home from study at Elam, Maughan was taking photographs of the landscape, as he frequently did, for possible use in his paintings. Dick Frizzell was one of his painting tutors and, in addition to van Gogh, had been the catalyst for Maughan's broadly painted landscapes at the time.

Maughan had eight shots left on his film when he got home, so he photographed his mother's garden to finish the roll. When the film was developed, Maughan 'fell into the garden'. The resulting eight photographs were to serve his painterly purposes for the next two years.

Maughan's parents began their involvement with gardens in the Manawatu when they worked with landscape architect David Irvine. Maughan's mother, Lesley Maughan, later became a landscape gardener and designer and taught at Massey University. Maughan describes the garden she made at Ashhurst with Bill, his father, as:

> *a fantastic combination of cottage garden with several perennial borders and many larger trees planted near the edge which are now very big. It was a huge project.*

Maughan made five large paintings of his parents' garden for his first solo exhibition in 1987 at Wellington's Brooker Gallery, where he had been invited to show following the impact of his work in an earlier student group exhibition. *Plume poppies*, a large triptych, was painted after this exhibition and left at Brooker as stock, although it was soon purchased by Glaxo Smith Kline. The Brooker exhibition was a sell-out, paying for the materials Maughan needed to paint his next exhibition, at the Gow Langsford Gallery, recently opened in Grey Lynn.

The photographs on which all these early paintings were based were taken in early summer. The poppies are coming through, as are the perennials and some early roses in the background. Maughan has emphasised the flatness of the picture plane and his viewpoint conforms to what one would expect to see in a simply taken photograph looking down on the plants with just a hint of foreground. The artist liked the grey-green foliage and enjoyed painting the details of the plants as he worked across the canvas.

Wellington garden with fence post

KARL MAUGHAN 1964–

KARL MAUGHAN DESCRIBES this painting as a 'found image'. He was staying with friends in Mount Cook, Wellington, and leaned over the fence early one morning to take a photograph of the neighbour's garden. When he came to make the painting, he found there was little to change.

The green square is the top of a fence post and there is a feeling of a diagonal pull away from it towards the sunlit patch of path.

Philip Trusttum's garden paintings, which he much admired, were an early influence on Maughan, as were those of Pat Hanly.

Ohinetahi

1994

KARL MAUGHAN 1964—

SIR MILES WARREN'S garden Ohinetahi, at Governors Bay on Banks Peninsula, has an important and venerable history. In 1858, Thomas Henry Potts (1824–1888), one of the country's foremost early conservationists and owner of Valehead Station, bought 255 acres (103 hectares) in Governors Bay from lawyer Sefton Moorhouse, to which he later added another 600 acres (242 hectares). Here Potts built the splendid neoclassical stone and wood mansion Ohinetahi and created the grounds with his gardener William Gray. Neglect by subsequent owners and natural disasters sadly ensured that little remains of Potts's original planting besides some camellias and some fine trees, including araucarias and unusual conifers on the northern boundary, which protect the garden from southerly winds.

Potts's original fernery, the first of its kind in New Zealand, was washed away by a flash flood, heavy snow in 1945 wrecked the orchard, and many huge trees were lost in the *Wahine* storm of 1968. Warren, one of New Zealand's foremost architects, has restored the house and established the fine formal gardens since 1977 with his sister and brother-in-law, Pauline and John Trengrove.

No nineteenth or early twentieth century paintings of Ohinetahi have come to light and, to Warren's knowledge, no one had painted Ohinetahi before Karl Maughan in the mid-1990s. The artist had visited Ohinetahi when in Christchurch for an exhibition and subsequently painted several views of the garden. Some of these works remained in Christchurch and others went into his 1994 Gow Langsford Gallery exhibition. In his review of the exhibition in the *New Zealand Herald* in May 1994, TJ McNamara wrote:

The work that comes closest to convincingly uniting path and flowers is Ohinetahi. Here the play of light and dark, the rich paint on sword-like leaves and particularly the lovely warm colour combinations pull everything together . . . virtuoso painting on a large scale.

Maughan painted the Ohinetahi paintings on a brown ground, which has been left visible in places. He liked the sepia tones and the 'spikiness' of the plants. One or two of this group of paintings combine elements of Ohinetahi and Monet's garden at Giverny, but in this example there are 'no tricks', Maughan says. The view is of the Red Garden, a square, formal, walled garden, its red-brick paths crossing at right angles under a gazebo-shaped climbing frame where a large stone font is positioned.

Surrender Rodney

KARL MAUGHAN 1964–

AUCKLAND ARTIST RODNEY Fumpston's garden in Morningside, Auckland, across the motorway from Western Springs, was considered one of the finest inner-city gardens of the late 1980s. As can be seen in Fumpston's own lithograph of the garden (page 227), as viewed from the house, it has a long reflecting pond with an architectural feature at the end, against the northern wall.

On the right of the pool Fumpston put in a fiery red garden, while on the left he planted a white and grey garden, partly inspired by Vita Sackville-West and Harold Nicholson's Sissinghurst in Kent. Maughan painted two groups of paintings of Fumpston's garden, of the red garden illuminated at night and the white garden, of which *Surrender Rodney* is one.

To add interest as well as for compositional purposes — to lock in the top of the painting — the artist has chosen to paint the last couple of metres of the long flowerbed where it meets the house and has included a glimpse of the closed French doors.

KARL MAUGHAN 1964—

KARL MAUGHAN'S FIRST paintings of Gordon and Annette Collier's magnificent and famous garden, Titoki Point, date from 1988. Some were included in that year's sell-out exhibition at Gow Langsford Gallery, as were paintings of Kathleen and Robin Lush's intimate Remuera garden, full of flowers and vegetables.

Gordon Collier, a descendant of New Zealand painter Edith Collier, began to create Titoki Point when his parents gave him and Annette some land as a wedding present in 1964. Gordon Collier's book on the garden was published in 1993 and Titoki Point now has a new owner.

Some 40 km from Taihape, the Titoki Point garden began to take shape on the remote and difficult hillside of which a glimpse remains in Maughan's view, just below and to the right of the homestead. The 1998 group of paintings of Titoki Point were all painted from photographs taken in 1987 and by this time, a decade later, the view was already obscured by the trees along the upper boundary.

In the catalogue of his 2008 exhibition at Te Manawa, Maughan summarised his objectives and working procedure:

The design and shape of the gardens give me an interplay of light, colour and structure. The photos are a visual reference. I often collage several to make a composite image, and work against the compression of perspective. Working with gardens over twenty years has meant the parts of the garden I am drawn to have become not so much a subject for paint, as a language to make paintings with.

Cross Hills

KARL MAUGHAN 1964–

RODNEY AND FAITH Wilson's 7 hectare garden Cross Hills, is near Kimbolton, 30 km northeast of Feilding. The garden's founder, Eric Wilson, purchased the original 240 hectare farm in 1938 and the development of the garden as one can see it today began in 1951 with the building of a new homestead. The success of the rhododendrons Wilson planted led to a decision in 1970 to make them a special feature, followed a little later by azaleas.

Maughan had painted rhododendrons first in his 1998 Titoki Point canvases. While living in London Maughan saw several major gardens featuring rhododendrons, including Stourhead (Wiltshire) and Hergest Croft (Herefordshire), as well as Kew Gardens and Richmond Park in London.

Although Cross Hills is not far from his childhood home in Palmerston North, Maughan had never visited and his mother took him there on one of his visits home from London.

Paths play an important role in the composition of Maughan's paintings. They literally lead the viewer into the picture but the artist also likes the sense of mystery and the certain edginess that they introduce.

One of Maughan's favourite conceits, though not represented in this selection of paintings, is to 'twin' some of his favourite gardens for both fun and effect. In one, Maughan takes a view of rhododendrons in the famous Hergest Croft on the English–Welsh border and grafts it into some rhododendrons from Cross Hills in the Manawatu.

Nigel Brown 1949—

MOST OF NIGEL Brown's work, generally produced in discrete series, has addressed New Zealand subjects: its history, its myths and its archetypes, whether the black singlet-wearing working man or personalities such as the poet James K Baxter. *Home gardener*, on the other hand, is ostensibly domestic-focused and its high key colour and happy and relaxed atmosphere are a reflection of the artist's positive outlook during the period in which this was painted. In 1986 Brown, his partner Sue McLaughlin and her two children had moved to Aroha Avenue in Sandringham, Auckland. Here, with a QEII Arts Council grant, he was able to build a studio.

Home gardener is one of several works in Brown's eponymous series from 1989, which were shown, with related prints, at Portfolio Gallery in 1990. All the *Home gardener* paintings show either McLaughlin or the artist at work in the garden, with their house in the background, their dog George and a lemon tree. One of the paintings features a watering can and trowel in the foreground; another shows Brown with a wheelbarrow and beyond him the tiny image of McLaughlin with a rake and bucket in front of the house.

Brown recalls that during the 1980s and 1990s 'the garden at Aroha Street gradually progressed through several stages, becoming more subtropical at the end, with corresponding Pacific themes' in his work.

Generally my idea of gardening is of labours of love and hard work. It may be struggle and may be that the man is an assistant to the woman.

A number of works and series by Brown include gardens or have gardening references, including a small bronze sculpture of a gardener; they all provide additional context for the *Home gardener* paintings. The most important were the *Lemon tree* paintings, shown in the sell-out exhibition at Barry Lett Galleries in 1977. They mark the first appearance of text in Brown's mature work, and brought him to the attention of a wider public for the first time. The paintings were inspired by Brown's planting of a lemon tree; although he did everything he could to ensure its survival, in the end it produced one fruit and died. Brown characterised the paintings as symbolising 'the pioneer struggle to break in the land and sustain its productivity'.

PAUL HARTIGAN 1953—

PAUL HARTIGAN'S POPULAR reputation was built up around his neon sculptures but, in addition to being a painter and printmaker, he has developed a significant body of work that is photo-based.

Big instant #2 is derived from a multi-exposure Polaroid photograph of Hartigan's mother's flower garden in New Plymouth. It was one of the works in Hartigan's 1989 exhibition at Real Pictures Gallery, Auckland, called *Big Instants*. It was shot on the rectangular Polaroid Spectra film, which followed the square format SX70 film that first appeared in 1972.

Hartigan was able to make multiple exposures — in this case four — by working out how to fool the Polaroid camera's unique automatic-ejection mechanism. He then made a 'copy-in-between' stage, a 4 inch x 5 inch Kodak Ektachrome transparency, which was required for the Cibachrome printing process.

Hartigan points out that 'with making that enlargement, and the two-stage process involved, comes a slight though perceptible difference in colour saturation, and in turn the image density.'

Hartigan was born and brought up in Brooklands, New Plymouth. His mother Mary was Lebanese; Hartigan describes her as:

an avid gardener with a deep love of cooking, [who] grew both vegetables and an esoteric array of (now unfashionable) colourful flowers at the sun-drenched little house: dahlias, gladioli, pansies and roses as well as giant sunflowers and opium poppies; a magnificent cacophony of 'pretty' flowers.

Later Hartigan's mother replaced the flowers at the front of her house with eggplants — then a rarity in New Zealand — which grew to a huge size and attracted a lot of interest.

Flowers and gardens have been infrequent inspirations for Hartigan but he retains a soft spot for the *Big instant* series because of the combination of the low-tech adaptation of the Polaroid camera's old-fashioned mechanical process and the advanced-looking photo-based imagery he was able to produce almost 20 years ago. He explains:

Mine is a painter's eye, not a photographer's, so my objectives are quite different. I do not seek to capture a singular definitive moment, aspect or character in a conventional way, my representation (or image) is more about a period of experience, intangible yet fulfilling, but without precise detail. I seek to represent a time-lapse sequence in one frame, three or four perspectives blended as one, a kind of frozen home movie, nostalgic, retrospective, slightly romantic even, an ideal.

IN 1989, PETER Siddell and his wife, the painter Sylvia Siddell, made their first visit to Europe. He had never seen major paintings by artists such as JMW Turner before, and was impressed by those he saw at the Tate Gallery and National Gallery in London.

He was especially taken with Turner's sunsets, and on his return to Auckland he got down to work immediately. *Western garden* was the culmination of a series of paintings, including sunsets, that he made at this time. The view from Siddell's studio, a horizon line that includes the Manukau Heads, is frequently incorporated in his paintings. *Western garden* is an eloquent embodiment of Siddell's working practice because it is, like virtually all of his paintings, a construct, a collage of seen and imagined images.

When *Western garden* was painted it was only a couple of years after the Siddells had bought their Mount Eden villa, its wonderful garden established by the previous owners. Here the artist observed the various flowers, plants and lemon tree but in the painting he has set them in an imagined location in front of a scoria wall, a common feature in Mount Eden.

While Siddell's painting style is really the antithesis of Turner's, Siddell is paying homage to Turner's big sunset scenes through the inherent romanticism of the view, the sun hanging over the horizon, its light filtered by the clouds and touched with a warm, nostalgic pink glow.

Lewis' garden at Darfield

1989

SUSAN WILSON 1951—

MENTION OF SUSAN Wilson's paintings usually conjures up thoughts of her intensely detailed but expressively painted portraits, including self-portraits and still lifes, which are also portraits of a kind. They often raise questions of personal and family identity and place, combining nostalgia and history.

Wilson's Canterbury family history lies behind her painting *Lewis' garden at Darfield*, made on a return visit to New Zealand from London in 1989. She explains:

It's my Uncle Lewis' vegetable garden in Darfield, Canterbury in winter. It has a water race running through it. And it's very much a view of a serious gardener's spring preparation. It was a garden I really loved with trout in the water race and a native bush corner. A botanist from Lincoln University made it and Lewis loved it too. He used to make tomato chutney when the crop was huge, even when he was in his eighties.

Her Wilson family forebears had been gardeners for the Kennedy family at the magnificent Culzean Castle on the South Ayrshire coast, southwest of Glasgow. They came to New Zealand to garden for the Deans family, who had homes at Riccarton, Christchurch (named after their home at Riccarton in Ayrshire, not far from Culzean) and Homebush Station, near Coalgate on the Canterbury Plains. They also gardened at Mona Vale in Christchurch. Wilson's family story, therefore, stretches back not only to early gardening in Canterbury but also to Scottish gardening and horticulture in the eighteenth century.

Accordingly, it is no surprise that gardens and gardening figure in Wilson's Canterbury childhood:

My father always grew vegetables and fruit for us. We never bought the stuff. He and Lewis, his brother, were Presbyterian clergyman gardeners. They grew vegetables at the rear of the church in Waikari and planted redcurrants in otherwise empty spots beside it.

In the 1960s Wilson's father grew a grapevine; it produced wonderful fruit and was a topic of conversation among his parishioners at a time when there was not a vine to be seen in Waipara, which was part of his parish.

Paradoxically, *Lewis' garden at Darfield* is a painting of a constructed garden; being winter, there is little in it that is 'natural'. The diagonal thrust of the composition — as if in echelon formation — of the trough, the climbing frame and the trellis signals the future results of the gardener's labour. The artist recalls that her uncle 'felt a little embarrassed that the garden was portrayed as being so bare but that was something I really liked — winter with spring approaching. It was cold and rainy!'

Wilson continues to paint occasional garden views, including nocturnes, of her London garden.

RODNEY FUMPSTON'S FIRST prints of garden subjects were made when he lived in Remuera, Auckland. His four popular *Garden view* etching aquatints of 1977 were followed by the suite of six etching aquatints called *Garden evening*, from 1979 to 1981. These prints brought Fumpston's work to a wider audience and their technical innovation helped establish his career as an exhibiting artist and one of the country's foremost printmakers.

In 1980 Fumpston moved from Remuera to Warwick Street in Morningside, across the motorway from Western Springs. Over the next few years he developed a marvellous garden that was the subject of a number of prints. Looking east from the rear of the house the viewer sees a reflecting pond extending down the middle of the garden to a verdigris architectural feature against the end wall. On either side of the lawn are deep herbaceous borders.

Several garden works followed Fumpston's move, including *Tropical garden I & II* (1983). His first prints of the Warwick Street garden were lithographs printed at Muka Studios in 1988–89, which were conventional in format.

However, when Fumpston came to make the *Night garden* lithographs and drypoints in 1993 he paradoxically chose a panoramic format for his views. As a result, although he has recorded everything as he saw it, by using the compositional device of foreshortening he gives the impression of a much larger, wider garden, with no fences or boundaries.

As *Night garden* is a nocturne, with no artificial light in the garden, Fumpston shows the abundant foliage of the white and silver plants picking up the available light. The water in the pond shows dark, and beyond the garden is the familiar silhouette of the Auckland skyline. The cat is the most obvious of the local fauna that Fumpston has included but there are also one or two moths and snails.

The artist has applied the marks in a painterly, calligraphic style by using tusche (lithographic ink), especially for the final colour, silver. Each of the flicks and loops is a brushstroke and together they create the effect of a vibrant, shimmering surface. Fumpston thought of this print as 'a garden animated by nature' in the spirit of the English artist Samuel Palmer.

Large pink roses

2002

PAMELA WOLFE 1950–

FLOWERS AND GARDENS were significant elements in Pamela Wolfe's earliest paintings, and became part of the South Pacific imagery that brought her to the attention of a wider public in the mid-1980s. By this time she was living in Freemans Bay, Auckland, where she developed her own garden, incorporating many old roses.

Wolfe's first exhibition of large still lifes with flowers, particularly roses, was *Grandiflora* at the Lane Gallery, Auckland, in 1995. At the time she was remaking her garden and she planted a 'Penelope' rose in memory of a friend who had recently died. When she painted these flowers her work now took on a more universal theme, looking back to Dutch still life compositions of the seventeenth century.

Specifically, Wolfe was interested in the *vanitas* aspect of Dutch still life, along with the dark, velvety backgrounds that makes the flowers and other objects glow as they catch the light from an unseen source. Essentially a subtly moralising reminder of life's transience and that beauty eventually fades, the reference to *vanitas* remained a feature of Wolfe's subsequent paintings to a greater or lesser degree.

Large pink roses was shown in her exhibition at the Dobson Bashford Gallery in Christchurch in 2002. It dates from a time when Wolfe was painting roses mostly from her own garden, such as 'Parade', the largest of the roses in this painting. Other roses came from the garden of her neighbour, garden writer and rose specialist Rose Thodey.

Wolfe's procedure is to collect and photograph potential subjects in the summer, usually around November, and paint in the winter. In this case she made the still life group and photographed it, then painted from the photograph with a few changes for compositional purposes.

It was significant for Wolfe to capture the moment when the flower was full blown—indeed, at the point of turning, with the edges starting to brown — adding colour and variety as well as an additional level of meaning.

2004

NANCY TICHBORNE 1942–

NANCY TICHBORNE FIRST showed signs of her painting ability when still at primary school in Hawera, and was encouraged by her teachers and parents throughout her secondary schooling in Dunedin. When she went to St Martin's School of Art in London in 1960 it was developing its reputation as one of the most innovative in Britain at that time. Tichborne studied fine art and considers Peter Blake and Joe Tilson among her favourite and most influential teachers there.

Okains Bay heritage was painted in 2004 and is of Judy and Kerry Thacker's garden, Kawatea, in Okains Bay, Banks Peninsula. Kawatea is a century-old homestead, beautifully restored, set in a mature garden and surrounded by farmland that has been worked by five generations of the family.

The romantic aspect of the scene, the way the light plays on the garden and the various textures were what initially attracted Tichborne. She explains that 'the wisteria and the old rose come out together down this way, in October–November, but the timing can vary', adding that Banks Peninsula is full of such 'little microclimates'. On the other side of the lawn are hydrangeas, rhododendrons and hostas.

When Tichborne has decided on a subject she makes sketches and photographs on the spot but paints all her finished works in the studio, where she can work listening to music and untroubled by insects, the scourge of the *plein air* painter.

Noise (Yellow)

2004

LEIGH MARTIN 1964–

LEIGH MARTIN STUDIED design in Christchurch and Brighton before enrolling at the Glasgow School of Art in 1990. At that time Martin was interested in realist painting and the art school had a reputation for New Figuration. He was also attracted to Glasgow because it was European City of Culture that year.

As a student, Martin would visit the Glasgow Botanic Gardens, especially Kibble Palace, its renowned temperate-zone glasshouse. He later realised that his preferred area was the New Zealand flora section. While in Glasgow Martin also met film director Derek Jarman, whose books *Modern Nature* and *Chroma* and garden at Prospect Cottage near Dungeness in Kent were influential on Martin's work.

Martin returned to New Zealand in 1995. This painting was included in his first solo exhibition, *Noise*, in 2004 at the Jensen Gallery.

At the time Martin was spending a lot of time developing his Grey Lynn, Auckland, garden. He became aware of the number of flower and garden images that surrounded him and began to photograph items that interested him, such as seed packets or illustrations in magazines, as well as actual flowers and plants in Western Springs lakeside park and other gardens. He was particularly attracted to close-up, intense and hyper-real images totally isolated from their surroundings or an identifying context. This interest coincided with the Elam School of Fine Arts' purchase of a Chameleon painting machine, which Martin decided to use to distance himself from the actual painting process.

Having selected a photograph to make a painting of, he converted it to digital CMYK (cyan, magenta, yellow, black) files. These were then used as the source material for the painting machine, which passes over the canvas and lays down oil paint for each colour. The artist gives the painting the finishing touch by applying a glaze using a large, purpose-made brush.

The machine is not 100 per cent accurate and any glitches in the source imagery are amplified by the machine's own flawed technology, which results in distortion or the 'noise' of the title. Accordingly, the final floral image is recognisable but subtly changed, for example through ghosting where the image has been repeated slightly out of registration.

In *Noise (Yellow)*, the floral appearance is unmistakable although the derivation of the imagery is ambiguous — it bears a resemblance to a specimen on a slide, seen through a microscope. The artist takes the idea of flowers through a previously processed image by means of a photograph and mechanically reproduces it, yet the finished painting manages to communicate a floral image and its direct associations with the garden, which was its initial inspiration.

PETER HACKETT 1960—

SINCE 2001, PETER Hackett has concentrated on paintings of wildflowers in the landscape, all of which he has titled *The honeymooners' bed*®. This for him 'evokes images of passionate lovemaking in a field of wild flowers'.

The subject matter is closely related to the artist's rediscovery of his love of oil paint. The series was inspired by 'the mass seeding of wildflowers along [Auckland's] southern motorway and the marriage of a close friend', for whom the first work of this title was painted. The artist intends the viewer of his paintings to experience 'notions of scent, texture, colour and the sublime, incomparable beauty of nature'.

Typical paintings by Hackett show drifts of brightly coloured flowers filling the picture space with little to distinguish the foreground and no indication of horizon. With this painting Hackett has taken a specific garden as his starting point: Beverley McConnell's renowned garden Ayrlies at Whitford, southeast of Auckland, which he visited in 2007 and 2008. The artist explains his motivation:

Ayrlies is more than just a garden, it is a life's work. I thought it impossible to depict such a vast and wonderful garden in a single painting so, out of homage to the man and woman that created it, I chose only to portray its intimacy.

Hackett's painting depicts a specific place in the garden, referred to as the top of the rose garden steps. He has chosen to focus not on the vista from the garden seat but the seat itself, which perhaps he imagines as a love seat, symbolising the garden's creators.

Beverley McConnell and her late husband Malcolm began work on their garden at Ayrlies, named after the McConnell family farm in Scotland, in 1964. In 1978, with the addition of three large ponds, the garden expanded from 1.2 hectares to 4. In 2000 the swamp below the homestead was transformed into a wetland area, linking the garden to the sea.

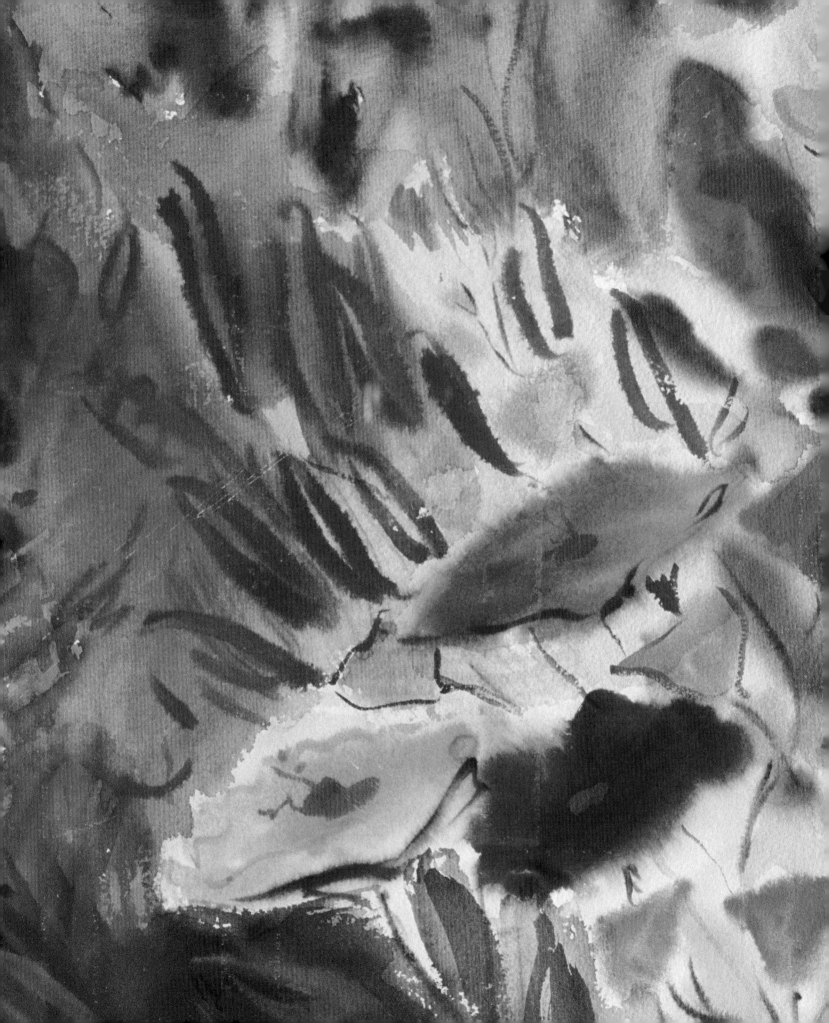

ARTIST BIOGRAPHIES

Jane Evans, *Summer garden I* (detail), see page 205

All measurements are in centimetres. For simplicity, the principal medium is given. Paper is the assumed support for all watercolours unless otherwise stated.

Artist unknown

The missionary settlement
Rangihoua on the
north side of the Bay of
Islands, New Zealand
Before 1832
Oil on wood panel
22.3 x 30.5
Rex Nan Kivell Collection
National Library of Australia

Gretchen Albrecht

1943–

GRETCHEN ALBRECHT was born and brought up in Auckland, where she attended the University of Auckland's Elam School of Fine Arts, graduating in 1963, and teachers' training college, graduating in 1966. She had her first solo exhibition at the Ikon Gallery, Auckland, in 1967 and subsequently exhibited in Auckland at the Barry Lett and Peter Webb galleries, as well as at the Brooke Gifford, Christchurch, and galleries in the other centres. She also showed at the Todd Gallery in London. She was the Frances Hodgkins Fellow at the University of Otago in 1981. Since 1985 Albrecht has shown at the Sue Crockford Gallery, Auckland. In 1986 her major retrospective exhibition *AFTERnature*, organised by the Sarjeant Gallery, toured the country. A print retrospective, *Crossing the Divide: A Painter Makes Prints*, toured in 1999. In 2002 a survey of 21 years' work, *Illuminations*, was organised by the Auckland Art Gallery and in 2005 *Returning* at the Dunedin Public Art Gallery surveyed 24 years of her hemispheres and ovals. Albrecht has been included in a number of New Zealand exhibitions overseas, including *Distance Looks Our Way* at Expo '92 Seville (1992) and *From the Edge: Contemporary Art from New Zealand*, first shown in Valencia in 2007. Albrecht was included in *Refractions and Shadows* at the Lemon Street Gallery, Truro, Cornwall, in 2008. In 2000 she was made a Companion of the Order of New Zealand.

Winter trees
1971
Watercolour
76.0 x 56.0
Signed and dated
Artist's collection
Reproduced with the kind permission
of the artist

Wekaweka garden
1971–2
Acrylic on canvas
150.0 x 1131.0
Private collection
Reproduced with the kind permission
of the artist

Rita Angus

1908–1970

RITA ANGUS, one of New Zealand's greatest modernist painters, was born in Hastings, grew up in Palmerston North and studied at the Canterbury College School of Art from 1927 to 1933. She was briefly married to a fellow student, Alfred Cook, and lived alone for the rest of her life. Although she exhibited widely throughout her life, especially with the Canterbury Society of Arts and The Group, she was resistant to selling her work and as a result her income was extremely meagre. At times she suffered from poor physical and mental health and the support of her parents was crucial at times especially, in 1943, to the purchase of a cottage at Clifton, near Christchurch, where she lived until moving to Wellington in 1954. Angus had her first solo exhibition there in 1957 and the following year visited Europe for the first time on an Association of New Zealand Art Societies Fellowship; in London she attended life classes at the Chelsea School of Art. In 1965 three of her paintings were shown in *Contemporary New Zealand Painting* at the Commonwealth Institute, London, sponsored by the QEII Arts Council. In 1968 and 1969 Angus's health was poor but she continued to work, especially on drawings of Wellington's Bolton Street Cemetery, a section of which was soon to be demolished. Her last solo exhibition was planned for the Bett–Duncan Studio Gallery in October 1970 and there was discussion of a retrospective at the Manawatu Art Gallery just before her death in January that year. A major biography by Jill Trevelyan was published in 2008.

Passionflower
1943
Watercolour
11.2 x 13.0
Signed and dated
Museum of New Zealand Te Papa
Tongarewa
Purchased 1998 with New Zealand
Lottery Grants Board funds
Reproduced with the kind permission of
the estate of Rita Angus

WATERLILIES
1950
WATERCOLOUR
28.6 X 38.6
SIGNED AND DATED
MUSEUM OF NEW ZEALAND TE PAPA
TONGAREWA
PURCHASED 1998 WITH NEW ZEALAND
LOTTERY GRANTS BOARD FUNDS
REPRODUCED WITH THE KIND PERMISSION
OF THE ESTATE OF RITA ANGUS

GARDEN, WAIKANAE
CA 1952
WATERCOLOUR
31.0 X 34.0
MUSEUM OF NEW ZEALAND TE PAPA
TONGAREWA
REPRODUCED WITH THE KIND PERMISSION
OF THE ESTATE OF RITA ANGUS

IRIS
1953
WATERCOLOUR
56.8 X 33.6
SIGNED AND DATED
FLETCHER TRUST COLLECTION
REPRODUCED WITH THE KIND PERMISSION
OF THE ESTATE OF RITA ANGUS

JOSEPH ANNABELL
1815–1893

JOSEPH ANNABELL was born in Mansfield, Nottinghamshire. He eloped with Mary Chambers (he was a Methodist and she a Quaker) from Heanour, Derbyshire, and they were married in 1839. In 1852 they travelled to Melbourne with their children, John and Mary, and in 1860 came to Napier, where Mary's brother had a farm at Te Mata. They built a house, Undercliff, on Te Mata Peak Station. Annabell, who had had some training as an artist in England, practised as a painter of portraits and horses, mainly painting from photographs. He died in Napier aged 78. His son John Annabell (1846–1919) — a surveyor and explorer — became the government surveyor.

TIFFEN HOUSE AND THE ORIGINAL
ST PAUL'S CHURCH
CA 1870
OIL ON CANVAS
39.5 X 59.5
SIGNED
HAWKE'S BAY MUSEUM AND ART GALLERY
GIFT OF MISS EM BOYLE, 1959

HAMAR HUMPHREY ARDEN
1816–1895
FRANCIS ARDEN
1841–1899

HAMAR ARDEN was born in England, the son of watercolourist the Reverend Francis Edward Arden, who was vicar of Gresham, near Cromer on the Norfolk coast. Hamar Arden arrived in Taranaki with his wife and five children in 1853, took up land in Bell Block and was for a while a partner in a brewing business. The Taranaki Wars forced the family to take refuge in New Plymouth and for a brief time they moved to Nelson. On their return to New Plymouth in 1861 Arden established himself as a professional artist. He was granted some confiscated land for his service with the Taranaki Volunteers.

Francis Arden (or Hamar Arden Jnr) was the elder of the two Arden sons who became artists. He served with the Military Settlers, the Volunteer Rifles and the Armed Constabulary before becoming a farmer. Around 1871 he began to work with his father in his Gill Street, New Plymouth, studio. He was invited by the Auckland Society of Artists to exhibit in its first exhibition that year, sending two paintings that the *Taranaki Herald* thought 'cannot but help attract considerable attention from connoisseurs in Auckland'.

UNTITLED [HOUSE AND GARDEN]
CA 1870
WATERCOLOUR
23.4 X 31.8
COLLECTION OF PUKE ARIKI
PURCHASED 1925

DEAR GRANNY ARDEN'S HOME IN
COURTNEY STREET, NEW PLYMOUTH
CA 1880
WATERCOLOUR
28.7 X 44.5
ALEXANDER TURNBULL LIBRARY

FRANCIS DILLON BELL

1822–1898

FRANCIS DILLON BELL was born and brought up in France. At 17 he joined the New Zealand Company through his relative Edward Wakefield and travelled to New Zealand in 1843. He was appointed as a magistrate in Nelson in 1846 and as resident agent for the New Zealand Company in New Plymouth the following year. In 1850 Governor George Grey appointed him commissioner of Crown lands, in 1853 he was elected to the Wellington Provincial Council, and in 1854 he was appointed to the Legislative Council. A fluent speaker of Maori, he became the Minister for Native Affairs in 1861, eventually retiring from politics in 1863. Bell was a competent watercolour painter and in 1865 he, JC Richmond and William Fox, all of whom had been ministers, exhibited at the New Zealand Exhibition in Dunedin. In 1849 Bell married Margaret Hort. One of their seven children was Francis Henry Dillon Bell, the first New Zealand-born prime minister of New Zealand. Bell was knighted in 1881.

THE HOUSE OF ALFRED LUDLAM ESQ., RIVER HUTT, NEW ZEALAND
1850
WATERCOLOUR
23.4 X 33.4
HOCKEN COLLECTIONS UARE TAOKA O HAKENA, UNIVERSITY OF OTAGO

DON BINNEY

1940–

DON BINNEY, one of New Zealand's most distinguished painters, took art lessons with John Weeks while still a schoolboy. He studied at the Elam School of Fine Arts at the University of Auckland from 1958 to 1961 and, after teacher training, taught art at Mount Roskill Grammar School. In 1963 Binney had his first solo exhibition, at the Ikon Gallery, Auckland. A QEII Arts Council Travel Fellowship in 1967 allowed him to travel to Europe, North America, Mexico and Central America. During 1971 Binney was visiting lecturer in Victoria University's extension department and in 1974 he became a tutor in painting at Elam. He continued to teach there in various positions until he became head of painting, a position he held until his retirement in 1998. Binney exhibits regularly at Artis Gallery, Auckland, and the Brooke Gifford Gallery, Christchurch. His biography by Damian Skinner, *Don Binney Nga Manu/Nga Motu: Birds/Islands*, was published by Auckland University Press in 2003 and a major survey exhibition, *Binney: Forty Years On*, was presented by the Auckland Art Gallery and toured to a number of regional art museums.

BACKYARD GARDEN II
1961
OIL ON BOARD
120.0 X 165.0
SIGNED AND DATED
ARTIST'S COLLECTION
REPRODUCED WITH THE KIND PERMISSION OF THE ARTIST

FAREWELL, CECIL ROAD
1985
DRY MEDIUM ON PAPER
37.0 X 53.0
SIGNED AND DATED
ARTIST'S COLLECTION
REPRODUCED WITH THE KIND PERMISSION OF THE ARTIST

CYPRIAN BRIDGE

1807–1885

CYPRIAN BRIDGE was born in Canada. His father was in the Royal Artillery and Bridge joined the 58th Regiment of Foot (Rutlandshire) in 1825, rising to major in 1842. He arrived in Auckland in 1845 and commanded the British forces in the Bay of Islands. He was appointed by Governor George Grey as resident magistrate and then in 1848 deputy registrar of births, deaths and marriages at Russell. He left New Zealand in 1850 to command the 58th at Chatham, later serving in Jersey and Ireland and being promoted to Brevet Lieutenant-Colonel in 1854 before retiring in 1860. The 58th left New Zealand in 1858.

VIEW OF AN ORDINARY NEW ZEALAND PA WITH POTATO PLANTATIONS AROUND IT
1845
WATERCOLOUR
22.5 X 30.0
ALEXANDER TURNBULL LIBRARY

NIGEL BROWN

1949–

NIGEL BROWN, one of New Zealand's best known figurative painters, was born in Invercargill, and in 2001 returned to Southland to live in Cosy Nook, near Riverton. He grew up in Tauranga and attended the Elam School of Fine Arts at the University of Auckland, where Colin McCahon was one of his tutors. On graduating in 1972, he had his first solo exhibition at Mollers Gallery, Auckland. An extensive traveller, he has visited the Pacific, Europe, the United States and most recently the former Soviet Union. In 1998 Brown was one of the inaugural visitors to the Antarctic under Creative New Zealand's Artists to Antarctica programme. He has received several QEII Arts Council grants and his commissions have included stained glass windows for Auckland's Holy Trinity Cathedral, completed in 1998. Brown has exhibited extensively throughout his career and has regular solo exhibitions at Warwick Henderson Gallery, Auckland. A book about his work by Gregory O'Brien was published in 1991.

HOME GARDENER
1989
OIL ON BOARD
120.0 X 80.0
SIGNED AND DATED
PRIVATE COLLECTION
REPRODUCED WITH THE KIND PERMISSION OF
THE ARTIST

CONSTANCE FREDERICA GORDON CUMMING

1837–1924

CONSTANCE CUMMING was born in Altyre, Morayshire, Scotland, the youngest daughter of Sir William Gordon Gordon-Cumming and his first wife, Eliza Maria. In 1867 she spent a year with a married sister in India, a trip that began 12 years of travel. She eventually settled back in Scotland, organising exhibitions of her watercolours and working up her various books. She was also increasingly engaged with the development of a typeface for blind and sighted Mandarin-speaking Chinese, as a result of visiting William Hill-Murray's school for the blind in Peking. In addition to *At Home in Fiji* (1881) her books include *Two Happy Years in Ceylon* (1892), *A Lady's Cruise in a French Man-of-War in the South Seas* (1882), *A Visit to the Granite Crags of California* (1884), *Wanderings in China* (1886) and *Fire Fountains of Hawaii* (1883). Cumming died in Crieff, Perthshire, in 1924.

SIR GEORGE GREY'S HOME ON
THE KAWAU
1877
WATERCOLOUR
41.4 X 60.5
AUCKLAND ART GALLERY TOI O TAMAKI
PURCHASED 1990

WILLIAM CUMMING

1933–2002

WILLIAM CUMMING was born in Hokitika. He trained first as a draughtsman, then as an engineering assistant with Transmission Line Construction, building high-voltage transmission cables for the state hydroelectric department. On his overseas experience he worked on engineering projects in Canada and the United States. Back in Christchurch he studied part time at the School of Fine Arts at Canterbury University until 1959, while working as an engineer for the Christchurch Drainage Board. In 1972 he was a finalist in the Benson & Hedges Art Award. From 1975 to 1984 Cumming joined an architectural practice and was co-director of Cowley Mills & Co Ltd. He then became a tutor at the School of Art and Design, Christchurch Polytechnic Institute of Technology, until his death in 2002. Cumming's first solo exhibition was at the Canterbury Society of Arts in 1969 and he continued to show there in solo and group exhibitions throughout his career. Cumming became interested in papermaking in the late 1980s and attended a course on it at the Tasmanian School of Art, Hobart in 1990. In 1998 he was awarded a Bachelor of Design degree from Christchurch Polytechnic Institute of Technology. His paper works, including paper sculptures, were exhibited at the Christopher Moore Gallery, Wellington, and at the Salamander and Brooke Gifford galleries in Christchurch. Cumming's background made him an ideal project manager and he assisted the Robert McDougall Art Gallery with the installation of major public sculptures, including those by Neil Dawson and Bing Dawe. He also undertook frame restoration and gilding in preparation for the opening of the new Christchurch Art Gallery. Cumming played an important role in the establishment of the Olivia Spencer Bower Foundation and the Olivia Spencer Bower Foundation Art Award.

GARDEN
1976
ACRYLIC ON CANVAS
45.0 X 45.0
SIGNED AND DATED
PRIVATE COLLECTION
REPRODUCED WITH THE KIND PERMISSION OF
MARY ADAMS-TAYLOR AND JEAN CUMMING
PHOTOGRAPH: JON HUNTER

JANE EVANS

1946–

JANE EVANS was born in Nelson, where she attended Nelson Girls' College. In 1965 she enrolled at the University of Canterbury School of Fine Art but was unable to continue beyond her first year because of an illness that would affect her on and off, sometimes seriously, throughout her career. She had her first exhibition at Chez Eelco in Nelson in 1966 before travelling to England, where she attended

Waltham Forest Art School for a year, before travelling in Europe and returning to Christchurch. In 1969 she visited the Bahamas, where she had an exhibition at Freeport, and returned to Nelson, where she continues to live. Another solo exhibition followed at Chez Eelco in 1972 and then, in 1974, Evans had the first of two sell-out exhibitions at the Lee Cramp Gallery, Auckland. In 1975 she won the Commonwealth Art Prize and, following the second Lee Cramp exhibition, spent three months in the UK. In 1979 she was the subject of a documentary by John Reid. Evans had several exhibitions through the 1980s, including a show in San Francisco and a major exhibition at the Denis Cohn Gallery, Auckland (*Jane Evans Recent Paintings*), both in 1985. In 1997 she was awarded the New Zealand Order of Merit and her biography by John Coley was published. In 2002 Evans painted her largest painting, a 4m wide view of vineyards, a commission for Montana Wines.

SUMMER GARDEN I
1985
GOUACHE ON PAPER
71.5 X 101.5
SIGNED AND DATED
FLETCHER TRUST COLLECTION
REPRODUCED WITH THE KIND PERMISSION OF
THE ARTIST

CLAUDIA POND EYLEY

1946–

Painter, art teacher and documentary film-maker CLAUDIA POND EYLEY was born in Matamata and brought up in Montreal and New York. She studied at the Elam School of Art at the University of Auckland, and following graduation in 1968 she trained at Auckland Teachers' College. Since 1973 Eyley has taught drawing in the School of Architecture at the University of Auckland. The founder of Visual Artists Against Nuclear Arms and a member of the Women Artists' Association in Auckland, Eyley was active through her art in the women's movement in the 1970s and 1980s. She travelled widely, collaborating in workshops and exhibiting in a wide range of exhibitions. In 1985 she had a two-person exhibition with Carole Shepheard at the City Gallery, Wellington. With her friend Robin White she collaborated on the book *28 Days in Kiribati*, 1987. Her many commissions include paintings for the Auckland High Court (1990), stained glass windows for St Mary's Church, Parnell, and a ceramic mural in Khartoum Place, Auckland, a collaborative work to mark the centenary of women's suffrage in New Zealand. It was completed in 1993, the year of her survey exhibition at the Auckland City Art Gallery in the *Unruly Practices* series. In 2007 Eyley completed *No Nukes is Good Nukes!*, a documentary she produced and directed about the anti-nuclear movement in New Zealand and the Pacific.

MOUNT EDEN GARDEN I
1979
ACRYLIC ON CANVAS
101.0 X160.0
ARTIST'S COLLECTION
REPRODUCED WITH THE KIND PERMISSION OF
THE ARTIST

MOUNT EDEN LANDSCAPE
1984
ACRYLIC ON CANVAS ON BOARD
254.0 X 206.5 (TRIPTYCH)
SIGNED AND DATED
UNIVERSITY OF AUCKLAND COLLECTION
REPRODUCED WITH THE KIND PERMISSION OF
THE ARTIST

SARAH FEATON

1848–1927

Little is known about the early life of SARAH FEATON (née Porter) other than that she was probably born in London, where she received some artistic training before travelling to New Zealand. In Auckland in 1870 she married Edward Featon (1840–1909), an English army captain who had arrived in New Zealand in 1860. In 1874 he was appointed a draughtsman in the government survey department and in 1875 they moved to Gisborne where he was made the first district lands officer, although he continued his military service too. It was probably in Gisborne that the Featons conceived and embarked on the project which eventually became *The Art Album of New Zealand Flora; being a systematic and popular description of the native flowering plants of New Zealand and the adjacent islands* (1887–79). Edward Featon retired in 1893 because of ill health but two years later was re-engaged by the survey department until 1900. The Featons had one son, Edwin (Teddy), who worked for a stock and station firm. In 1918 Sarah Featon sold the original paintings she had made for the book to the Dominion Museum in order to reduce her mortgage. She remained in Gisborne, where she continued to paint copies of her botanical studies and occupied herself with various crafts.

PIKIARERO (CLEMATIS HEXASEPALA)
CA 1880
WATERCOLOUR ON GREEN-TONED PAPER
SET DOWN ON CARD
29.0 X 24.0
MUSEUM OF NEW ZEALAND TE PAPA
TONGAREWA
PURCHASED 1919

IVY FIFE
1905–1976

IVY FIFE was born in Christchurch and studied at the Canterbury College School of Art, where Francis Shurrock was among her teachers, from 1920 to 1931. In 1934 she became a member of the college staff and taught there until her retirement in 1959, teaching design, embroidery and plant forms in the junior school, and later landscape painting at the senior level. In 1951 Fife was included in the International Women's Art Club exhibition, part of the Festival of Britain in London, and in 1954 she was appointed to the Robert McDougall Art Gallery Advisory Panel. In 1957 she was included in the Auckland City Art Gallery's annual exhibition *Eight New Zealand Painters*. Fife exhibited regularly at the Canterbury Society of Arts and other main-centre annual art society exhibitions. A major retrospective featuring 78 of her works was being organised by the Robert McDougall Art Gallery at the time of her death; it was held in 1977.

SUNFLOWER
1964
OIL ON BOARD
58.0 X 79.0
SIGNED
AIGANTIGHE ART GALLERY, TIMARU
BOUGHT WITH FUNDS FROM THE GEORGE
SEVICKE JONES TRUST 1965

JAMES FITZGERALD
1869–1945

Edinburgh-born JAMES FITZGERALD was brought up in London, where he served his apprenticeship as a lithographic artist. He emigrated to New Zealand in 1903, settling in Auckland, where he was responsible for the art department of the *New Zealand Herald*. Twenty years later and now a successful commercial artist, Fitzgerald relocated his Medusa Studio to Christchurch. He exhibited at the New Zealand Academy of Fine Arts, the Auckland Society of Arts and the Canterbury Society of Arts and was widely known for his etchings.

SUMMER EVENING IN THE CITY
1935
OIL ON BOARD
49.0 X 72.0
SIGNED
PRIVATE COLLECTION
PHOTOGRAPH COURTESY OF FERNER
GALLERIES

WILLIAM FOX
1812–1893

WILLIAM FOX was New Zealand's second premier. Born in Westoe near Durham, England, he studied at Oxford. Soon after being called to the Bar in 1842 he emigrated with his wife Sarah to New Zealand, where he became editor of the *New Zealand Gazette and Wellington Spectator*. He was appointed the Nelson agent of the New Zealand Company before becoming its principal agent in Wellington in 1848. In 1855 he was elected a member of the House of Representatives for Wanganui. During his long political career he was premier four times, served as colonial secretary and attorney-general and was opposition leader. His most important achievement was bringing peace to Taranaki by sorting out its complex land claims. He retired in 1875 and was knighted in 1879.

W. FOX'S HOUSE, NELSON
1848
WATERCOLOUR
23.8 X 34.5
HOCKEN COLLECTIONS, UARE TAOKA O
HAKENA
UNIVERSITY OF OTAGO

LOWER WESTOE RANGITIKEI 1860
1860
WATERCOLOUR ON BROWN PAPER
39.8 X 27.2
ALEXANDER TURNBULL LIBRARY

LOWER WESTOE RANGITIKEI 1860
1860
WATERCOLOUR ON BROWN PAPER
38.7 X 26.0
ALEXANDER TURNBULL LIBRARY

WESTOE RANGITIKEI 1872
1872
WATERCOLOUR
25.5 X 41.3
ALEXANDER TURNBULL LIBRARY

RODNEY FUMPSTON

1947–

RODNEY FUMPSTON was born in Fiji and came to New Zealand with his mother at around the age of seven, when his parents separated. After secondary school in the Waikato he attended the University of Canterbury for two years, then enrolled at the Elam School of Fine Arts at the University of Auckland, where he took a Bachelor of Fine Arts degree and then a Master's in 1972. He had his first solo exhibition, of etchings, at the Auckland Society of Arts in 1972. Fumpston then went to London's Central School of Art and Design where he studied advanced printmaking in 1973 and 1974. On his return he helped establish the printmaking studio at the Auckland Society of Arts. From 1978 onwards Fumpston exhibited annually in all the main centres. He received two QEII Arts Council grants: in 1980 for overseas study and in 1991 a major visual arts award. Fumpston began teaching part time at the Auckland Society of Arts in 1985 and in 1995 he was appointed senior lecturer in printmaking at Elam, a position he held for 10 years. A survey exhibition, *Fumpston One Decade*, was organised and toured from 1983 to 1985 by the New Zealand Art Gallery Directors Council. The survey *Etchings, Mezzotints, Lithographs 1982–1992* was presented in 1992 by The Lane Gallery, which also showed *Pacific Woodcuts* in 1996, with an essay by Jim and Mary Barr. In 2004 a major retrospective, *Fumpston Prints 1973–2003*, was organised by the Sarjeant Gallery, Wanganui. Fumpston has also had solo exhibitions in the UK and Australia.

NIGHT GARDEN
1993
LITHOGRAPH
50.0 X 100.0
COLLECTION OF THE ARTIST
REPRODUCED WITH THE KIND PERMISSION OF
THE ARTIST

CHARLES GOLDIE

1870–1947

CHARLES GOLDIE was born in Auckland. His father, a successful timber merchant, was a politician and mayor of Auckland. His mother, Maria, was the daughter of Auckland miller and baker Charles Frederick Partington. On leaving school he studied part time with Louis Steele and probably at Kennett Watkins's Auckland Free School of Art. He became a member of the Auckland Academy of Art in 1889 and its secretary in 1892. In 1893 he went to Paris to study at the Académie Julian in William Bouguereau's studio. He was back in Auckland by mid-1898 and shared a studio with Steele, with whom he collaborated on the famous painting *The arrival of the Maori in New Zealand* (1899). In 1900 he exhibited six portraits, including images of Maori, at the Auckland Society of Arts, an exhibition that marked the beginning of his professional career. Until 1919 Goldie exhibited a succession of the portraits of Maori that

established his widespread reputation and for which he is best known today. In 1920 he left Auckland, apparently destined for Paris. On arriving in Sydney he married Olive Cooper, an Auckland milliner. They returned to Auckland in 1923 after Goldie experienced a bout of illness; he remained in poor health throughout the 1920s, probably the result of lead poisoning. A commission from Governor-General Lord Bledisloe for a painting relating to Waitangi later inspired a productive period of painting, mostly adaptations of his earlier successful portraits. In the 1930s he exhibited at the Royal Academy, London, and the Paris Salon, and in 1935 he was presented with the King George V Silver Jubilee Medal and made an OBE. In 1939 he gave two paintings to the Auckland Art Gallery in memory of his mother. Goldie stopped painting in 1941.

CLEMATIS
1886
OIL ON WOOD PANEL
76.0 X 29.0
PRIVATE COLLECTION
PHOTOGRAPH: KALLAN MACLEOD

MURRAY GRIMSDALE

1943–

MURRAY GRIMSDALE, a painter, sculptor, illustrator and ceramic artist, was born in Dunedin and grew up in Christchurch. He attended the School of Fine Arts at the University of Canterbury from 1959 to 1963, where he studied painting with Bill Sutton and Rudi Gopas and illustration with Russell Clark. After graduating he moved to Auckland for teacher training, which he did not complete, instead working as a set designer for television and then for his partner, fashion designer Annie Bonza. In 1970 Grimsdale had a two-person exhibition with the Australian artist Mike Brown, *Bloodlust in the Boondocks*, at Barry Lett Galleries, Auckland. In 1971 he went to London, where he installed exhibitions at the Camden Arts Centre, then was a display artist and cover designer for a record distribution company. On his return to New Zealand in 1974 he settled in Pakiri where he met and, in 1976, married May Higgott (the painter Hariata Ropata Tangahoe). After their separation in 1981, Grimsdale took primary responsibility for their two children. In 1982 he moved to Mt Eden with his partner Whanaupani (Bunny) Thompson. From 1971 until 1997, when he began to suffer from RSI, he was an illustrator for the *School Journal*. Grimsdale made eight visits to Vanuatu from 1990 to 1995 to teach book illustration under a scheme established by the Ministry of Foreign Affairs and Trade. In 1997 the Rotorua Museum of Art and History presented a retrospective exhibition, *Murray Grimsdale: Three Decades Hard Labour*. Grimsdale has illustrated 30 books, particularly books for children, and in 1997 won the Russell Clark Award for Illustration with *George's Monster*, written by Amanda Jackson. His best-known mural, at the Leys Institute Community Library in Auckland, depicts scenes of Ponsonby.

THE ARTIST'S GARDEN, PAKIRI
1977
OIL ON CANVAS
92.5 X 76.5
SIGNED AND DATED
THE GARDEN PARTY COLLECTION
REPRODUCED WITH THE KIND PERMISSION OF THE ARTIST
PHOTOGRAPH: KALLAN MACLEOD

PETER HACKETT

1960–

PETER HACKETT was born in Auckland and brought up in Rotorua. After high school, he travelled to Paris to study at the Paris American Academy where his tutors included Camilo Otero, Suzanne Runacher and Rafael Madhavi, who established the Bastille annual open studios. While in Paris he was included in the 1980 *Salon des Artistes Francaises*. Hackett returned to New Zealand in the early 1980s to study at the Auckland Society of Arts under Rodney Fumpston and Carole Shepheard. He exhibited regularly in group shows, shared exhibitions and solo shows in the 1980s and 1990s, including at the Auckland Society of Arts, the Portfolio and Chiaroscuro galleries, as well as the TVH Gallery, Sydney. Since 2003 Hackett has shown annually at Fishers Fine Arts in Auckland, Wellington and Christchurch. He was a finalist in several major art awards including the Nola Holmwood Memorial Portrait Prize (1989), the Team McMillan Art Award (1990) and the Ida Eise Art Award (1991). He lives and paints in rural north Auckland.

THE HONEYMOONERS' BED®
2008
OIL ON CANVAS
120.0 X 170.0
PRIVATE COLLECTION
REPRODUCED WITH THE KIND PERMISSION OF THE ARTIST

ANNE HAMBLETT

1915–1993

ANNE HAMBLETT was born in 1915 in Mosgiel, where her father was the Anglican vicar. She attended Otago Girls' High School from 1929 to 1934 and was a scholarship student at the King Edward Technical College until 1938. Hamblett met her future husband, Colin McCahon, when he entered art school the previous year. With friends, including Doris Lusk, Hamblett set up in a professional studio in Dunedin and she made commissioned illustrations for the medical school. She showed in the 1937 exhibition of the Otago Art Society, where she continued to exhibit until the mid-1940s. In July 1942 she had a solo exhibition at the French Maid Café, Wellington. That year she and McCahon were married and in 1943 they moved to Nelson, where the first of their four children was born, and also made her first book illustrations, for *At the Beach* by Aileen Findlay. In 1945 the McCahons returned to Dunedin, where Hamblett showed her last oil painting at that year's OAS annual exhibition. From 1951 to 1957 her illustrations appeared in the *School Journal*. The McCahons moved to Auckland in 1953, where Colin McCahon took up a position at the Auckland City Art Gallery. In the late 1960s and 1970s Hamblett developed an interest in hand-made ceramics, but she had to put this aside to look after McCahon during his last illness.

POPPIES
CA 1937
OIL ON COMPOSITION BOARD
45.6 X 45.2
SIGNED
HOCKEN COLLECTIONS, UARE TAOKA O HAKENA, UNIVERSITY OF OTAGO
GIFT OF JOHN AND ETHEL MCCAHON, 1973
REPRODUCED WITH THE KIND PERMISSION OF THE MCCAHON FAMILY TRUST

PATRICK HANLY

1932–2004

PAT HANLY was born in Palmerston North where, after two years at Palmerston North Boys' High School, he worked as an apprentice hairdresser for four years. He also studied art at Queen Elizabeth Technical College. Encouraged by his teacher, Allan Leary, in 1952 Hanly attended the Canterbury College School of Art, where he met his future wife, Gillian Taverner. He graduated in 1956 and had his first exhibition, with Taverner and Bill Culbert, at Wellington's Architectural Centre Gallery. Before leaving Christchurch in 1957 Hanly organised *Young New Zealand Artists* at the Durham Street Gallery, then followed Taverner to London where he worked in a nightclub and in theatre. Hanly and Taverner married in 1958. In 1959 Hanly had a work in *Young Contemporaries* and a solo exhibition at the Comedy Gallery and was a finalist in the John Moores biennial exhibition, Liverpool, with one of his *Showgirl* paintings. In 1960 a grant allowed him to study in Florence and then, in 1961, in Holland. The Hanlys returned to Auckland in 1962 and Pat Hanly found a part-time position teaching drawing at the School of Architecture, which he held for the rest of his career. Hanly began to exhibit regularly, first at the Ikon Gallery, then at the Barry Lett and RKS galleries in Auckland, Peter McLeavey in Wellington and Brooke Gifford in Christchurch. In 1974 Hanly was given his first retrospective at the Dowse Art Gallery, Lower Hutt, and the show then toured the main centres. There were numerous other solo exhibitions including *Hanly: The Painter as Printmaker* (1981), *Women by Hanly* (1988) and *Hanly Trust Paintings* (1996–1998). In the mid-1990s, by then showing the first signs of Huntington's, Hanly ceased painting.

'INSIDE' THE GARDEN
1969–1970
ENAMEL AND OIL ON HARDBOARD
120.0 X 120.0
COLLECTION OF TE MANAWA MUSEUMS TRUST
PURCHASED BY MANAWATU ART GALLERY
FOR THE AWAPUNI JAYCEE CENTENARY
COLLECTION, 1971
REPRODUCED WITH THE KIND PERMISSION OF
GIL HANLY

GARDEN ENERGY
1972
OIL AND ENAMEL ON HARDBOARD
91.4 X 91.4
PRIVATE COLLECTION
REPRODUCED WITH THE KIND PERMISSION OF
GIL HANLY

UNTITLED
1981
CRAYON AND WATERCOLOUR ON PAPER
64.0 X 58.5
SIGNED AND DATED
PRIVATE COLLECTION
REPRODUCED WITH THE KIND PERMISSION OF
GIL HANLY
PHOTOGRAPH: KALLAN MACLEOD

NEON GARDEN
1984
WATERCOLOUR
61.5 X 54.0
SIGNED AND DATED
THE GARDEN PARTY COLLECTION
REPRODUCED WITH THE KIND PERMISSION OF
GIL HANLY
PHOTOGRAPH: KALLAN MACLEOD

PAUL HARTIGAN
1953–

PAUL HARTIGAN was born in New Plymouth. He studied at the Elam School of Fine Arts at the University of Auckland from 1971 to 1973, graduating with a Diploma in Fine Arts. In 1973 he went to Melbourne and trained in commercial screenprinting, including hand-printed wallpaper. After his return to Auckland in 1974 he established Snake Studios, a silkscreen printing business producing fabrics, t-shirts and artist print editions. In 1977 he travelled throughout Australia, Asia, Europe and the United States and on his return took a job at the Auckland Museum as an assistant display artist. His first solo exhibitions were *Modernesque* at Galerie Legard, Wellington, and *Picturesque* at Barry Lett Galleries, Auckland, in 1979. He subsequently had solo exhibitions at RKS and Artis, Auckland, and at Janne Land and Tinakori Gallery, Wellington. Around 1980 Hartigan became a full-time artist and designer and in 1981 received a QE II Arts Council major visual arts project grant that enabled him to establish Gone On Neon, which produced neon fine-art works, as well as installations for corporate and individual clients. Gone on Neon closed in 1990. From 1994 to 1996 Hartigan was a lecturer at Elam, first in printmaking and then in painting. In 1987 Hartigan received the first of several public and corporate commissions: *Whipping the wind*, Wellington. Others since then include *Pathfinder* (1997, Govett-Brewster Art Gallery), *Nebula Orion* (2001, Orion NZ Ltd, Christchurch), *Signal/Echo* (2001, New Lynn Community Centre) and *Colony* (2004, University of Auckland).

BIG INSTANT #2
1989
CIBACHROME PRINT
63.5 X 80.0
COLLECTION OF THE ARTIST
REPRODUCED WITH THE KIND PERMISSION OF
THE ARTIST

CHARLES HEAPHY
1820–1881

CHARLES HEAPHY was a surveyor, explorer, soldier, public servant, member of Parliament and — like his father — an artist. Born in London, he became a draughtsman for a railway company and in 1837 entered the Royal Academy Schools, London. In 1839, now a draughtsman for the New Zealand Company, he arrived in New Zealand and was appointed assistant surveyor in Port Nicholson. He explored the West Coast and the Buller River with William Fox before taking up a surveyor's position with the colonial government in Auckland. Through the 1850s he held a number of minor government positions before enrolling in the Auckland Volunteer Rifles and being commissioned as a lieutenant in 1863. In 1864 he was awarded a Victoria Cross for bravery in an incident in the Waikato War. Heaphy briefly

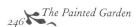

represented Parnell in the House of Representatives and held several more minor government positions. His health failed in 1881 and he died in Brisbane.

THE HOME OF MR & MRS WILLIAM
BISHOP, MAITAI VALLEY
1844
WATERCOLOUR
24.4 X 32.1
ALEXANDER TURNBULL LIBRARY
GIFT OF MISS H NICHOLLS, 1984

MABEL HILL
1872–1956

MABEL HILL was born at Cox's Creek, Auckland, and moved with her family to Wellington in 1876, where her father established his business as a hatter on Lambton Quay. Instead of having a traditional secondary school education, Hill enrolled in 1886 at the Wellington School of Design (later Wellington Technical College) to study art. When her training was finished in 1891 she became an instructor and a colleague of James Nairn, who joined the staff that year to teach still-life painting and life drawing. Hill attended Nairn's life-drawing classes. In 1898 she married printer John McIndoe and moved to Dunedin, where they raised four children. (Unusually for the times, Hill retained her maiden name as her professional name throughout her career.) McIndoe died in 1916 and Hill lived in Dunedin for much of the rest of her life, continuing to paint. She also travelled and was based in London from 1930 to 1935. She returned to the United Kingdom after the war and lived at East Grinstead, near her son Archibald McIndoe, the pioneering plastic surgeon.

CHRYSANTHEMUMS
1896
WATERCOLOUR
52.0 X 66.0
SIGNED AND DATED
PRIVATE COLLECTION
REPRODUCED WITH THE KIND PERMISSION OF
THE ESTATE OF ELIZABETH MASON
PHOTOGRAPH: CHRIS COAD PHOTOGRAPHY

REED STREET, OAMARU
1915
WATERCOLOUR
30.0 X 52.0
PRIVATE COLLECTION
REPRODUCED WITH THE KIND PERMISSION OF
THE ESTATE OF ELIZABETH MASON
PHOTOGRAPH: ALAN DOVE

ASTERS AND ARABIS
1917
WATERCOLOUR
12.0 X 17.0
PRIVATE COLLECTION
REPRODUCED WITH THE KIND PERMISSION OF
THE ESTATE OF ELIZABETH MASON
PHOTOGRAPH: ALAN DOVE

FOR THE PASSER-BY
1917
WATERCOLOUR
18.0 X 12.0
PRIVATE COLLECTION
REPRODUCED WITH THE KIND PERMISSION OF
THE ESTATE OF ELIZABETH MASON
PHOTOGRAPH: ALAN DOVE

GENERAL MCARTHUR
1917
WATERCOLOUR
18.0 X 12.0
PRIVATE COLLECTION
REPRODUCED WITH THE KIND PERMISSION OF
THE ESTATE OF ELIZABETH MASON
PHOTOGRAPH: ALAN DOVE

JOHN HOLMWOOD
1910–1987

JOHN HOLMWOOD was born in Wellington and his first art lessons were with Linley Richardson at his Saturday morning classes. At the age of 14 Holmwood was apprenticed to the Railways Advertising Studios; he also attended evening classes at Wellington Technical College. During the Depression he was transferred to Christchurch and Dunedin and in 1934 he took a year's leave of absence to design posters for an advertising agency in Hong Kong. After his return to the Wellington office he also began to teach drawing part time at the Technical College. At the outbreak of the Second World War he joined the army, serving in a camouflage unit in the Pacific. On leave he married designer Nola Findlay, whose commercial design studio he joined at the conclusion of the war, when he also began to paint regularly for the first time. The Holmwoods closed their business in 1969 to travel and on their return John Holmwood was elected president of the Auckland Society of Arts. After Nola's death in 1972 he moved to England, where he remarried. He ceased painting in 1976 because of poor eyesight. A major retrospective exhibition at the Auckland Society of Arts was held in 1984.

THE GARDENER
1956
OIL ON CANVAS
122.0 X 76.2
SIGNED AND DATED
COLLECTION OF RICHARD AND MARGARET
HOLMWOOD
REPRODUCED WITH THE KIND PERMISSION OF
THE HOLMWOOD FAMILY
PHOTOGRAPH: ROGER HYND

JOHN BARR CLARK HOYTE

1835–1913

JOHN HOYTE is thought to have been born in London. From a middle-class background, he is likely to have studied drawing and perhaps watercolour painting as a teenager. Before emigrating to New Zealand in 1861 Hoyte worked in the sugar industry in the West Indies. By 1862 he was teaching English and art at the Church of England Grammar School, Auckland, appointed to the position by the Reverend John Kinder. He also taught art privately. Hoyte resigned in 1864 but returned as drawing master after a four-year break. He taught at Auckland Grammar School from 1869 to 1876. His move to Dunedin that year is considered to be the result of disaffection with the Society of Artists, which he had helped establish in 1869 and of which he had been secretary for a time. In 1879 Hoyte and his family moved to Sydney; except for a spell in Melbourne from 1888 to 1892 he remained in Sydney until his death. Hoyte was associated with the establishment of the Art Society of New South Wales and was its president in 1880. He won a silver medal at the Melbourne Society of Arts in 1875.

AUCKLAND HARBOUR AND RANGITOTO
ISLAND FROM THE GARDEN OF HARRY
COBLEY'S HOUSE
CA 1870
WATERCOLOUR AND CHINESE WHITE
33.3 X 53.1
SIGNED
ALEXANDER TURNBULL LIBRARY
GIFT OF MISS J PACEY, 1964

HARRY COBLEY'S HOUSE, DEVONPORT,
AUCKLAND
CA 1870
WATERCOLOUR AND CHINESE WHITE
33.3 X 53.1
SIGNED
ALEXANDER TURNBULL LIBRARY
GIFT OF MISS J PACEY, 1964

CHARLES IGGLESDEN

1832–1920

CHARLES IGGLESDEN was born in Bombay, India and came to New Zealand via Australia in 1855, settling in Wanganui. He moved to Wellington on receiving his commission as a lieutenant in the Wellington Militia in 1868. In 1870 he moved to Nelson, where he was a surveyor. On his retirement in 1903 he returned to Wellington. Besides being a highly competent artist, Igglesden was also an architect and photographer.

VIEW LOOKING FROM CAPTAIN
SHARP'S GARDEN, WELLINGTON
1868
WATERCOLOUR
38.4 X 51.9
ALEXANDER TURNBULL LIBRARY

CAPTAIN SHARP'S RESIDENCE
1868
WATERCOLOUR
37.0 X 50.0
FLETCHER TRUST COLLECTION
PHOTOGRAPH: CHRIS COAD PHOTOGRAPHY

MINNIE IZETT

1862–1924

MINNIE IZETT was born Mary O'Neill in Dunedin. In 1881 she moved with her parents to Wanganui, where she spent most of her life. She and her first husband, bookseller and stationer Leonard Jones, were married in 1884 and had a daughter in 1886. Jones died the following year. Wanganui's Sarjeant Gallery holds her watercolours of Hampton Court, Florence, Naples and Monte Carlo, and it is speculated that she travelled to London to study with Sir James Linton, and then on to the Continent. On her return she became an art teacher, exhibiting her students' work in her studio and in 1901 her own work, in the inaugural exhibition of the Wanganui Arts and Crafts Society. In 1903 she married journalist Andrew Pattle Izett. By 1907 she was honorary secretary of the Wanganui Arts and Crafts Society and her husband was a committee member. Izett and Ivy Copeland taught artist Edith Collier at the Wanganui Technical School.

A New Zealand garden
CA 1905
Watercolour on paper over board
75.0 X 55.5
Signed
Gift of the artist, 1924
Collection of Sarjeant Gallery
Te Whare O Rehua Whanganui

Flower piece
1933
Oil on canvas
45.5 X 44.1
Signed
Hocken Collections, Uare Taoka o
Hakena, University of Otago
Gift of Mr RE Kennedy, Dunedin, 1988
Reproduced with the kind permission of
the Robert Kennedy estate

Richard Seymour Kelly

1820–1873

RICHARD KELLY was born in Ireland and emigrated to Australia where he was a draughtsman in the Victorian Public Works Department. He moved to Dunedin in 1861, accompanied by his Cornish wife Elizabeth (née Nancarrow), following the discovery of gold in Otago. In December 1863 he was in Christchurch, where he sketched the opening of the first section of the Lyttelton to Christchurch railway, and by 1866 he was working as a draughtsman in the government survey office in Palmerston, Otago. He died in Christchurch.

Dunedin 1862 from the zig-zag of
Graham Street, between High and
Maclaggan streets
1862
Watercolour and gum arabic
40.0 X 58.7
Signed
Hocken Collections, Uare Taoka o
Hakena, University of Otago

Rodney Kennedy

1909–1989

RODNEY KENNEDY was born in Dunedin. After attending Otago Boys' High School he enrolled at the Dunedin School of Art, full time between 1928 and 1929, then part time in 1930. Kennedy became a close friend of Toss Woollaston, whom he would visit in Nelson each summer. In 1936 Kennedy arranged Woollaston's first solo exhibition. Kennedy worked as an illustrator at the University of Otago Medical School and became increasingly interested in theatre; he designed his first production in 1938. A pacifist, Kennedy refused military service and was imprisoned and then detained as an agricultural worker for the duration of the Second World War, returning to Dunedin in 1945. In 1948, he became a drama tutor at the University of Otago. That year, with his friend Charles Brasch, he organised an important Colin McCahon exhibition at the Dunedin Public Library. In 1955 he was a delegate to an international theatre conference and toured Europe. He continued to teach at Otago until 1971 and was later the director of the Globe Theatre in Dunedin.

John Kinder

1819–1903

JOHN KINDER was born in London and as a teenager took lessons from Edwin Aaron Penley, an established watercolour painter who wrote several books on watercolour technique. After attending Cambridge University from 1838 to 1845, he trained for the Anglican ministry and was ordained in 1848. Accepting an invitation from Bishop George Selwyn, Kinder travelled to New Zealand in 1855 to become the headmaster of the new Church of England Grammar School in Auckland. As well as teaching he was the first vicar of St Mark's, Remuera, and then of St Andrew's, Epsom. Kinder married Celia Brown in 1859. They did not have children of their own but adopted the orphaned children of Kinder's brother. In 1869 he was appointed master of St John's College at Meadowbank, Auckland, resigning in 1880. Kinder, who was awarded a Doctorate of Divinity by the Archbishop of Canterbury in 1873, was an indefatigable traveller around New Zealand, sketching, painting and, from 1859, taking photographs. He was a founding member of the Auckland Society of Artists in 1869 and exhibited at its first exhibition two years later. Kinder died at his Remuera home, Woodcroft.

Auckland, from the veranda of
Mr Reader Wood's cottage
1856
Watercolour
29.0 X 24.7
Auckland Art Gallery Toi o Tamaki
Gift of Harry Kinder, 1937

Pikiarero (Clematis paniculata)
CA 1865
Albumen on paper
13.6 X 8.8
Auckland Art Gallery Toi o Tamaki
Purchased 1983

SAINT JOHN'S COLLEGE
1878
WATERCOLOUR AND GOUACHE OVER PENCIL
26.0 X 35.8
AUCKLAND ART GALLERY TOI O TAMAKI
PURCHASED 1989

VIEW FROM WOODCROFT, REMUERA,
AUGUST 16, 1888
1888
WATERCOLOUR
25.4 X 35.5
PRIVATE COLLECTION

MARTHA KING
1802/3–1897

Little is known about MARTHA KING before she emigrated from Ireland in her late thirties with her sister, Maria, and brother, Samuel. They came from Cork, where their father was a Protestant minister; their mother's maiden name was Popham, a distinguished County Cork family. The Cork Mechanics Institute gave classes for architects and craftsmen and the Society of Arts, later absorbed by the Royal Cork Institution, had a school from around 1818, so there were opportunities for a young woman to study drawing at least. The Kings arrived on the *London* in December 1840 to take up land they had purchased in Wanganui from the New Zealand Company, establishing their home in two raupo whare in February 1842. The two women opened a school and Samuel was soon appointed to the first in a succession of government positions. Following a dispute between Samuel King and the captain of the Wanganui peacekeeping force, they moved to New Plymouth in 1847. Martha King died there in 1897, aged 94. She left her estate to the Recreation Grounds Board, which used the realised funds to reduce the mortgage on land purchased for what would eventually be Pukekura Park.

RIIABDOTIIAMNUS solandri OR NEW
ZEALAND GLOXINIA
1842
WATERCOLOUR
37.5 X 27.6
ALEXANDER TURNBULL LIBRARY

MARY KING
1829–1907?

MARY KING was the daughter of Thomas McDonnell (1788–1864) and was brought to the Hokianga by her family on the *Sir George Murray* in 1831. She married Captain William Magrath King (1825–1859) of the Royal Artillery, commander of the British army in Auckland, and the couple lived in Jermyn Street, Auckland (near what is now Anzac Avenue). Captain King died serving in Malta in 1859 and in 1876 she married Stephen William Elmes. Her date of death is uncertain but she was still alive in London in at least 1907.

HOUSE OF CAPTAIN KING, R.A.,
JERMYN STREET, AUCKLAND
1858
WATERCOLOUR
14.7 X 24.2
ALEXANDER TURNBULL LIBRARY

GWEN KNIGHT
1888–1974

GWEN KNIGHT was born in Wellington, but when she was four her family moved to Hunters Hill, Sydney. Knight, who had shown musical promise at school, studied at the Sydney Conservatorium of Music. After her father's death she returned to New Zealand to study physiotherapy in Dunedin and then moved back to Wellington. She spent a little time in Masterton before leaving for Europe around 1929, the year she first exhibited at the New Zealand Academy of Fine Arts (she was elected an artist member in 1938). She studied at Heatherley's in London, Hans Hofmann's school in Munich, and at the Academy Ranson with Roger Bissière and the Académie Lhote in Paris. In the mid-1930s, while travelling with fellow New Zealand painter Maud Burge, she met Frances Hodgkins in St Tropez and again in Ibiza, where Knight lived for six years. When in London she showed at the Leicester and Redfern galleries, the latter run by New Zealander Rex Nan Kivell. Knight returned to New Zealand in 1948, first settling in Mahina Bay and then Eastbourne, Wellington. She became a member of the lively scene around the Helen Hitchings Gallery and continued to exhibit in Wellington, Masterton, Napier, Levin and Palmerston North until the early 1970s.

SUZIE'S GARDEN
CA 1969
OIL ON CARDBOARD
50.0 X 69.0
COLLECTION OF THE NEW DOWSE
GIFT OF MURIEL MOODY
REPRODUCED WITH THE KIND PERMISSION OF
CARMEN LEES
PHOTOGRAPH: MARK MARRIOTT

ERIC LEE-JOHNSON
1908–1993

ERIC LEE-JOHNSON was born in Suva, Fij, and arrived in New Zealand with his family in 1912. He attended the Elam School of Fine Arts at Auckland University from 1924 to 1927 and then embarked on a career as an award-winning designer and commercial artist, first with Wilson & Horton, then with the SH Benson advertising agency in London, where he exhibited photographs and showed with the South London Group. On his return to Wellington he worked as copywriter for advertising agency Ilott's. In 1942, after two and a half years in a tuberculosis sanatorium, he moved to Auckland, then Piha and Mahurangi. By 1948 he was living at Pakanae, near Omapere in the Hokianga. In 1945 Lee-Johnson had a joint exhibition with Rex Fairburn at the Auckland Society of Arts and in 1948 to 1949 he had his first solo exhibitions in Dunedin, Wellington and Tauranga. In 1956, the year his photographs of the famous Opononi dolphin were published worldwide, Lee-Johnson was the subject of a National Film Unit documentary by Maurice Shadbolt and an illustrated biography by Eric McCormick. In 1960 Lee-Johnson married his third wife, Elizabeth MacDonald, and they moved to Waihi, then Howick, Auckland, in 1985. In 1981 the Waikato Art Museum presented and toured a large retrospective exhibition, and in 1993 the Auckland City Art Gallery presented a retrospective exhibition of his photographs. Lee-Johnson's *No Road to Follow: Autobiography of a New Zealand Artist* was published posthumously in 1994.

POMPALLIER HOUSE, RUSSELL
1955
WATERCOLOUR AND PASTEL
38.8 X 52.6
SIGNED AND DATED
NEW ZEALAND HISTORIC PLACES TRUST, POMPALLIER
REPRODUCED WITH THE KIND PERMISSION OF THE ERIC LEE-JOHNSON ESTATE
PHOTOGRAPH: STEPHEN WESTERN

COLIN LOVELL-SMITH
1894–1960

COLIN LOVELL-SMITH won a scholarship to the Canterbury College School of Art, where he studied in 1908–09 before working for his father's printing firm, Smith and Anthony, continuing his art studies part-time. Suffragist Kate Sheppard married his father, William, when she was 78. Lovell-Smith saw service in the First World War with the New Zealand Expeditionary Force at Gallipoli as a draughtsman with the Royal Engineers on the Balkan front, and in France with the New Zealand Engineers. In 1919 he resumed his career and re-enrolled at the School of Art. In 1922 he married Rata Bird, a fellow student. In 1927 he was appointed to the staff of what was now a special school of the Canterbury University College. From 1945 to 1946 he was the school's acting director, then served as director from 1947 until his retirement in 1960. He was an exhibiting member of the Canterbury Society of Arts and served on its council from 1936 to 1955 and as president from 1953 to 1955. In 1951 he was elected a Fellow of the Royal Society of Arts. He was included in the 1940 National Centennial Exhibition of New Zealand Art. In 1985 the Rotorua Art Gallery organised a joint exhibition of Colin and Rata Lovell-Smith's paintings.

CANTERBURY GARDEN
CA 1934
OIL ON BOARD
44.2 X 57.0
G J MOYLE COLLECTION
REPRODUCED WITH THE KIND PERMISSION OF NAN LOVELL-SMITH

RATA LOVELL-SMITH
1894–1969

After leaving Christchurch Girls' High School, RATA LOVELL-SMITH (née Bird) attended Christchurch Training College and took drawing classes at the Canterbury College School of Art before taking up primary school teaching. She returned to art school part time from 1917 to 1923, studying under Leonard Booth and Richard Wallwork. There she met Colin Lovell-Smith, whom she married in 1922. Rata Lovell-Smith then taught at the School of Art until 1945. She was included in the 1940 National Centennial Exhibition of New Zealand Art. Lovell-Smith exhibited at the Canterbury Society of Arts from 1924 until shortly before her death, served as the society's president in the mid-1950s, and was also a regular exhibitor with The Group. In 1961 a retrospective exhibition of her work was presented at the Durham Street Gallery, Christchurch. She continued to paint still lifes and landscapes, including some of Queensland made on her visits there in 1961 and 1963. In 1985 the Rotorua Art Gallery organised a joint exhibition of Rata and Colin Lovell-Smith's paintings.

SOUTH WINDOW
CA 1948–9
OIL ON CANVAS
47.2 X 39.5
SIGNED
CHRISTCHURCH ART GALLERY
TE PUNA O WAIWHETU
PURCHASED 1949
REPRODUCED WITH THE KIND PERMISSION OF NAN LOVELL-SMITH

DORIS LUSK

1916–1990

DORIS LUSK was born in Dunedin, where she attended Otago Girls' High School. In 1934 she enrolled at King Edward Technical College, holding her her first exhibition in 1936 with fellow artist Dick Seelye. She completed art school in 1939 and the following year had her first solo exhibition in her Moray Place studio. Lusk worked as a ticket writer and taught art at two private schools. In 1942 she married engineer Dermot Holland and moved to Christchurch, where she exhibited with The Group for the first time in 1943 and then regularly through to the 1950s. She was a member of the close-knit artistic and literary community around the Caxton Press and the magazine *Landfall*. In 1966 Lusk had a retrospective exhibition at the Dunedin Public Art Gallery and began teaching drawing at the University of Canterbury School of Fine Arts until her retirement in 1981. In 1996 the Robert McDougall Art Gallery presented a major exhibition: *Landmarks: The Landscape Paintings of Doris Lusk*. Lusk was also a potter, taught at Risingholme Community Centre, and was president of the Canterbury Potters' Association from 1970 to 1972. She was president of the Canterbury Society of Arts in 1982.

MIXED FLOWERS

1940

OIL ON BOARD

47.3 X 42.0

SIGNED AND DATED

HOCKEN COLLECTIONS, UARE TAOKA O HAKENA, UNIVERSITY OF OTAGO

GIFT OF CHARLTON EDGAR FOR THE MONA EDGAR COLLECTION, 1963

REPRODUCED WITH THE KIND PERMISSION OF THE DORIS LUSK ESTATE

STEWART MACLENNAN

1903–1973

STEWART MACLENNAN studied at the King Edward Technical College in his home city of Dunedin under William Allen and Robert Field. He first worked as a commercial artist before beginning studies at the Royal College of Art, London, where he became an associate in 1938 and met and married Dorothy Kenwright. He continued his studies in 1939 on a scholarship and was elected to the National Register of Designers. On his return to New Zealand he taught art at Wairarapa College. In 1946 he was appointed education officer at the National Art Gallery and then, in 1948, the gallery's first director — becoming the first professional art museum director in the country. He retired in 1968 and was made an OBE in 1969. Maclennan's teachers at the Royal College included Paul and John Nash, Eric Ravilious, Edward Bawden and Edward McKnight Kauffer, and Maclennan's fine draughtsmanship,

facility with watercolour and graphic technique across a variety of print mediums reflect their influence. Maclennan is best known for his delightful and vivid prints, especially wood engravings, of birds, flowers and other subjects from nature.

WELLINGTON SUBURBAN GARDEN

CA 1960

WATERCOLOUR

55.4 X 68.3

MUSEUM OF NEW ZEALAND TE PAPA TONGAREWA

GIFT OF THE NATIONAL BANK OF NEW ZEALAND, 1962

REPRODUCED WITH THE KIND PERMISSION OF THE STEWART BELL MACLENNAN ESTATE

ALBIN MARTIN

1813–1888

ALBIN MARTIN was born in 1813 at Stour Provost, Dorset, the son of the parish minister. From Salisbury Grammar School he went to Cambridge University, but he left in 1832 when his father died, and became a pupil of the distinguished painter John Linnell. He married Jemima Kempe in 1841, and the couple travelled overland to Naples, where Martin painted for over a year. By the time the Martins emigrated to New Zealand in 1851 they had six children. Martin bought farmland near the Tamaki River on which he built their home, Stour House. They farmed there until 1882, when they moved to Arthur Street, Ellerslie, probably because of his deteriorating health. He died suddenly in 1888 and was buried in Panmure. In 1871 Martin was one of the founding members of the Society of Artists, Auckland, exhibiting in four of the five society exhibitions and with the Auckland Society of Arts from 1881. Martin represented Franklin on the Auckland Provincial Council, was a regular contributor on art to the *New Zealand Herald* and was one the trustees who supervised James Mackelvie's great art bequest to Auckland. Martin was a fine and productive painter, a *petit maître*, in the European manner. His New Zealand oeuvre comprises oil paintings, mostly quite small, and watercolours of Auckland and its environs, especially East Tamaki.

GARDEN AT EAST TAMAKI

CA 1865

OIL ON PAPER

21.9 X 32.0

MACKELVIE TRUST COLLECTION, AUCKLAND ART GALLERY TOI O TAMAKI

LEIGH MARTIN

1964–

LEIGH MARTIN was born in Hamilton and as a teenager moved to Christchurch, where he studied design in 1980 and 1981 at Christchurch Polytechnic. Martin went to London in 1985 and after gaining UK residency in 1988 took the foundation certificate in art and design at Brighton Polytechnic. In 1990 he enrolled at the Glasgow School of Art, where he received several prizes and scholarships. On completing his Bachelor of Fine Arts degree in 1993 he received the prestigious Christie's Prize and stayed on to complete his post-graduate diploma in painting in 1995. Martin participated in the DAAD (German Academic Exchange Service) group study tour of Berlin and Dresden in 1994. Martin returned to New Zealand and was senior tutor in painting at the Elam School of Fine Arts from 1995 until 2006. He won the Ida Eise Award at Auckland Society of Arts in 1996. He also lectured at Auckland University of Technology from 1998 to 2001. Martin was included in the 2000 *Art and Industry Biennial* at the Physics Room, Christchurch, and the 2001 *Prospect Biennial*, *Close Ups of the Horizon*, City Gallery, Wellington. From 2006 to 2007 he was a lecturer in the Design School at Unitec, Auckland. Martin's first group exhibition was *New Art in Scotland* at Glasgow's Centre of Contemporary Art. His first solo exhibitions were in 1998: *Immersion* was shown at the Jonathan Smart Gallery, Christchurch, and *Dissolve*, his Christchurch high street project, was shown at Gow Langsford Gallery, Auckland, where he showed before moving to the Jensen Gallery in 2004.

NOISE (YELLOW)
2004
OIL ON LINEN
137.0 X 137.0
COLLECTION OF THE ARTIST
REPRODUCED WITH THE KIND PERMISSION OF THE ARTIST

KARL MAUGHAN

1964–

KARL MAUGHAN was born in Wellington and grew up in the Manawatu, first living on a farm near Colyton, then in Palmerston North and finally, in 1977, in Ashhurst. From Freyberg High School Maughan went to the Elam School of Fine Arts in 1983, graduating in 1986. In 1987 he decided not to complete his master's degree and had his first solo exhibition at the Brooker Gallery, Wellington, followed by his first Auckland show in 1988 at Gow Langsford Gallery, where he has subsequently exhibited every year or two. Both exhibitions sold out. Maughan moved in 1994 to London, where he married novelist Emily Perkins and where their three children were born. Maughan had several studios around the East End and his London successes included being a finalist in the 1997 John Moores biennial painting prize at the

Walker Art Gallery, Liverpool, purchases by the Saatchi Collection and the Arts Council of England and, in 1999, the production of a six-panel work for display at a Habitat store, *A clear day*, which was later purchased by the Museum of New Zealand Te Papa Tongarewa. Maughan, who returned to New Zealand in 2005, now lives and paints in Grey Lynn, Auckland, and exhibits at Gow Langsford Gallery, Auckland; Tinakori (now Paige Blackie Gallery), Wellington; and Martin Browne Fine Art, Sydney. In 2007 to 2008 Te Manawa, the regional museum in Palmerston North, presented a mid-career survey of Maughan's paintings: *Karl Maughan: A Clear Day*.

PLUME POPPIES
1987
OIL ON CANVAS
200.0 X 300.0
GLAXO SMITH KLINE NZ LTD
ON LOAN TO TE MANAWA
REPRODUCED WITH THE KIND PERMISSION
OF THE ARTIST
PHOTOGRAPH: DAVID LUPTON

WELLINGTON GARDEN WITH FENCE POST
1991
OIL ON CANVAS
137.0 X 183.0
PRIVATE COLLECTION
REPRODUCED WITH THE KIND PERMISSION
OF THE ARTIST

OHINETAHI
1994
OIL ON CANVAS
122.0 X 183.0
PRIVATE COLLECTION
REPRODUCED WITH THE KIND PERMISSION
OF THE ARTIST

SURRENDER RODNEY
1996
OIL ON CANVAS
152.4 X 213.0
PRIVATE COLLECTION
REPRODUCED WITH THE KIND PERMISSION
OF THE ARTIST

LANDSCAPE WITH LAWN
1998
OIL ON CANVAS
123.0 X 243.0
PRIVATE COLLECTION
REPRODUCED WITH THE KIND PERMISSION
OF THE ARTIST

CROSS HILLS
2004
OIL ON CANVAS
178.0 X 275.0
COLLECTION OF TE MANAWA
MUSEUMS TRUST
REPRODUCED WITH THE KIND PERMISSION
OF THE ARTIST

COLIN McCAHON

1919–1987

COLIN MCCAHON, New Zealand's foremost twentieth-century century painter, grew up in Dunedin and attended Russell Clark's Saturday morning art classes. In 1937 he enrolled at the Dunedin School of Art, where he studied for two years. In 1939 McCahon became a member of the Otago Art Society and in 1940 he was a guest exhibitor with The Group in Christchurch, later becoming a member and exhibiting there until 1977. In 1942 McCahon married fellow artist Anne Hamblett and they lived in Christchurch from 1948 to 1953. McCahon's first important exhibition was held at the Wellington Public Library and later at the Lower Hutt Library in 1948. Later that year another exhibition was held at the Dunedin Library. It was followed in 1949 by a joint exhibition with his friend Toss Woollaston at the Helen Hitchings Gallery, Wellington, and in Auckland. In 1953 the McCahon family moved to Auckland on the promise of a job at the Auckland City Art Gallery, where he became curator and eventually keeper in 1956. In 1958 he went on a study tour of the USA and in 1960 the family moved from Titirangi to Grey Lynn. From 1964 to 1971 McCahon taught painting at the Elam School of Fine Arts and then became a full-time painter except for some part-time teaching and summer schools. McCahon began to exhibit at the Barry Lett Galleries, Auckland, in 1965 and with the Peter McLeavey Gallery, Wellington, from 1969. A sequence of exhibitions in public art museums — a retrospective at the Auckland Art Gallery in 1972, an exhibition of his religious paintings at the Manawatu Art Gallery in 1975 and the *Necessary protection* series at the Govett-Brewster Art Gallery in 1977 — started to bring McCahon to a wider public attention. In 1984 *Colin McCahon: I Will Need Words* was shown at the Sydney Biennale and at the Edinburgh Festival and Gordon Brown's major study *Colin McCahon: Artist* was published. At the time of McCahon's death the Auckland City Art Gallery was in the process of organising a major

survey exhibition that, in 1988, became *Colin McCahon: Gates and Journeys*, later shown in a reduced form in Christchurch, Wellington and Dunedin.

HOUSE IN TREES, TITIRANGI
1953
OIL ON CARDBOARD
53.3 X 60.8
SIGNED AND DATED
AUCKLAND ART GALLERY TOI O TAMAKI
GIFT OF UNA PLATTS, 2003
REPRODUCED WITH THE KIND PERMISSION
OF THE COLIN McCAHON RESEARCH AND
PUBLICATION TRUST

TREVOR MOFFITT

1936–2006

TREVOR MOFFITT was born in Gore and attended Southland Technical College, Invercargill, before moving to Christchurch in 1955 to study at the University of Canterbury School of Fine Arts, where he won the Rosa Sawtell life painting prize. After graduation in 1957 he trained as a teacher in Auckland, followed by an honours year back at the School of Fine Arts. In 1960 he returned to Southland Technical College to teach and had his first solo exhibition at the then Invercargill Public Art Gallery. In 1961 he married Alison Hamilton and became a member of and began exhibiting with The Group. In 1962 he took up a position at Timaru Girls' High School, where he taught until moving to Burnside High School, Christchurch, in 1966, later becoming head of art and senior dean. From 1969 to 1975 Moffitt was the art critic for *The Press*. In 1987 he retired from teaching to paint full time, travelling to Europe in 1989 to deliver a commission in The Netherlands. Moffitt exhibited regularly in all the main centres throughout his career. In 1986 a survey of paintings 1960–1985 was presented at the Eastern Southland Gallery, Gore. Moffitt's biography by Chris Ronayne was published in 2006.

PRUNING ROSES
1980
OIL ON BOARD
61.0 X 61.0
CHRISTCHURCH ART GALLERY TE PUNA
O WAIWHETU
PRESENTED BY MR J SUMMERS WITH
ASSISTANCE FROM 'EVERYMAN FUND', 1982
REPRODUCED WITH THE KIND PERMISSION OF
TORUN MOFFITT

JAMES NAIRN
1859–1904

JAMES NAIRN was born in Lenzie, a few miles north-east of Glasgow, Scotland. As an apprentice architectural draughtsman he studied part time at the Glasgow School of Art from 1879 to 1883. He was a member of the Glasgow Art Club and exhibited at the Glasgow Institute of Fine Arts and the Royal Scottish Academy, Edinburgh. Nairn was one of the Glasgow Boys, an informal group of progressive painters in Glasgow who were influenced by European painting, and he also exhibited with the recently formed New English Art Club in London in 1889. Ill health prompted a visit to New Zealand in 1890 and after a solo exhibition in Wellington he was invited to establish a life drawing class at the Wellington Technical College. He became a full-time staff member and remained at the college until his untimely death from peritonitis. Although a member of the New Zealand Academy of Fine Arts and on its council (1890–1903), he established the more progressive Wellington Art Club in 1892, which promoted *plein air* painting and used Pumpkin Cottage at Silverstream, near the Hutt River, as a base.

AUTUMN BLOOMS
1899
OIL ON CANVAS
61.3 X 76.1 X 21.0
SIGNED AND DATED
MUSEUM OF NEW ZEALAND TE PAPA TONGAREWA
GIFT OF MISS SARA LEETHAM, 1939

MOUNT VICTORIA, WELLINGTON
1900
WATERCOLOUR
37.5 X 26.4
SIGNED AND DATED
HOCKEN COLLECTIONS, UARE TAOKA O HAKENA, UNIVERSITY OF OTAGO
GIFT OF MISS M B SCOTT, 1962

GARDEN SCENE — WOMAN BENEATH TREES
CA 1900
OIL ON CANVAS
28.5 X 23.5
COLLECTION OF TE MANAWA MUSEUMS TRUST

JOHN OAKLEY
1901–1977

After graduating from the Canterbury College School of Art, JOHN OAKLEY visited Europe in 1935, returning at the outbreak of war to teach art at Marlborough College and Napier Boys' High School. From 1946 to 1966 he was a highly regarded lecturer at the Canterbury College School of Art. Though crippled by childhood polio, he was a remarkably active man: a painter, a gardener and garden designer, the author of *Paintings of Canterbury 1840–1890* (1969) and art reviewer for *The Press*, a councillor and president of the Canterbury Society of Arts and a heritage activist.

GARDEN
1976
OIL ON BOARD
76.0 X 102.2
SIGNED AND DATED
CHRISTCHURCH ART GALLERY TE PUNA O WAIWHETU
PURCHASED 1976
REPRODUCED WITH THE KIND PERMISSION OF SARAH TURBOTT, KERRY OAKLEY, PHILIP OAKLEY AND CHRIS OAKLEY

FANNY OSBORNE
1852–1934

FANNY OSBORNE was born in Auckland, the first of 13 children of Scotsman Neill Malcolm and his London-born wife Emily, who had arrived in New Zealand in 1851. In 1859 the family moved to Rosalie Bay on Great Barrier Island, northeast of Auckland, where Malcolm became a partner in a cattle-farming business. In 1873 Fanny eloped with Alfred Osborne, a well-educated Englishman. The couple returned to Great Barrier and settled in Tryphena, where Osborne took over a land grant from his father. The Osbornes followed in the Malcolms' footsteps by having 13 children of their own. Osborne appears not to have begun painting until after the turn of the century. It is possible that two paintings of New Zealand native flowers published in colour supplements to *Brett's Christmas Annual* in 1911 and 1922 were by Osborne. Alfred Osborne died in 1920 and, suffering from arthritis, Fanny Osborne spent the last four years of her life in the care of two of her daughters in Auckland.

HOUHERE, LACEBARK
(HOHERIA POPULNEA)
CA 1916
WATERCOLOUR
28.0 X 19.0
AUCKLAND WAR MEMORIAL MUSEUM TAMAKI
PAENGA HIRA
GIFT OF MRS AW MOODIE, 1956

ALAN PEARSON

1929–

ALAN PEARSON was born in Liverpool, England. He left school to work on the railways and did his national service in the RAF. In 1951 he emigrated to Australia, where he drove bulldozers on the Snowy River hydroelectric scheme before moving to New Zealand in 1954, initially to work as a seaman. He enrolled at the Wellington Technical College to study art, continuing at the University of Canterbury School of Fine Arts and then at the Royal College of Art, London. Pearson returned to New Zealand in 1966, settling first in Auckland, where he had his first solo exhibition in 1969, and then Christchurch. Since that time Pearson has exhibited annually in New Zealand. Widely travelled, he divides his time between Queensland, where he built a house and studio in 2001, and Auckland. In 1999 the Robert McDougall Art Gallery, Christchurch, presented a major retrospective exhibition curated by Neil Roberts: *Heaven and Blood: Painting and Drawing by Alan Pearson 1959–1999.*

LYTTELTON GARDEN
1974
OIL ON BOARD
62.0 X 62.0
SIGNED AND DATED
PRIVATE COLLECTION
REPRODUCED WITH THE KIND PERMISSION OF
THE ARTIST
PHOTOGRAPH: KALLAN MACLEOD

ROBERT PROCTER

1879–1931

ROBERT PROCTER spent his childhood in Dalkeith, Edinburgh, Scotland and came with his family to New Zealand in March 1887. He studied at the Canterbury College School of Art from 1892 to 1899. From 1894 he also took private lessons with Petrus van der Velden. He was a member of and exhibited with the Canterbury Society of Arts until 1903, by which time he had left for Europe, probably via Melbourne. There are indications of his being at the Royal Academy of Fine Arts in Antwerp and in 1905 he was on the roll at the Académie Julian in Paris.

Signed paintings suggest that he was in Rome and Venice in 1904 and 1905. He had returned to New Zealand by 1906, when he was on the CSA council and had work in that year's New Zealand International Exhibition in Christchurch. In 1914 Procter was in Southern Italy sketching, then England and Scotland, possibly for family reasons, but he was back in New Zealand in 1915, first in Christchurch, then teaching at the Elam School of Fine Arts in Auckland. He married the following year and continued to teach at Elam until 1921. In 1928 Procter moved to Melbourne, where he was appointed to a teaching position at the Working Men's College (later the Melbourne Institute of Technology) and was a member of the Victorian Arts Society. In 1931 he collapsed while teaching and died in hospital. In 1932 a retrospective exhibition was held at the Seddon Galleries in order to assist his widow Elizabeth and their children.

THE VERANDAH
CA 1921–6
OIL ON CANVAS
64.5 X 49.1
SIGNED
ROTORUA MUSEUM OF ART AND HISTORY
TE WHARE TAONGA O TE ARAWA

JAMES ROSS

1948–

Artist, art writer, editor and curator JAMES ROSS was born in Gillingham, Kent, England and came to New Zealand in 1959. He studied at the Elam School of Fine Arts from 1966 to 1969. Ross had his first solo exhibitions at the Barry Lett Galleries, Auckland in 1974 and Elva Bett Gallery, Wellington in 1975. He was the art critic for the *Sunday Herald* in 1974–75. In 1979 a QEII Arts Council award allowed him to travel to the United States and Europe. In 1980 Ross won the Nola Holmwood Memorial Portrait Prize at the Auckland Society of Arts. He worked in New York for six months in 1982–83, followed by a residency at Victoria College, Prahran, Melbourne in 1984, following which he had a solo exhibition at Realities Gallery, Melbourne in 1985. In 1988 Ross was included in the Auckland City Art Gallery's exhibition *NZXI*, which toured to the Art Gallery of New South Wales and the Museum of Contemporary Art, Brisbane. Ross played a major role in the organisation of *Distance Looks Our Way*, an exhibition of New Zealand art in Seville, Spain, in 1993 which also travelled to The Netherlands and toured New Zealand. Recent solo exhibitions include Bath Street Gallery, Auckland, in 2003 and solo and group exhibitions at Robert Steele Gallery, New York. In 2007–08 Ross was one of six artists featured in *From the Edge*: *Contemporary Art from New Zealand* in Valencia, Spain, also shown in Hong Kong. In 2007 *James Ross: The Red Studio — Small Paintings and Sculpture 1982–2006* was shown at the Gus Fisher Gallery, University of Auckland. Ross was the editor of the three-volume catalogue of The Gibbs Collection, privately published in 1995.

THE PATH D
1974
OIL ON PANEL
44.5 X 44.5
COLLECTION OF THE ARTIST
REPRODUCED WITH THE KIND PERMISSION OF
THE ARTIST

CEDRIC SAVAGE

1901–1969

CEDRIC SAVAGE was born in Christchurch and attended the Canterbury College School of Art from 1916 to 1918, studying sculpture, painting and modelling. His first job, in the early 1920s, was working as a modeller on the new Parliament Buildings in Wellington; he then moved to Sydney and worked as a modeller on the State Theatre, among other buildings. Savage took up painting and moved to Fiji from 1930 to 1933, where he taught at a local school before returning to Sydney, and further developing his reputation for architectural modelling, carving and design. After war service with the New Zealand forces, in 1945 he settled in Takaka, and devoted himself to painting full time. He exhibited at the New Zealand Academy of Fine Arts, Wellington, from 1931 to 1969 (he was on its council in the 1940s) and the Canterbury Society of Arts. In 1949 he became a member of the Group of Nine, which included Evelyn Page and TA McCormack. In 1955 Savage moved to Europe, living mostly in southern Spain, Italy, Greece and the Aegean Islands, making the occasional return visit to New Zealand. In the late 1950s he exhibited in the Paris Salon, the Royal Academy and other exhibiting societies and in 1956 the New Zealand government presented the Queen Mother with one of his New Zealand landscapes. In 1961 he was awarded first prize in the Kelliher Art Award for *Summer, Hawke's Bay*. He died in Greece.

VIEW THROUGH TO SAVAGE'S GARDEN
CA 1953
OIL ON CANVAS
74.5 X 70.0
SIGNED
PRIVATE COLLECTION
REPRODUCED WITH THE KIND PERMISSION OF
BRAD SAVAGE

ALFRED SHARPE

1836–1908

ALFRED SHARPE was born in Liverpool, England, where his father was a merchant and art collector. Sharpe attended art school in Birkenhead and accompanied his father to exhibitions and private collections. In 1859 he emigrated to New Zealand and settled on Crown-granted land near Whangarei. In 1866 he moved to Auckland and from 1871 began exhibiting with the newly founded Auckland Society of Artists, as well as sending paintings to Wellington, Sydney and Melbourne. He worked as an architectural draughtsman and part-time teacher and exhibited in a Queen Street stationer's, organising art unions with his paintings as prizes. By 1880 Sharpe was profoundly deaf, but this in no way diminished his productivity. From 1884 to 1887 he exhibited with the New Zealand Art Students Association, of which he was a leading member. He was a prolific writer, his articles appearing in the *New Zealand Herald* and *Auckland Weekly News*. In 1887 Sharpe moved to Newcastle, New South Wales, where his younger brother lived. He worked as an architect, designing the city's major parks, and continued to paint landscapes of Newcastle and its environs.

THE GARDEN FRONT OF SIR GEORGE
GREY'S MANSION AT KAWAU
1884
WATERCOLOUR
38.0 X 62.0
SIGNED AND DATED
FLETCHER TRUST COLLECTION

PETER SIDDELL

1935–

PETER SIDDELL was born in Grey Lynn, Auckland, and after leaving Mount Albert Grammar School took up an electrical apprenticeship. In 1963 he retrained as a teacher. Around 1965 Siddell began to paint watercolours of the places he visited while tramping and climbing and began to read about art. He began to paint more seriously after building himself a studio in 1969. In 1971 and 1972 Siddell won the painting competitions at Auckland's Easter Show. Around that time one of his paintings was brought in for framing, and as a result Siddell was given his first solo exhibition at Moller's Gallery, Auckland, in 1973. Soon afterwards he began to paint full time, exhibiting at Barry Lett Galleries, Auckland. In 1976 the Auckland City Art Gallery purchased *Homecoming*. He has had two survey exhibitions, in 1986 at the Robert McDougall Art Gallery, Christchurch, and in 1988 at the Fisher Gallery, Pakuranga. Since 1994 Siddell has exhibited at Artis Gallery in Parnell, Auckland. In 2002 Artis presented *Peter Siddell: Landscape*, which toured seven public art museums throughout the country.

WESTERN GARDEN
1989
OIL ON CANVAS
66.0 X 101.0
SIGNED AND DATED
PRIVATE COLLECTION
REPRODUCED WITH THE KIND PERMISSION OF
THE ARTIST

WILLIAM MEIN SMITH

1799–1869

WILLIAM MEIN SMITH was born in Cape Town in South Africa but brought up in England, where he rose to the rank of captain in the Royal Artillery. In 1839 he became the first surveyor-general for the New Zealand Company and arrived in Wellington in 1840. He laid out Petone and Thorndon, surveyed country sections and mapped the harbours of the east coast of the South Island. In 1845 he moved to the Wairarapa and, as a successful runholder, contributed to the establishment of New Zealand's wool and beef industries. He represented Wairarapa on the Wellington Provincial Council from 1858 to 1865. Smith was a talented artist, and his 1842 panorama of Wellington was one of the lithographs in *Illustrations to 'Adventure in New Zealand'* published in London in 1845. He was a committee member of the Literary, Scientific and Philanthropic Institute, a member of the Wellington Horticultural Society and a prize-winning gardener.

F A MOLESWORTH, NEWRY, PORT NICHOLSON, NZ

1844
WATERCOLOUR
24.0 X 34.1
ALEXANDER TURNBULL LIBRARY

OLIVIA SPENCER BOWER

1905–1982

Born in St Neots, Cambridgeshire, England, OLIVIA SPENCER BOWER and her twin sister came to New Zealand with their mother, the painter Rosa Spencer Bower (née Dixon) in 1920. She studied at the Canterbury College School of Art, after which she attended the Slade School of Art, where her mother had been a student, and the Grosvenor School of Modern Art in London. After travelling in Europe, in late 1931 she returned to live at her family's farm at Swannanoa, North Canterbury. She was a member of the New Zealand Society of Artists, showed with the Canterbury Society of Arts (of which she was the first woman president) and from 1936 exhibited with The Group. In 1943 Spencer Bower moved to Auckland to study at Elam but returned to Canterbury to care for her elderly mother. In 1960 she visited the Pacific Islands and from 1963 to 1966 toured Europe. The Robert McDougall Art Gallery presented a retrospective exhibition of Spencer Bower's paintings in 1977. Spencer Bower established a foundation principally to support the development of emerging artists.

THE UNTIDY VERANDA

CA 1935–8
WATERCOLOUR
37.5 X 46.7
SIGNED
AIGANTIGHE ART GALLERY
GIFT OF MR AND MRS AN HOPE
REPRODUCED WITH THE KIND PERMISSION OF
THE ESTATE OF OLIVIA SPENCER BOWER

MARGARET STODDART

1865–1934

MARGARET STODDART was born near Lyttelton, Banks Peninsula; her father, a former station owner, was a naturalist and farmer, her mother had been a governess and teacher. After schooling in Edinburgh, Stoddart attended the Canterbury College School of Art from 1882. In 1885 she was elected to the council of the newly established Canterbury Society of Arts. In 1894 she went to Melbourne, where she had a successful exhibition, and in 1897 she travelled around England and Europe, meeting Frances Hodgkins and Dorothy Richmond in St Ives in 1902. She took classes and exhibited widely, including at the Royal Academy and the Paris Salon. She returned to New Zealand in 1906 and was a full-time painter until her death, regularly exhibiting in the Canterbury Society of Arts exhibitions. The society showed a major survey of 196 of her works on 1928 by way of a tribute. Stoddart was vice president of the society from 1931 until her death.

GARDEN, CHRISTCHURCH

CA 1912
WATERCOLOUR AND BODYCOLOUR OVER
CHARCOAL
25.4 X 35.4
SIGNED
HOCKEN COLLECTIONS, UARE TAOKA
O HAKENA, UNIVERSITY OF OTAGO

OLD HOMESTEAD, DIAMOND HARBOUR

CA 1913
WATERCOLOUR AND BODYCOLOUR OVER
CHARCOAL
38.3 X 49.4
SIGNED
CHRISTCHURCH ART GALLERY TE PUNA
O WAIWHETU

GODLEY HOUSE, DIAMOND HARBOUR
CA 1913
WATERCOLOUR AND BODYCOLOUR OVER
CHARCOAL
38.2 X 50.5
SIGNED
CHRISTCHURCH ART GALLERY TE PUNA
O WAIWHETU

HOUSE IN A SUMMER GARDEN
CA 1928
WATERCOLOUR
24.5 X 34.5
SIGNED
FORRESTER GALLERY
GIFT OF THE NORTH OTAGO ART SOCIETY

WINIFRED KERR TAYLOR

1868–1964

WINIFRED KERR TAYLOR was one of eight surviving children of leading early Auckland businessman Allan Taylor (1832–1890) and his second wife Sophia. Allan Taylor was born in India, where his father was in the army, and educated in Edinburgh. In 1848 he followed his two brothers who had earlier emigrated to New Zealand. Aged only 16, he bought 270 acres (109 ha) of land at Mount Albert, eventually acquiring over 500 acres (200 ha). Taylor spent two years in California before returning to New Zealand to pursue a career in farming and business. He went to England in 1860, married, and returned in 1862 to supervise the building of the Alberton farmhouse. His first wife died the following year. Taylor married Kaitaia-born Sophia Davis in 1865. In addition to the land in Mount Albert, Taylor had several thousand acres at Waimauku, some of which is still in family ownership. Taylor was an auditor of the Bank of New Zealand and a director of the colonial board of the New Zealand Loan and Mercantile Agency Company. He was also prominent in Auckland's civic affairs, a member of the Provincial Council and chairman of the Mount Albert Highway Board. In the 1880s the family added Kerr, Taylor's middle name, to their surname to differentiate themselves from Allan's two brothers. When Allan Taylor suddenly died in 1890 following New Zealand's banking collapse, his widow inherited hefty debts. She and three daughters, including Winifred, stayed on at Alberton, in due course selling off land. Sophia Kerr Taylor died in 1930 and the daughters made their last subdivision in the 1950s. Winifred was survived by her sister Muriel, who died in 1972 and left Alberton, now just the house and 0.6 hectares, to the New Zealand Historic Places Trust.

ALBERTON AND THE FRONT GARDEN
1888
GOUACHE
27.0 X 18.5
DATED
PRIVATE COLLECTION
PHOTOGRAPH: STEVE BURGESS
REPRODUCED WITH THE KIND PERMISSION OF
THE NEW ZEALAND HISTORIC PLACES TRUST

NANCY TICHBORNE

1942—

Painter and illustrator NANCY TICHBORNE was born in Levin and attended Otago Girls' High School. In 1959 she was awarded a scholarship that enabled her to study at St Martin's School of Art in London from 1960 to 1962. She returned briefly to Dunedin, where she had her first solo exhibition, then moved to Hong Kong, working as a fashion illustrator for the *South China Morning Post* and as a fashion designer. Tichborne returned to New Zealand in 1970 and settled in Rotorua, establishing herself as a landscape designer. Since 1980, when she illustrated *The Cook's Garden*, Tichborne has been in demand as an illustrator, especially for gardening and food books. In 1981 she received the AW Reed Memorial Book Award for illustration. She designed four stamp issues for New Zealand, the Pitcairn Islands and Bhutan. Since 1985 she and her husband Bryan have published calendars illustrated with her paintings as well as books, videos and DVDs on watercolour painting.

OKAINS BAY HERITAGE
2004
WATERCOLOUR
35.0 X 45.0
SIGNED
PRIVATE COLLECTION
REPRODUCED WITH THE KIND PERMISSION OF
THE ARTIST

PHILIP TRUSTTUM

1940–

PHILIP TRUSTTUM was born in Raetihi in the central North Island but grew up in Canterbury, attending the School of Fine Arts at the University of Canterbury, where Rudi Gopas was a strong influence. In 1964 he married fellow student Mary Lee Cresswell. In 1965 he was one of the 15 artists in *Contemporary Painting in New Zealand* at the Commonwealth Institute in London, and as a result Kees Hos gave him his first solo exhibition at the New Vision Gallery, Auckland, in 1966. Subsequently Trusttum represented New Zealand at the 1982 Sydney Biennale. He has had gallery and art museum exhibitions annually since 1969, most recently at the galleries of Warwick Henderson, Auckland; CoCa, Christchurch; and Janne Land, Wellington. A survey exhibition, *Selected Works 1962–79*, was organised by the Sarjeant Gallery, Wanganui, in 1980. Trusttum was awarded a prestigious Pollock–Krasner Foundation grant in 2000.

CHRISTCHURCH HOUSES

1973
OIL ON BOARD
90.0 X 58.5
ARTWORKS COLLECTION, CHRISTCHURCH
POLYTECHNIC INSTITUTE OF TECHNOLOGY
REPRODUCED WITH THE KIND PERMISSION OF
THE ARTIST

VANILLA TREE AND HOUSES

1973
OIL ON BOARD
120.4 X 105.5
SIGNED AND DATED
PRIVATE COLLECTION
REPRODUCED WITH THE KIND PERMISSION OF
THE ARTIST
PHOTOGRAPH COURTESY OF FERNER GALLERIES

BACK GARDEN NO. 47

1973
OIL ON BOARD
50.0 X 84.0
THE JAMES WALLACE ARTS TRUST
REPRODUCED WITH THE KIND PERMISSION OF
THE ARTIST

PETRUS VAN DER VELDEN

1837–1913

Dutch painter PETRUS VAN DER VELDEN arrived in Christchurch in 1890 and quickly established his reputation with striking paintings of the Otira Gorge, one of which was bought for the Dunedin Public Art Gallery in 1892. His growing renown, however, was not matched by increased earnings and in 1898 he and his family moved to Sydney in search of greater financial success. Though his wife died, the artist stayed on in Sydney until January 1904, when he returned to Wellington accompanied by Australia Wahlberg, whom he married in February. His posthumous portrait of Richard Seddon was destroyed in a fire at Parliament Buildings in 1907. Later there were several self-portraits and landscapes but most were versions of the Otira Gorge paintings that had established his reputation. One was bought by the Auckland Art Gallery.

A GARDEN IN TINAKORI ROAD,
WELLINGTON

1908
WATERCOLOUR
51.0 X 64.0
SIGNED AND DATED
ALEXANDER TURNBULL LIBRARY

A LOIS WHITE

1903–1984

LOIS WHITE was born in Auckland, the youngest of four children of the architect Arthur White and his wife Annie, who were devout Methodists. After attending Epsom Girls' Grammar School, where she excelled at art and swimming, she studied at the Elam School of Fine Arts from 1923 to 1927. She then taught for eight years at Takapuna Grammar School, before becoming first a part-time and from 1935 a full-time tutor at Elam, until her retirement in 1963. White exhibited regularly at the Auckland Society of Arts from the 1930s into the 1950s and from 1948 with the New Group, which she helped to form in that year. While White's paintings were often singled out for praise in group shows it was not until 1977, when she was 74, that the Peter McLeavey Gallery held the first comprehensive solo exhibition of her work, which finally brought her to the attention of galleries and collectors. In 1961 she travelled to Europe with her friend the painter Ida Eise. Auckland Art Gallery presented a major retrospective of her art in 1994, *By the Waters of Babylon: The Art of A. Lois White*.

BACK DOOR
1958
OIL ON BOARD
60.0 X 44.6
SIGNED
AUCKLAND ART GALLERY TOI O TAMAKI
PURCHASED 1987
REPRODUCED WITH THE KIND PERMISSION OF
ALISON DISBROWE

VIOLET WHITEMAN

1873–1952

VIOLET WHITEMAN (née Sells) was born in Guildford, Surrey, England and studied in London with W Frank Calderon and Stanhope Forbes and at Sir Herbert von Herkomer's art school in Bushey, Hertfordshire. She had one work exhibited at London's Royal Academy Summer Exhibition in 1903 and two paintings with the Society of Women Artists in 1907. Following her marriage in 1905, she lived in Leominster, Herefordshire, where she and her husband bred pedigree Hereford cattle and thoroughbred horses, some of which they raced. In 1926 they emigrated to New Zealand, where one of their sons was living, and bought a small farm at Kaitoke, near Wanganui. Whiteman also kept a flat in Wanganui and a separate studio. She was on the advisory committee of the Sarjeant Gallery and active in the Wanganui Arts Society, serving on its committee twice. Whiteman exhibited regularly with the Wanganui Society of Arts and with the Canterbury Society of Arts in the 1930s, and in 1944 she held a retrospective exhibition of her paintings.

VIEW OF THE DUNCAN FAMILY GARDEN,
DURIE HILL, TOWARDS WANGANUI
CA 1940
WATERCOLOUR
26.5 X 34.0
SIGNED
PRIVATE COLLECTION
PHOTOGRAPH COURTESY OF JONATHAN GRANT
GALLERIES
REPRODUCED WITH THE KIND PERMISSION OF
JOHN WHITEMAN

SUSAN WILSON

1951–

Susan Wilson was born in Dunedin and trained as a neurosurgical nurse, travelling in 1976 to London, where she studied painting at Camberwell School of Art and the Royal Academy. In 1987 Wilson travelled to Cassino, Italy, where her father had served during the Second World War; the visit resulted in a major series of self-portraits and in 1994 the *Cassino revisited* paintings. Among her awards and residencies are the Italian Government Borso di Studio in Venice and the Veneto (1984) and the Richard Ford Award to work in the Prado Museum (1985). In 1989 Wilson had a large solo exhibition at the Robert McDougall Art Gallery, Christchurch. Wilson received an Abbey Scholarship to live at the British School at Rome in 1992 and won the Regional Artists Prize in 2003 and 2005. Wilson's most recent solo exhibitions were at the Judith Anderson Gallery, Auckland (2001) and Browse and Darby, London (2005).

LEWIS' GARDEN AT DARFIELD
1989
OIL ON LINEN
71.0 X 91.5
PRIVATE COLLECTION
REPRODUCED WITH THE KIND PERMISSION OF
THE ARTIST

PAMELA WOLFE

1950–

PAMELA WOLFE was born in Reading, England, and came to Auckland as a small child. She grew up in Howick and attended the Elam School of Fine Arts from 1969 to 1971, when she graduated with a Diploma in Fine Art. She lived in Christchurch from 1973 until 1976, the year she had her first solo exhibition, at the Labyrinth Gallery. She subsequently showed at the Brooke Gifford, RKS and Lane galleries and, since 1998, mainly at Artis, Parnell. Wolfe was twice a finalist in the Benson & Hedges Art Award and won the Nola Holmwood Memorial Portrait Prize in 1985 and the Team McMillan Art Award in 1987. She has illustrated several children's books written by her husband Richard.

LARGE PINK ROSES
2002
OIL ON CANVAS
122.0 X 198.0
PRIVATE COLLECTION
REPRODUCED WITH THE KIND PERMISSION OF
THE ARTIST

GLOSSARY

ART SCHOOLS

The colony's first art school, the Dunedin School of Art (from 1894 the Otago School of Art and Design) was established by the provincial government in 1870, with David Con Hutton as its director. It was later absorbed by the King Edward Technical College. The short-lived Otago Art Academy was established in 1894 by Petrus van der Velden, John Perrett and Laurence Wilson.

Elam School of Art and Design, later Elam School of Art, was established in 1890 following the bequest of JE Elam. It later became Elam School of Fine Arts, University of Auckland.

The Canterbury College School of Art was established in 1881, becoming, in 1931, Canterbury University College of Art. It is now known as the School of Fine Arts, University of Canterbury. It is frequently referred to as Ilam after the suburb in which the campus is now situated.

The art school in Wellington was established as the School of Design in 1886; it later became the School of Art, Wellington Technical College.

ART SOCIETIES

The art societies that developed throughout New Zealand in the latter half of the 19th century were essentially exhibiting organisations, democratically run by councils elected by their members.

The Auckland Society of Artists was the first to be established, in 1869, with biennial exhibitions held in 1871, 1873, 1875, 1877 and 1879, when it was dissolved. A new organisation, the Auckland Society of Arts (ASA), was founded in 1880 and held its first exhibition in April 1881. It was dissolved in the 1990s.

The Otago Society of Artists, becoming the Otago Art Society (OAS) shortly afterwards, was established in 1875.

In 1863 a Society of Fine Arts was proposed (and a School of Design) but it would not be until 1880 that the Canterbury Society of Arts (CSA) was established. Its first annual exhibition was held in 1881.

In Wellington in 1882 the Fine Arts Society of New Zealand was established. It became the Wellington Art Society in 1883 and in 1889 the New Zealand Academy of Fine Arts (NZAFA), holding its first annual exhibition in 1892.

BLEDISLOE MEDAL

The Bledisloe Medal was awarded to the painter of the best landscape in the annual exhibition of the Auckland Society of Arts, and was named after Lord Bledisloe, former governor-general of New Zealand, who established the award. It was first made for a painting by Archibald Nicoll in 1932.

CENTENNIAL EXHIBITION

The National Centennial Exhibition of New Zealand Art, a survey with 355 exhibits, was part of the New Zealand Centennial Exhibition from 1939 to 1940 in Wellington. It was organised by the artist, writer and later parliamentary historian, Alexander (AH) McLintock.

KELLIHER ART AWARD

The Kelliher Art Award was established in 1956 by (Sir) Henry Kelliher (Dominion Breweries) to encourage New Zealand artists to portray the natural beauties of New Zealand. It was held almost annually until 1977.

LA TROBE SCHEME

After successfully modernising the Wellington Technical College, in 1919 William La Trobe became Head of Technical Education at the Department of Education. With a view to revitalising the teaching of art in New Zealand, in the mid-1920s he established a programme to attract qualified art teachers from Britain, among them Robert Field.

NEW ZEALAND ART STUDENTS ASSOCIATION

This association was formed in 1883 in Auckland as an alliance of artists and students 'to encourage a taste for the faithful representation of the country, scenery, and life of New Zealand, which had beauties and climate shared by no other land in the world'. It also organised sketching trips. The last of its three exhibitions was in 1886.

THE GROUP

The Group was established in 1927 by former students of the Canterbury College School of Art, Christchurch, as an alternative exhibiting body to the Canterbury Society of Arts. The more progressive artists from the region and throughout the country were invited to exhibit at its annual exhibitions. In 1933 it re-formed as the New Zealand Society of Artists (NZSA) 'to expand the boundaries of art expression and appreciation'. In 1936, it once again re-formed as The Group and maintained its vitality into the early 1960s.

WELLINGTON ART CLUB

The Wellington Art Club was formed in 1892 around James Nairn to encourage sketching and painting *en plein air*. It held lectures and provided a forum for critiquing members' work. Pumpkin Cottage, Silverstream, in the Hutt Valley, was its rural headquarters. The activities of the club began to wind down around 1902. However, under Frederick Sedgwick it was later revived and its artists are sometimes referred to as the Silverstream School.

Selected bibliography

THIS BIBLIOGRAPHY lists the main publications consulted during the preparation of this book. However, only the most important and informative solo exhibition catalogues are listed for individual artists. Biographies of individual artists published on-line in the *New Zealand Dictionary of Biography* are not listed, neither are most articles on individual artists in *Art in New Zealand* and *Art New Zealand*, as there are published indexes for both these periodicals. Other sources of information are press cuttings, articles, minor exhibition catalogues and ephemera gathered in the artist files maintained by the Auckland Art Gallery's EH McCormick Research Library.

Anyone writing about gardens in New Zealand from a historical viewpoint could not get very far without reference to these three volumes, to which I am particularly indebted: Matthew Bradbury et al., *A History of the Garden in New Zealand* (Viking, Auckland, 1995), Winsome Shepherd, *Wellington's Heritage: Plants, Gardens and Landscape* (Te Papa Press, Wellington, 2000), and Thelma Strongman's *The Gardens of Canterbury: a History (*AH & AW Reed, Wellington, 1984).

REFERENCE AND PERIODICALS

Art in New Zealand, Whitcombe and Tombs, Christchurch, 1928–1944

Art New Zealand, Auckland, Art Magazine Press, 1975–

Christchurch Art Gallery, on-line catalogue and information sheets.

McGahey, K, *The Concise Dictionary of New Zealand Artists: painters printmakers sculptors*, Gilt Edge Publishing, Wellington, 2000.

McLintock, AH, ed., *An Encyclopaedia of New Zealand*, RE Owen, Government Printer, Wellington, 1966.

New Zealand Dictionary of Biography, Ministry of Culture and Heritage, Wellington.

The Yearbook of the Arts in New Zealand, Whitcombe and Tombs, Christchurch, 1945–1949.

GENERAL MONOGRAPHS AND ARTICLES

Aitken, R, *Gardenesque: a celebration of Australian gardening*, Miegunyah Press, Melbourne, 2004.

Alberton 1863, New Zealand Historic Places Trust Pouhere Taonga, 2008.

Alfrey, N et al., *Art of the Garden: the garden in British art, 1800 to the present day*, Tate, London Publishing, London, 2004.

Allen, R, *Motif and Beauty: the New Zealand Arts and Crafts architecture of Basil Hooper*, Harptree Press, Dunedin, 2000.

Annesley, M, *As the Sight is Bent: an unfinished autobiography*, Museum Press, London, 1964.

Blunt, W and Stearn, WT, *The Art of Botanical Illustration*, Antique Collectors' Club, Woodbridge, 1994.

Bradbury, M, ed., *A History of the Garden in New Zealand*, Viking, Auckland, 1995.

Brierley, S, *The Story of Mansion House*, Hauraki Gulf Maritime Park Board, Auckland, 1985.

Brookes, B, ed., *At Home in New Zealand: houses, history, people*, Bridget Williams Books, Wellington, 2000.

Brown, GH, *Visions of New Zealand: artists in a new land*, David Bateman, Auckland, 1988.

Brown, W, *100 New Zealand Paintings*, Godwit Press, Auckland, 1995.

Burgess, M, 'Human Nature: the garden's shifting role as subject, medium, art or craft' in *Art New Zealand*, No 112, Spring 2004.

Butterworth, S, *The Suter: one hundred years in Nelson*, Nikau Press, Nelson, 1999.

Carman, K, *Emily's Garden: the colonial New Zealand garden of a Suffolk Lady*, Random Century, Auckland, 1990.

Cassidy, J, King, J and Nunn, P, *White Camellias: a century of women's art making in Canterbury*, Robert McDougall Art Gallery, Christchurch, 1993.

Caughey, E and Gow, J, *Contemporary New Zealand Art 1*, David Bateman, Auckland, 1997.

Caughey, E and Gow, J, *Contemporary New Zealand Art 2*, David Bateman, Auckland, 1999.

Caughey, E and Gow, J, *Contemporary New Zealand Art 3*, David Bateman, Auckland, 2002.

Caughey, E and Gow, J, *Contemporary New Zealand Art 4*, David Bateman, Auckland, 2005.

Collier, G, *Gordon Collier's Titoki Point*, Moa Beckett, Auckland, 1993.

Darwin, C, *Voyage of the 'Beagle'*, J M Dent & Sons, London, 1959.

Davis, J King, *History of St John's College, Tamaki, Auckland, New Zealand*, Abel Dykes, Auckland, 1911.

Dawson, B, *Lady Painters: the flower painters of early New Zealand*, Viking, Auckland, 1999.

Elias, A, *New Zealand Still Life and Flower Painting 1880–1940*, PhD thesis, University of Auckland, Fine Arts Library, 1991.

Fell, D, *Great Gardens of New Zealand*, David Bateman, Auckland, 2003.

Frederikse, F and Panoho, R, *Landscape into Garden*, Sarjeant Gallery, Wanganui, 1988.

Froud, J, *Oceana or England and her Colonies*, Longmans Green, London, 1886.

Griswold, M, *Pleasures of the Garden: images from the Metropolitan Museum of Art*, Metropolitan Museum of Art and Harry N Abrams, New York, 1987.

Holcroft, M, *The Shaping of New Zealand*, Paul Hamlyn, Auckland, 1974.

Husslein-Arco, A et al., *Gartenlust: der Garten in der Kunst*, Belvedere, Vienna, 2007.

Impelluso, L, *Gardens in Art*, J. Paul Getty Museum, Los Angeles, 2007.

Jackson, P, Roberts, N and Strongman, L, ed., *Images of Home and*

Garden, Robert McDougall Art Gallery, Christchurch, 1991.

Kay, R and Eden, T, *Portrait of a Century: the history of the New Zealand Academy of Fine Arts, 1882–1982*, Millwood, Wellington, 1983.

Kerr, D, *Amassing Treasures for All Times: Sir George Grey, colonial bookman and collector*, Oak Knoll Press, Delaware; Otago University Press, Dunedin, 2006.

Kirker, A, *New Zealand Women Artists: a survey of 150 years*, Craftsman House, Sydney, 1993.

Leach, H, *1000 Years of Gardening in New Zealand*, Reed, Wellington, 1984.

Lee, M, '*Flower piece*: reflections on an exhibition of flower paintings' in *Bulletin of New Zealand Art History*, vol.18, 1997.

Matthews, B, *Gardens of New Zealand*, Lansdowne Press, Auckland, 1983.

McQueen, H, *The Earth's Deep Breathing: garden poems by New Zealand poets*, Godwit, Auckland, 2007.

Milbank, B, *Kindred Spirits: the Wanganui Arts Society Centenary 1901–2001*, Sarjeant Gallery, Wanganui, 2001.

Minson, M, *Encounter with Eden: New Zealand 1770–1870: paintings & drawings from the Rex Nan Kivell Collection, National Library of Australia*, National Library of New Zealand, Wellington, 1990.

Oakley, J, *Paintings of Canterbury 1840–1890*, AH & AW Reed, Wellington, 1969.

O'Brien, G, *Lands and Deeds: profiles of contemporary New Zealand painters*, Godwit, Auckland, 1996.

Platts, U, *The Lively Capital: Auckland 1840–1865*, Avon Fine Prints, Christchurch, 1971.

Platts, U, *Nineteenth Century New Zealand Artists*, Avon Fine Prints, Christchurch, 1980.

Registration Proposal: Rangihoua Historic Area, Rangihoua and Wairoa Bays, Bay of Islands, New Zealand Historic Places Trust Pouhere Taonga, Wellington, 2007.

Sampson, F, *Early New Zealand Botanical Art*, Reed Methuen, Auckland, 1985.

Shaw, H, 'Northern Star' in *Heritage*, New Zealand Historic Places Trust, No 108, Autumn 2008.

Shaw, P, *Why Go to the Riviera: images of Wellington*, Godwit, Auckland, 2003.

Shepard, D, ed., *Between the Lives: partners in art*, Auckland University Press, Auckland, 2005.

Shepherd, W, *Wellington's Heritage: plants, gardens and landscape*, Te Papa Press, Wellington, 2000.

Sinclair, A and Thodey, R, *Gardening with old roses: a New Zealand guide*, Godwit, Auckland, 1993.

Stanhope, Z. et al., *Botanica*, Adam Art Gallery, Victoria University of Wellington, Wellington, 2001.

Stapylton-Smith, M, ed., *Diamond Harbour: portrait of a Community*, Diamond Harbour Community Association, Christchurch, 1993.

Strachan, S and Tyler, L, *Ka Taoka Hakena: treasures from the Hocken Collections*, Otago University Press, Dunedin, 2007.

Strange, G, *Brief Encounters: some uncommon lawyers*, Clerestory Press, Christchurch, 1997.

Strongman, T, *The Gardens of Canterbury: a history*, AH & AW Reed, Wellington, 1984.

Vial, J, *Avant-garde Painting in New Zealand and Australia 1884–1904*, MA thesis, Victoria University of Wellington, 1993.

Ward, J, *Information Relative to New Zealand Compiled for the Use of Colonists*, Capper Press reprint, Christchurch, 1975.

White, E, *My New Zealand Garden, By a Suffolk Lady*, AD Willis, Wanganui, 1902.

Wolfe, R, *Battlers, Bluffers and Bully-Boys: how New Zealand's prime ministers have shaped our nation*, Random House, Auckland, 2005.

ARTIST MONOGRAPHS AND ARTICLES

ALBRECHT, GRETCHEN

Brownson, R, Kisler, M and Fletcher, B, *Gretchen Albrecht: illuminations*, Auckland Art Gallery, Auckland, 2002.

Gill, L, *Gretchen Albrecht*, Random Century, Auckland, 1991.

Gill, L and Pound, F, *Afternature: Gretchen Albrecht, a survey — 23 years*, Sarjeant Gallery, Wanganui, 1986.

ANGUS, RITA

Cochran, V and Trevelyan, J, *Rita Angus: live to paint & paint to live*, Godwit, Auckland, 2001.

McAloon, W and Trevelyan, J, eds., *Rita Angus: life and vision*, Te Papa Press, Wellington, 2008.

Day, M et al, *Rita Angus*, National Art Gallery, Wellington, 1982.

Trevelyan, J, *Rita Angus: an artist's life*, Te Papa Press, Wellington, 2008.

BINNEY, DON

Skinner, D, *Don Binney: Nga Manu/Nga Motu — Birds/Islands*, Auckland University Press, Auckland, 2003.

BRIDGE, CYPRIAN

Blackley, R, 'Lance-Sergeant John Williams: military topographer of the northern war' in *Art New Zealand*, No 32, Spring 1984.

BROWN, NIGEL

O'Brien, G, *Nigel Brown*, Random Century, Auckland, 1991.

EVANS, JANE

Coley, J, *Jane Evans*, Hazard Press, Christchurch, 1997.

EYLEY, CLAUDIA POND

Johnston, A, *Unruly Practices 2. Claudia Pond Eyley*, Auckland City Art Gallery, Auckland, 1993.

FIFE, IVY

Muir, B, *Ivy Fife Retrospective Exhibition 1938–1976* (No 66, 16 February–18 March 1977), Robert McDougall Art Gallery, Christchurch, 1977.

FOX, WILLIAM
Sotheran, C, 'The Later Paintings of William Fox' in *Art New Zealand*, No 11, Spring 1978.
Trevelyan, J, *Picturing Paradise: the colonial watercolours of William Fox from the collections of the Alexander Turnbull Library and the Hocken Library*, National Library of New Zealand, Wellington, 2000.

FUMPSTON, RODNEY
Bogle, A, *Fumpston One Decade*, Sarjeant Gallery, Wanganui, 1983.
Rankin, E, *Fumpston Prints 1973–2003*, Sarjeant Gallery, Wanganui, 2004.

GOLDIE, CHARLES
Blackley, R, *Goldie*, Auckland Art Gallery and David Bateman, Auckland, 1997.

GRIMSDALE, MURRAY
Coley, J, 'Perspectives: painted journal' in *The Press*, Christchurch, May 18, 2005.
Walker, T, 'Murray Grimsdale: Three Decades Hard Labour' in *Art New Zealand*, No 83, Winter 1997.

HAMBLETT, ANNE
Entwisle, P, 'Anne Hamblett', unpublished biographical essay, Hocken Library, 1991.

HANLY, PATRICK
Haley, R, *Hanly: a New Zealand artist*, Hodder & Stoughton, Auckland, 1989.
Millar, D, *Patrick Hanly Retrospective*, Dowse Art Gallery, Lower Hutt, 1974.
O'Brien, G, 'The Don Quixote of Mt Eden: Pat Hanly 1932–2004' in *The New Zealand Listener*, October 16, 2004.HOLMWOOD, JOHN
Holmwood, J, 'Untitled biographical memoir' 17 May 1982, in the artist's file, Auckland Art Gallery Library.

HILL, MABEL
Douglas, B, *Pictures in a New Zealand Garden*, Alexander McCubbin, Melbourne, 1921.
Mason, E and Vial, J, 'Mabel Hill 1872–1956: a memoir', *Bulletin of New Zealand Art History*, Vol. 11, 1990.
www.mabelhill.net

KINDER, JOHN
Brownson, R, Blackley, R, Dunn, M and Shaw, P, *John Kinder's New Zealand*, Auckland Art Gallery/Godwit, Auckland, 2004.
Dunn, M, *John Kinder: paintings and photographs*, SeTo, Auckland, 1985.
Dunn, M, *Lakes, Shores and Mountain Crags: the Ferrier-Watson album of watercolours by John Kinder*, Kinder House Society, Auckland, 2007.

KING, MARTHA
Long, M, 'Martha King. botanical artist', in *The Summer Book 2*, Port Nicholson Press, Wellington, 1983.

LEE-JOHNSON, ERIC
Fairburn, G and Mackle, T, *Eric Lee-Johnson Exhibition*, Waikato Art Museum, Hamilton, 1981.
Lee-Johnson, E, *No Road to Follow*, Godwit, Auckland, 1994.
McCormick, EH, *Eric Lee-Johnson*, Pauls Book Arcade, Hamilton, 1956.

LOVELL-SMITH, RATA
Elias, A, 'Rata Lovell-Smith', MA thesis, University of Auckland, 1979.

LUSK, DORIS
Beaven, L and Banbury, G, *Landmarks: the landscape paintings of Doris Lusk*, Robert McDougall Art Gallery/Hazard Press, Christchurch, 1996.

MACLENNAN, STEWART
Mackle, T, 'Stewart Bell Maclennan: the man for the job' in *Journal of New Zealand Art History*, Vol, 26, 2005.

MARTIN, ALBIN
Blackley, R and Platts, U, *Albin Martin*, Auckland City Art Gallery, Auckland, 1988.

MARTIN, LEIGH
Smith, A, 'Leigh Martin: Noise', Jensen Gallery, unpublished essay, 2004.

MAUGHAN, KARL
Jennings, N, *Karl Maughan: a clear day*, Te Manawa, Palmerston North, 2007.
Wolfe, R, 'Interflora: Karl Maughan paints in the face of nature' in *Art New Zealand*, No 97, Summer 2000–2001.

MCCAHON, COLIN
Simpson, P, *Colin McCahon: the Titirangi years, 1953–1959*, Auckland University Press, Auckland, 2007.

NAIRN, JAMES
Hearnshaw, V, 'James McLauchlan Nairn: a catalogue of works', in *Bulletin of New Zealand Art History*, Special Series No 3, Dunedin 1997.
Hearnshaw, V, 'The Glasgow Boy "Downunder": James Nairn's New Zealand years, 1890–1904' in *Journal of the Scottish Society of Art History*, 2004.

OSBORNE, FANNY
Goulding, J, *Fanny Osborne's Flower Paintings*, Heineman, Auckland, 1983.

PEARSON, ALAN
Roberts, N et al., *Heaven and Blood: painting and drawing by Alan Pearson 1959–1999*, Robert McDougall Art Gallery, Christchurch, 1999.
Trussell, D, *Alan Pearson: his life and art*, Hazard Press, Christchurch, 1991.

PROCTER, ROBERT
King, L, *Robert Field Procter: New Zealand artist 1879–1931*, L King, Auckland, 2002.

ROSS, JAMES
Johnston, A and Pound, F, *NZXI*, Auckland City Art Gallery, Auckland, 1988.
Rowe, N, 'Exhibitions — Wellington: James Ross, Barbara Strathdee' in *Art New Zealand*, No 16, Winter 1980.

SAVAGE, CEDRIC
Pauli, D, 'Not Accepting Oblivion: the career of Cedric Savage', in *Journal of New Zealand Art History*, The Hocken Collections Uare Taoka o Hakena University of Otago, Vol 28, 2007.

SHARPE, ALFRED
Blackley, R, *The Art of Alfred Sharpe*, Auckland City Art Gallery, Auckland, 1992.

SIDDELL, PETER
Dunn, M, *Peter Siddell: landscape*, Artis Gallery, Auckland, 2002.
Roberts, J, *Peter Siddell: from the isthmus — 1994*, Artis Gallery, Auckland, 1994.

SPENCER BOWER, OLIVIA
Mitchell, A, *Retrospective: Olivia Spencer Bower*, Robert McDougall Art Gallery, Christchurch, 1977.

STODDART, MARGARET
King, J, *Flowers into Landscape: Margaret Stoddart 1865–1934*, Robert McDougall Art Gallery, Christchurch, 1997.

TRUSTTUM, PHILIP
Brown, GH and Leech, P, *Philip Trusttum: selected works 1962–1979*, Sarjeant Gallery, Wanganui, 1980.
Ross, J, 'Philip Trusttum's Paintings of the Seventies', in *Art New Zealand*, No 6, June/July 1977.
Schulz, D. 'Everyday Opinions', in *The New Zealand Listener*, 6 December 1980.

VELDEN, PETRUS VAN DER
Wilson, TLR, *Petrus van der Velden*, Reed, Wellington, 1976.

WHITEMAN, VIOLET
Wilkinson, C, 'Violet Emily Whiteman (née Sells) 1873–1952', unpublished essay, Sarjeant Gallery Library, Wanganui, 1999.

WILSON, SUSAN
Wolfe, R, 'Worlds Apart: recent painting by Susan Wilson', in *Art New Zealand*, No 103, Winter 2002.

WOLFE, PAMELA
Coney, H and Field, J, *Pamela Wolfe*, Artis Gallery, Auckland, 2006.

ACKNOWLEDGEMENTS

THE AUTHOR IS fortunate to have received such generous and widespread support from the art museum and art history community in the preparation of this book. I am greatly in the debt of everyone who helped and, if errors remain, they are entirely of my own making. I am especially grateful to those busy independent art historians — writers and consultants — who not only shared their enthusiasm for many of the artists and paintings in the book but also freely gave of their knowledge and responded to the kites flown and boats pushed out with patient indulgence. They are all listed below but I would like particularly to offer the following my heartfelt thanks — they know that they made my life that much easier by their timely and helpful responses: Peter Entwisle, Jill Trevelyan, and especially the generous and indefatigable Neil Roberts with his unparalleled knowledge of Canterbury art. My friend Richard Wolfe, his own deadlines notwithstanding, was unfailing with his assistance.

As far as personnel are concerned our institutions are in good shape and I cannot praise highly enough the timely and encouraging support I have received. However, I hope that I will not put the noses of the others listed below out of joint if I highlight the following here, to whom I owe a special debt: Marian Minson helped me on my way by reviewing with me the Turnbull Library's potential holdings and was always quick to respond to my many queries, and Ewen Cameron, Caroline McBride, Rendell McIntosh, Tony Mackle, Denis Rainforth, Warwick Smith and Linda Tyler went well beyond what I could have hoped for. I trust the book is more informative as a result.

All the artists were exceptionally generous in their help and their enthusiasm for the project. Equally helpful and encouraging were the families of those late artists whose paintings remain vivid reminders of their full creative contributions to our art historical narrative.

The following family historians were immensely helpful: Donald and Carole Mason, Ian Maclennan, Beverley Woolley, Sarah Turbott, Rob Douglas and Barbara Simpson.

It has been the greatest of pleasures to have worked once again with Nicola Legat and her team at Random House and designer Nick Turzynski of RedInc.

The author and publisher are extremely grateful to all the copyright holders for their permission to reproduce paintings, especially Karl Maughan for the cover image. Paintings in copyright at the time of publication have been reproduced with the kind permission of the artist, the artist's estate or the copyright holder. Every effort has been taken to establish and contact copyright holders.

The author and publisher are extremely grateful to the following for their kind permission to include extracts from letters that they own and letters for which they own copyright: the Rita Angus Estate, the McCahon family to quote from letters from Anne Hamblett and Colin McCahon, the Caselberg Estate and the Hocken Library.

Individuals I wish to thank are: John Adam, Gretchen Albrecht, Bill Angus, Don Binney, Alan and Eileen Bisset, Roger Blackley, Gordon H Brown, Nigel Brown, Warwick Brown, Victoria Carr, John and Fay Coley, Roger Collins, Joanne Drayton, Michael and Patsy Dunn, Rob and Sue Douglas, Jim and Robyn Douglas, Malcolm Douglas, Ann Elias, Peter Entwisle, Jane Evans, Claudia Pond Eyley, Jonathan Field, Rodney Fumpston, Steve Greenwood, Murray Grimsdale, Peter Hackett, Gil Hanly, Paul Hartigan, Vickie Hearnshaw, Richard and Margaret Holmwood, Louise Johnstone, Hamish Keith, Julie King, Leo King, Professor Helen Leach, Barry Lett, Anna Lim, Jeremy Lowe, Graham McGregor, Bill McIndoe, Ian Maclennan, Beverley McConnell, Peter Malcouronne, Leigh Martin, Donald and Carole Mason, Karl Maughan, Bill Milbank, Richard Morphet, Michael Newell, Alan Pearson, John Perry, Neil Roberts, James Ross, Peter Siddell, Barbara and Lindsay Simpson, Peter Simpson, John Stacpoole, Lara Strongman, Rose Thodey, Nancy and Bryan Tichborne, Jill Trevelyan, Philip Trusttum, Sarah Turbott, Linda Tyler, Jane Vial, Emma Louise Weston, John Whiteman, Cunitia Wilkinson, Hamish Wilson, Ian Wilson, Susan Wilson, Pamela Wolfe, Richard Wolfe, Philip Woollaston, Beverley Woolley.

Institutions I wish to thank are: Fiona Ciaran, Aigantighe Museum of Art, Timaru; Elizabeth Meek, Marian Minson, Margaret Morris, Alexander Turnbull Library; Abby Sisam, Artis Gallery; Catherine Hammond, Caroline McBride (EH McCormick Research Library) Ron Brownson, Auckland Art Gallery; David Verran, Staff of Grey Lynn Community Library, Auckland City Libraries; Ewen Cameron, Mei Nee Lee, Auckland War Memorial Museum; Julie Catchpole, Anna-Marie White, The Bishop Suter Art Gallery; Tim Jones, Peter Vangioni, Christchurch Art Gallery; Warren Feeney, Rachel Slade, CoCa, Christchurch; Natalie Coup, Helena Walker, Dunbar Sloane Ltd; Genevieve Webb, Dunedin Public Art Gallery; Caro Geelen, Susan Hislop, Helene Phillips, Ferner Gallery; Peter Shaw, Fletcher Trust Collection; Warwick Smith, Forrester Gallery, Oamaru; Murray Gray, Gone West Books; Gary Langsford, Gow Langsford Gallery; Sarah Snelling, Hawke's Bay Museum and Art Gallery; Martin Jones, Kate Martin, Rendell McIntosh, Stuart Park, John Webster, New Zealand Historic Places Trust; Donald Kerr, Hocken Library, University of Otago; Lucy Clark, Natalie Poland, Hocken Pictorial Collections, University of Otago; Anna Mangnall, Department of Internal Affairs; John Gow, John Leech Gallery; Jonathan Gooderham, Jonathan Grant Galleries; Bryan Harold, Moa Hunter Books; Victoria Boyack, Jonathan Mane-Wheoki, William McAloon, Tony Mackle, Joanna Moore, Museum of New Zealand Te Papa Tongarewa; Tony Billing, Judy Buttery, Napier City Council; Andrew Clifford, Linda Tyler, Centre for New Zealand Art Research and Discovery, University of Auckland; Bev Eng, Tim Walker, The New Dowse; Neil McCormick, New Zealand Academy of Fine Arts; Kelvin Day, Ruth Harvey, Ron Lambert, Puke Ariki; Cherie Meecham, Rotorua Art Museum; Denis Rainforth, Sarjeant Gallery; Nicola Jennings, Te Manawa; Gail Keefe, Fine Arts Library, University of Auckland; Simona Albanese, James Wallace Arts Trust; Warwick Henderson, Warwick Henderson Gallery; Scott Pothan, Whangarei Art Museum.

INDEX

Italicised numbers denote a featured painting.